# NEW YORK CITY with Kids
## 2001-2002

**ELLEN R. SHAPIRO**

PRIMA PUBLISHING
3000 Lava Ridge Court • Roseville, California 95661
(800) 632-8676 • www.primalifestyles.com

# For Steven,
## who always sits beside me

Illustrations and maps by Nathaniel Levine; Photographs by Ellen R. Shapiro

**Library of Congress Cataloging-in-Publication Data**
Shapiro, Ellen.
    New York City with kids, 2001–2002 / Ellen Shapiro
      p.  cm.—(Traveling with kids series)
    Includes index.
    ISBN 0-7615-2940-3
    1. New York (N.Y.)—Guidebooks. 2. Family recreation—New York (State)—New York—Guidebooks. 3. Children—Travel—New York (State)—New York—Guidebooks. I. Title. II. Series.
    F128.18.S425 2000
    917.47'10444—dc21                       00-050170

01 02 03 04 HH 10 9 8 7 6 5 4 3 2 1
Printed in the United States of America

---

## How to Order
Single copies may be ordered from Prima Publishing, 3000 Lava Ridge Court, Roseville, CA 95661; telephone (800) 632-8676 ext. 4444. Quantity discounts are also available. On your letterhead, include information concerning the intended use of the books and the number of books you wish to purchase.

**Visit us online at www.primalifestyles.com**

# Contents

## Chapter 6  Dining                                        305

## Chapter 7 Shopping 381

# List of Maps

# List of Quick Guides

# List of Indexes

# Abbreviations and Icons

| | | | | |
|---|---|---|---|---|
| BR | Brooklyn | | MTE | Midtown East |
| BX | Bronx | | MTW | Midtown West |
| CH | Chelsea | | Q | Queens |
| CT | Chinatown | | SH | SoHo |
| EV | East Village | | SI | Staten Island |
| FD | Financial District | | TBC | TriBeCa |
| GD | Garment District | | TD | Theater District |
| GP | Gramercy Park/Flatiron | | TS | Times Square |
| GV | Greenwich Village | | UES | Upper East Side |
| LES | Lower East Side | | US | Union Square |
| LI | Little Italy | | UWS | Upper West Side |
| MT | Midtown | | WV | West Village |

 City Fact

 Helpful Hint

 Money-Saving Tip

 Learning Tip

 Insider's Tip

# Acknowledgments

New Yorkers can be the most generous people in the world, and I was the grateful beneficiary of that generosity when I researched and wrote this book. I'd like to thank all the people who were so giving of their time, expertise, and support: Liz Tober, for her insightful teenage advice into shopping and dining. The many hotel reservationists and front-desk clerks who took time out from selling rooms (and making money) to help me when I needed a fact or crucial hotel tidbit. The hotel managers (especially Victoria Barr and Marcel Fohlinger), for the hours spent taking me around to see every aspect of their hotels' facilities and answering my endless stream of questions—all on short notice. The many helpful museum employees and public-relations representatives, especially Mary Record, Helen Lazzaro, Sari Becker, Ned Kulakowski, Curtis Stallworth, and Michael Norris. Professor Richard Sugarman, for his sense of humor and continued moral support. Everyone, friends and strangers, who contributed advice for the Insider Tips. The team at Prima, especially Jamie Miller and Tara Mead, for having the vision to turn my manuscript into this beautiful, soon-to-be new bestseller, and Ben Dominitz for his continued support behind the scenes. Robert and Mazi, the art geniuses, for their insight on museums and knowledge of galleries and peaceful public spaces. Andrew and Addie for their excellent strategies for crowd-avoidance with kids. My neighbors Ken and Jane for always having the answer. My cousin Jane, for her moral support and watchful eye regarding city shopping trends and fashion. My mother, Sue, for her clippings, brochure collecting, and generous sharing of her excellent and extensive early childhood insights. My brother Jonathan, because he's an idea guy. My father, Jack, and brother Michael for their love and low-key support. My mother-in-law, Penny, for sharing her city wisdom. Feller Publicity, for the countless hours of hard work executed on a moment's notice and at all hours of the day and night. Also Heidi Lynne, Buster, and LeClair, just for being you.

And most of all, to my husband and editorial assistant, Steven Shaw, for his critical eye and his never-ending support and for putting up with me when I spin myself into a whirling dervish of stress. Truly, I could not do it without you, nor would I ever want to.

# Introduction

This is the best time in history to be a kid in New York City. Today's New York is a shining, clean, safe metropolis and one of the most family-friendly cities on the planet. The Gotham of the twenty-first century is eminently walkable, loaded with history, culturally enriching, endlessly diverse, and teeming with arts, activities, entertainment, and food for every taste and budget.

This book will help you and your family get the most out of New York. My goal in writing was to make it the clearest, most comprehensive, and most current guide to New York City for families with children *in every age group*. I built this book from the ground up, relying only on up-to-the-minute sources, interviews with dozens of parents and children, and thousands of hours of research—not to mention a lifetime of living in and around New York City. Paying special attention to the needs of all kinds of children—from toddlers to teens, as well as the adults who travel with them—I've included hundreds of activities, shops, restaurants, hotels, events, and resources for children of all ages.

Before we start our journey, let's take a look at New York City, present, past, future, and throughout the year.

# New York City Today: The Greatest Show on Earth

In four centuries, there has never been a better time to visit New York. Tourism is at an all-time high, the economy is booming, construction is growing (up, of course!), and every nook and cranny of the City is blossoming as a result.

🍎 By far the most significant news for vacationing families is New York's recent major drop in crime. Safety in New York City has been improving by leaps and bounds over the past few years, and things continue to get better. All major categories of crime—including murder, rape, robbery, and auto theft—are at their lowest points in three decades, and New York is now by far the safest large city in America.

🍎 Moving into the twenty-first century, New York City remains the national capital of the arts, banking, publishing, finance, accounting, advertising, fashion, and law. It's home to the United Nations, and many major overseas corporations choose New York as their base of U.S. operations. More Fortune 1000 companies are headquartered in New York than anywhere else in the country.

🍎 Most of the action happens on a tiny island, Manhattan, which is only 22.7 miles square—probably smaller than your hometown. The total area of all five boroughs of New York City (Manhattan, Brooklyn, Queens, the Bronx, and Staten Island) is just 301 square miles. Yet the City has 6,374.6 miles of streets and had nearly 36.7 million tourists from across the country and around the globe visited last year. They spent more than $21 billion.

🍎 A newly revitalized Grand Central Terminal (commonly known as Grand Central Station) has exceeded the expectations of even the most optimistic New Yorkers: It has become one of the premier dining and shopping destinations in the world. This, combined with other recently completed projects—like the World Financial Center, the Bridgemarket, and the Chelsea Piers—has brought the City an unprecedented rate of renewal and expansion.

℮ The new Rose Center for Earth and Space is the American Museum of Natural History's greatest addition in decades—and one of the City's greatest architectural accomplishments. In addition to the completely revamped Hayden Planetarium, other new attractions include the Gottesman Hall of Planet Earth, the Cullman Hall of the Universe, and the Big Bang Theater, where visitors are transported back to the beginning of time.

℮ With 714 miles of track, 469 stations, and 6,089 subway cars, New York's subway system is the world's largest. The subways run 24 hours a day and carry 1.2 billion passengers a year, while the City's public bus system consists of 300 routes and carries 600 million people a year (by far the most in the nation) on 4,200 buses.

℮ With immigrants continuing to pour in, the City boasts a plethora of ethnic neighborhoods, plus more than 100 ethnic newspapers, including 25 catering to the Russian community alone. The languages spoken in the streets and on the subways range from Spanish, Arabic, Urdu, and Korean to Chinese, Hindi, Hebrew, and Russian.

℮ A major boost to the City's image, economy, and celebrity status, the film industry plays an important role in the New York economy. Some 60 to 90 productions are filmed daily, with a total of 22,851 aggregate shooting days. Just walk around the City any day of the week, and you're bound to bump into a film crew, walk onto a set, or spy a star.

@ In cultural terms, you can't do better than 150 museums, 38 Broadway playhouses, scores of off-Broadway and off-off-Broadway productions, more galleries than museums, and thousands of concerts, performances, and special events—and that's just the beginning.

# Timeline of New York City History

New York is the economic capital of the world today, but that's nothing new. For almost as long as European settlers have been in North America, New York has been the center of the action.

**9000 B.C.–A.D. 1524:** The area now known as New York City was occupied only by Native Americans.

**1524:** Giovanni da Verrazano, a Florentine explorer hired by the French to chart the northeastern coast of North America, was the first European to visit New York.

**1609:** English explorer Henry Hudson rediscovered New York on a mission to find the Northwest Passage. He claimed the area for his employer, the Dutch East India Company. When Hudson reported back on the beauty of Manhattan and its ample natural treasures (furs, birds, and fruits), New York made an indelible impression on Europe.

**1626:** The area was established as a Dutch fur-trading post, eventually called New Amsterdam. Peter Minuit, the director of the Dutch East India Company, purchased the island from local tribes for goods worth 60 guilders (about $24; though some historians dispute this account).

**1653:** New Amsterdam became a city with a population of 800.

**1664:** New Amsterdam became the British colony of New York. Under British rule, Manhattan (then known as New York) gained prominence because of the shipping industry—it had an excellent natural harbor, extensive riverfront property for building piers, and easy access to the open ocean. The entire city occupied only the area that today runs from Wall Street (named because it was the site of a wall built to protect against invasion) to the southern tip of Manhattan.

**1775:** The first bloodshed in the struggle for independence occurred in New York, when the Sons of Liberty, a local patriotic group, clashed with British soldiers. One of the Sons of Liberty was killed, and several were wounded.

**1783:** The British surrendered to the revolutionary colonists. George Washington said farewell to his generals in his historic speech at Fraunces Tavern (which you can still visit today).

**1789:** George Washington was sworn in as president of the United States of America on the balcony of Federal Hall on Wall Street. New York's population was 33,000. New York remained the nation's capital until 1790.

**1792:** The stock exchange was founded.

**1811:** John Randel Jr., an engineer, headed up a commission that mapped out all the streets from Houston Street to 155th Street, before most of them were even built. With minor modifications (like the addition of Central Park), this is the rectilinear grid we see in New York today. Below Houston Street, the streets still run on the old meandering Dutch plan, which is why it's so hard to find your way around down there!

**1820:** New York's population grew to 250,000.

**1825:** The Erie Canal opened, connecting New York City, via Albany, with Buffalo, the Great Lakes, and the Western territories, and guaranteed New York's commercial preeminence for years to come.

**1863:** During the Civil War, Irish immigrants began the "draft riots," in response to a provision that allowed wealthy men to pay $300 to avoid military service. The rioters soon turned against the City's black citizens, who they blamed for the war and also for taking many jobs. More than ten black men were lynched in the streets, and a black orphanage was burned to the ground.

**1870:** The American Museum of Natural History was founded.

**1880:** New York's population reached 1.1 million. The Metropolitan Museum of Art opened.

**1883:** The Brooklyn Bridge was completed.

**1892:** The Ellis Island Immigration station first started registering immigrants on Friday, 1 January 1892. Famous immigrants to pass through its doors included Bob Hope, Marcus Garvey, Irving Berlin, and the von Trapp family.

**1898:** The five boroughs—Manhattan, Queens, the Bronx, Brooklyn, and Staten Island—voted to become incorporated into the entity of Greater New York.

**1912:** Scheduled to dock in New York at the end of her maiden voyage, the *Titanic's* tragedy prevented her from ever reaching the City's shores. Of the 2,200 passengers aboard the *Titanic,* 675 were rescued by a Cunard liner, which delivered the passengers to the very same dock at which the *Titanic* was supposed to arrive.

**1923:** Babe Ruth hit his first home run in Yankee Stadium in the first game ever played there.

**1930:** The population reached 7 million, thanks in large part to immigration.

**1939:** The World's Fair was held in Flushing Meadows, Queens.

**1969:** The Jets and the Mets won the Superbowl and the World Series, respectively.

**1970s:** After years of mismanagement, New York City plunged into financial crisis.

**1973:** The World Trade Center opened.

**1993:** Rudolph Giuliani was elected mayor. He is widely credited with being the impetus for New York's current economic boom and improved public safety.

# Looking Forward

The City That Never Sleeps is also the city that never rests on its laurels. Never still *or* silent, the City is always changing and evolving. New York is looking ahead with grand ambition. From expanding and updating the classics, like the Museum of Modern Art and Radio City Music Hall, to revitalizing long-neglected neighborhoods, like Harlem, the City's growth and booming economy promise to preserve New York's position as a world leader among cities.

Massive expansion in New York's already enormous public transportation system is on the way:

@ The Port Authority of New York and New Jersey is planning $2.5 billion in construction and projects at Newark and Kennedy International Airports, intended to ease congestion, shorten passenger waits, and create thousands of jobs.

@ The Metropolitan Transit Authority recently approved a 5-year, $17.2-billion plan, which will include new trains and buses and two entirely new subway lines. The new construction will include a rail link to La Guardia Airport.

@ A $484-million project is underway to convert the majestic Farley Post Office Building (the twin of the original Penn Station) into a Penn Station annex. Construction is scheduled to last just over 2 years, and the results promise to be spectacular.

New York's neighborhoods continue to improve:

@ Times Square, no longer the seedy area it was only ten years ago, will keep getting brighter, cleaner, and safer with each passing year. Developments in the area include fresh hotels like the Doubletree and the Westin New York (with as many as 450 and 850 rooms, respectively); the Forest City Ratner entertainment complex (which will include 25 movie screens, shops, and Madame Tussaud's Wax Museum); B. B. King's 550-seat Blues Room music club and restaurant; the World Wrestling Federation's WWF New York restaurant; corporate headquarters of companies including Viacom, MTV, VH-1, ABC-TV's *Good Morning America,* Condé Nast Publishing, and Reuters; the new ESPN Zone dining and entertainment complex; and the $25-million, 8-story NASDAQ sign—the world's largest video screen.

@ Harlem, a thriving cultural center during the 1920s and 1930s, is now on the up and up. New shopping centers and suburban-sized grocery stores have been built and even more is underway, along with scheduled face-lifts for famous favorites like the Apollo Theater, Minton's Playhouse, the Art Deco Lenox Lounge, and the Renaissance Ballroom. Residents are sprucing up many of the beautiful, aging brownstones that line the streets.

And construction efforts continue to amaze:

@ The Museum of American Folk Art is in the process of constructing a $20-million, 6-story, 30,000-square-foot building (to be completed by the end of 2001). It is the City's first major new art museum construction since 1966.

@ The Museum of Jewish Heritage—A Living Memorial to the Holocaust (established in 1997) is planning an 80,000-square-foot expansion (costing $45 million) to be completed by 2002.

@ New York Studios, a multimillion-dollar, Hollywood-style sound stage complex, is coming to the Brooklyn Navy Yard. The site, which has often been used for film location shoots in the past, will feature eleven sound stages ranging in size from 12,000 to 40,000 feet.

Please feel free to send your comments and corrections to ellen@nycwithkids.com and visit the Web site at www.nyc withkids.com.

# CHAPTER 1

# Planning the Journey

## When to Go

Everybody has a favorite time of year in New York, but it's highly debatable whether there's a best time to go. If you asked me, I'd say it depends primarily on your priorities.

@ I'm very sensitive to the weather, which can be a major concern when traveling with small children. My personal favorite seasons in New York are spring and fall, when it's delightfully cool but sunny, and your choice of activities is virtually unlimited. Then again, New York has a relatively moderate, temperate climate year-round. Even the worst days of summer and winter are quite bearable compared with equatorial and arctic extremes.

@ If you want to enjoy the outdoors, winter may not be your best bet; at the same time, winter is the best season for sales, to see the Christmas windows, and to take in all of New York's holiday spectacles. There's nothing like

Christmas or New Year's in New York, but these are also the most expensive times to be in the City.

⊜ If you're looking to avoid the crowds, there's no better time than summer, when the theaters, museums, and restaurants are emptiest (though all is relative—most out-of-towners, no matter what time of year they visit, would be astonished to hear locals remark that "the City is so empty"). Summer is also great for taking advantage of New York's multitude of free, outdoor concerts, performances, and activities at the parks and museums. Your chance of getting a great discounted package air-and-hotel deal is typically best in summer.

⊜ If you have special interests, check the calendar of events on the following pages, research your desired activities and events (see chapter 5), and plan your trip accordingly.

## The Year in New York City

Here's a look at the major, recurring events that happen year-in, year-out in New York City. Tens of thousands of other activities and events are going on all the time in New York (see chapter 5), but most don't adhere to such a strict calendar—you'll have to research them close to the time you'll be visiting. Not all of the events listed here are specifically for kids—though many are. This is more to give you an idea of the rhythm of the City, to help you plan as well as possible and think about your trip.

### January

The big post-holiday sales get going at the major department stores and also at many smaller shops.

The New York National Boat Show (lasting ten days) at the Javits Center exhibits the latest in boats, related equipment, and sea-worthy toys (212-216-2000).

Leading dealers in the field of so-called visionary art—also sometimes called naïve art or art of the self-taught—exhibit their wares at the Outsider Art Fair, at the Puck Building in SoHo (212-777-5218).

## February

The New York Yankees Fan Festival celebrates both the team and the fans. Meet team players, past and present, test your swing, or participate in a memorabilia auction (718-293-4300).

Chinese New Year celebrations, which are spread over the course of two weeks, include lots of noisy fireworks, banquets, and the historic paper-dragon dance that winds through Chinatown (212-484-1222).

During the Westminster Kennel Club Dog Show, as many as 3,000 dogs strut their stuff at the annual event at Madison Square Garden (800-455-3647). It is the second-longest-running animal event in the country (after the Kentucky Derby).

*14 February:* The Empire State Building is the site of the Valentine's Day Marriage Marathon, when couples marry on the observation deck (212-736-3100).

The Annual Empire State Building Run-Up is an invitational event wherein 150 runners run, push, scramble, and wheeze up the 1,576 stairs to the 86th-floor observation deck.

## March

The St. Patrick's Day parade is one of the longest running (and recently most controversial) events in New York City.

## Favorite Spring Activities and Attractions

1. Going to a Yankees or Mets baseball game (p. 295)
2. Walking over the Brooklyn Bridge (p. 175)
3. Watching the arrival of the Ringling Bros. circus animals (p. 284)
4. Renting and rowing a boat in Central Park (p. 255)
5. Taking a Circle Line cruise around Manhattan (p. 65)
6. Sitting at an outdoor café (ch. 6)
7. Visiting the Bronx and Brooklyn botanic gardens (pp. 238, 244)
8. Going to the Central Park Easter Egg Hunt (p. 250)
9. Watching the St. Patrick's Day parade (p. 4)
10. Stopping by Macy's Flower Show at Rockefeller Center (p. 182)

The parade starts at 11:30 A.M. at 44th Street, goes up Fifth Avenue, and turns on 86th Street for the finish.

The International Asian Art Fair is held, with dealers from around the world showing art and artifacts from the Middle East, Southeast Asia, and the Far East (212-642-8572).

### Late March–Early April

The Ringling Bros. and Barnum & Bailey Circus arrives in New York each spring, and, upon its arrival, the animals are walked (around midnight) from Penn Station to Madison Square Garden, where the circus takes place.

The Triple Pier Expo (Piers 88, 90, and 92) is a big antique event, but if you miss it in the spring, there's a showing in November as well (212-255-0020).

## April

The Macy's Flower Show takes place each year in Rockefeller Center the week before Easter.

The Easter Parade goes up Fifth Avenue and ends at St. Patrick's Cathedral, at 51st Street and Fifth Avenue.

Antiquarian Book Fair is held at the Seventh Regiment Armory (featuring first editions, rare volumes, manuscripts, autographs, letters, atlases, drawings, prints, and maps, with prices ranging from low double digits well into five digits and beyond).

The Major League baseball season kicks off (running through September or October, if we're lucky): New York Yankees in the Bronx (718-293-6000); New York Mets at Shea Stadium, in Queens (718-507-8499).

*Pausing for the National Anthem at Yankee Stadium*

## May

The Cherry Blossom Festival blooms at the Brooklyn Botanic Garden (718-622-4433).

Bike New York is the The Great Five Borough Bike Tour, a 42-mile ride that begins in Battery Park and ends with a ride across the Verrazano-Narrows Bridge (212-932-0778).

The International Fine Art Fair includes works from the Renaissance to the twentieth century.

Congregation Shearith Israel (the Spanish and Portuguese Synagogue, the oldest congregation in America) sponsors a Sephardic Fair (212-873-0300).

Tap Dance Extravaganza events are held around Manhattan (718-597-4613).

***Memorial Day Weekend (and following three weekends)***
Washington Square Outdoor Art Exhibit is an arts-and-crafts fair with hundreds of exhibitors in and around the park (212-982-6255).

## June

The Texaco New York Jazz Festival (212-219-3006) sponsors 350 performances of classic, acid, Latin, and avant-garde jazz at clubs and public spaces around town.

Lesbian and Gay Pride Week features the world's biggest annual gay pride parade, a film festival, and countless other events.

National Puerto Rican Day Parade is the largest of its kind in the United States.

JVC Jazz Festival New York is a huge jazz event featuring jazz greats and unknowns all around town.

***Late June–Early July***
The Washington Square Music Festival features free outdoor concerts on Tuesday evenings with classical, jazz, and big band sounds (212-431-1088).

***June–August***
Midsummer Night Swing, a fabulous outdoor dance event at Lincoln Center's Fountain Plaza, offers open dance and nightly lessons (212-875-5766).

Bryant Park Film Festival. Monday night movies in Bryant Park are a huge social scene and happening event—and there are free, mostly classic, movies.

## Favorite Summer Activities and Attractions

1. Riding the carousel in Central Park (p. 254)

2. Watching the Fourth of July fireworks on the East River (p. 9)

3. Strolling through, shopping, browsing, and snacking at neighborhood street fairs (ch. 4–7)

4. Stopping for ice cream at Serendipity or the Chinatown Ice Cream Factory (pp. 346, 347)

5. Going to free summer concerts in Central Park (p. 253)

6. Strolling along the boardwalk, visiting the beach, and riding on the Ferris wheel at Coney Island (and don't miss a hot dog from Nathan's and a visit to Philip's Candy next door) (p. 89)

7. August sales—shopping at the big department stores (and the small stores too) (chapter 7)

8. Checking out the tall ships during Fleet Week (leading up to the Fourth of July) (p. 9)

9. Taking in free Monday night movies in Bryant Park (p. 7)

10. Attending U.S. Open tennis tournament (p. 298)

Central Park SummerStage features free events on weekday evenings and blues, Latin, pop, African, country, dance performances, opera, and readings on weekends (212-360-2777).

Shakespeare in the Park (212-539-8500; 212-539-8750 seasonal phone at the Delacorte Theater), sponsored by the Joseph Papp Public Theater at Central Park's Delacorte Theater, tackles the Bard and other classics, often with a star performer or two from the big or small screen.

The New York Philharmonic gives free concerts around the City's parks (212-875-5656).

Celebrate Brooklyn features pop, jazz, rock, classical, klezmer, African, Latin, and Caribbean music and theatrical performances, at the band shell in Prospect Park in Brooklyn (718-855-7882 ext. 52). And it's all free.

### Early July–Mid-August

The Museum of Modern Art. Classical music, performed by students of the Julliard School, is presented in the Summergarden on Friday and Saturday evenings (212-708-9400).

## July

### Independence Day

Great Fourth of July Festival's downtown festivities include live entertainment, arts and crafts, and a parade from Bowling Green to City Hall.

South Street Seaport Fourth of July festival.

East River Fireworks Fourth of July fireworks. The best you're likely to see—ever! Vantage points are best from 14th to 41st Streets along the FDR Drive (which is closed to cars for the event) and the Brooklyn Heights Promenade.

Lincoln Center Festival features classical and contemporary music concerts, dance, stageworks, and non-Western arts.

*Tall Ships on the Hudson River, Fourth of July*

## August

Along with January, this is the big time for clearance sales in New York City. Clothing, electronics, and everything else get marked down all over town.

Lincoln Center Out-of-Doors (212-875-5108) is a series of music, dance, and family-oriented events lasting almost the entire month.

Harlem Week is the world's largest African American and Hispanic festival, where events include concerts, gospel performances, the Black Film Festival, and Taste of Harlem Food Festival (212-862-7200).

Mostly Mozart. Music festival at Lincoln Center includes free afternoon concerts and evening concerts for a fee (212-875-5103).

Brooklyn County Fair is just like fairs in the country (718-689-8600).

### *Late August–Early September*

U.S. Open Tennis Tournament is held at Flushing Meadows-Corona Park in Queens (800-524-8440).

### *Labor Day Weekend*

West Indian American Day Parade is New York's largest parade (held in Brooklyn) and only one of the many events that occur on this day. Festivities begin Friday night with salsa, reggae, and calypso music at the Brooklyn Museum and end Monday afternoon with a huge parade—floats, costumed dancers, stilt walkers—nothing is missing. And don't forget about the West Indian food and music (212-484-1222).

## September

Feast of San Gennaro honors the patron saint of Naples with this fabulously colorful event on Mulberry Street in New York's Little Italy.

Broadway on Broadway is a free two-hour outdoor concert in Times Square.

New York Is Book Country is an event held along Fifth Avenue, between 48th and 57th Streets, during which publishers set up shop so you can see their upcoming wares, meet authors, play games, and sometimes even get free stuff (212-207-7242).

*Late September–Early October*
The New York Film Festival is the City's most prestigious annual film event (212-875-5610).

## October

The International Fine Art and Antique Dealers Show is one of the world's finest shows (212-642-8572).

Greenwich Village Halloween Parade is a must-do event, at least once (914-758-5519).

*October–April*
New York Rangers hockey is at home at Madison Square Garden.

New York Knicks basketball is at home at Madison Square Garden.

## November

The New York City Marathon is a citywide event for runners and spectators alike that draws runners from all over the world. Participants run through all five boroughs before finishing up in Central Park.

Veteran's Day Parade heads down Fifth Avenue to the United War Veterans Council of New York County.

The Fall Antiques Show is held at the Seventh Regiment Armory (212-777-5218).

## Favorite Autumn Activities and Attractions

1. Cheering the New York City Marathon (first Sunday of November) (p. 11)

2. Viewing the Thanksgiving Day Parade (p. 12)

3. Checking out the changing leaves in Central Park from the top of the Empire State Building (p. 177)

4. Going to Old Home Day at Historic Richmond Town (third Sunday in October, on Staten Island)

5. Observing the Halloween Parade in Greenwich Village (p. 11)

6. Taking a trip to the Union Square Greenmarket (to buy fresh cider, apples, and donuts) (p. 373)

7. Seeing the new fall fashions at the City's trendiest boutiques (chapter 7)

8. Checking out the San Gennaro Festival in Little Italy (September) (p. 85)

9. Going to KidAround Downtown (special programs for kids ages 3 to 12)

10. Celebrating at the New York Is Book Country Fair (September) (p. 11)

### Thanksgiving Day

The Macy's Thanksgiving Day Parade is a favorite New York event (as is now the "balloon stroll" the night before, where city folk gather to watch the balloons being inflated before the big event). Gigantic balloons coast down Central Park West, starting at 77th Street and finishing up at Macy's at Herald Square.

### November–January

The Radio City Christmas Spectacular features the fabulous Rockettes at home at Radio City Music Hall (212-247-4777).

## *Thanksgiving Weekend Through New Year*

Christmas windows are a New York City tradition. The best decorations are usually seen at:

- Saks Fifth Avenue (611 Fifth Ave. at 49th St.)
- Lord & Taylor (424 Fifth Ave. at 38th St.)
- Bloomingdale's (Lexington Ave. at 59th St.)
- F.A.O. Schwarz (767 Fifth Ave. at 58th St.)
- Barneys (660 Madison Ave., between 60th and 61st Sts.)
- Macy's (Broadway at 34th St.)

It's best to start at 58th Street and stroll down Fifth Avenue until you hit Saks (stopping at Rockefeller Center, St. Patrick's Cathedral, etc.), stroll up the other side of Fifth to 57th, and then walk over to Madison to see Barney's windows and the other shops along Madison Avenue (like the Polo stores at 72nd St.). Macy's requires a special detour further downtown.

## December

Kwanzaa Fest is the world's largest celebration of African American culture and includes entertainers, cultural exhibits, and attractions for children (718-585-3530).

*Radio City Music Hall*

## Favorite Winter Activities and Attractions

1. Ice-skating in Rockefeller Center (p. 182)
2. Viewing the Christmas windows along Fifth Avenue (p. 13)
3. Watching the Radio City Christmas Spectacular Show (p. 280)
4. Attending Nutcracker Ballet at Lincoln Center (p. 281)
5. Drinking hot chocolate at Serendipity (p. 347)
6. Visiting the Living Nativity at St. Stephen's Church and the giant Menorah lighting (p. 15)
7. Exploring Grand Central Station, indoors, where it's warm (p. 179)
8. Seeing the Christmas tree at Rockefeller Center (p. 182)
9. Going to a hockey or basketball game at Madison Square Garden (p. 296)
10. Buying (and eating) roasted chestnuts, hot pretzels, and honey-roasted peanuts from street vendors

Handel's Messiah usually begins at 7:30 P.M., Cathedral of St. John the Divine (212-316-7540; 212-662-2133), and runs for several performances; call for dates.

Midnight Mass on Christmas Eve, Cathedral of St. John the Divine, has music for choir, brass, and organ; a sermon; and candle lighting. The service usually begins at 10:30 P.M.; call for details (212-316-7540).

Midnight Mass is also held on Christmas Eve at St. Patrick's Cathedral (212-753-2261).

The giant Chanukah Menorah lighting is at Fifth Avenue and 59th Street.

The Rockefeller Center Christmas tree, one of the tallest in the country, makes headlines annually when it is first lit—it's an event that draws thousands of spectators each year.

### New Year's Eve

The ball drops in Times Square.

Midnight Run is a 5-mile fun run sponsored by the New York Road Runners Club (212-860-4455).

Fireworks.

And at least a hundred other New Year's Eve events.

## New York Weather

The following table shows 70-year average temperature and precipitation ranges for New York City.

| Month | Low (°F) | High (°F) | Rain (in.) | Snow (in.) |
|---|---|---|---|---|
| January | 26 | 38 | 3.11 | 7 |
| February | 26 | 42 | 3.08 | 8 |
| March | 38 | 51 | 4.1 | 5 |
| April | 40 | 65 | 3.76 | 1 |
| May | 49 | 74 | 3.46 | 0 |
| June | 59 | 82 | 3.15 | 0 |
| July | 67 | 84 | 3.67 | 0 |
| August | 66 | 84 | 4.32 | 0 |
| September | 56 | 79 | 3.48 | 0 |
| October | 46 | 70 | 3.24 | 0 |
| November | 37 | 48 | 3.77 | 1 |
| December | 30 | 46 | 3.68 | 5 |

*Source:* The Weather Channel (www.weather.com)

## Research and Resources

Throughout this book, in the relevant chapters, I've listed Web sites, newspapers, magazines, and specialty publications that will help you plan specific activities and events, such as sports, arts, shopping, and transportation. In addition, here are some general resources that can help you to plan your trip and learn a little bit about New York before you visit:

@ New York City has three major newspapers: *The New York Times* (www.nytimes.com), *New York Post* (www.ny post.com), and *New York Daily News* (www.nydaily news.com). Of these, the *Times* is the best for activity and event listings. In particular, the Friday *New York Times* "Weekend" section has extensive arts and entertainment listings, as well as a special "Family Fare" section listing kid-appropriate events. The *Post* and *News,* although not as valuable for trip planning, are excellent introductions to the local attitudes and issues of New York City, as is the *New York Observer* (www .observer.com).

@ Two free newspapers, the *Village Voice* (www.vil lagevoice.com) and *New York Press* (www.nypress.com), also offer extensive local event listings as well as in-your-face New York opinions. They are available on many street corners, from clearly marked dispensers.

@ *New York Magazine* (www.nymag.com) and *Time Out New York* (www.timeoutny.com) are the best weekly magazines for local listings, with, in my opinion, *Time Out* being slightly better. Both are often available in Barnes & Noble and Borders bookstores across the country. *Where Magazine* (www.wheremagazine.com) also has excellent listings, and you'll probably find a free copy waiting in your hotel room. *The New Yorker* magazine has less comprehensive listings, but is the most literary of the local weeklies. If you have a teen who's interested in reading what some of New York's most articulate voices have to say about a variety of issues, you should grab a copy.

@ Families may want to take a look at some of the local publications geared toward New Yorkers with kids: *New York Family* (www.parenthoodweb.com), *Big Apple Parent* (www.parentsknow.com), and *ParentGuide* (www.parentguidenews.com).

@ On the Web, the most extensive general New York information comes from www.newyork.citysearch.com, which lists all manner of events, shops, theaters, restaurants, and more. The www.nytoday.com site, which is an outgrowth of the *New York Times,* also has good information, especially on restaurants.

@ Two other important Web sites are those of the New York Convention and Visitors Bureau (www.nycvisit.com) and the New York City Government (www.ci.nyc.ny.us). Both contain a wealth of information—practical and educational—for visitors.

@ For local television and radio news, check out NY1 News (www.ny1.com, Channel 1 on most New York City cable TV systems) and 1010 WINS AM radio (www.1010wins.com).

@ The above resources could keep you busy for months, but if you have special interests, you can also pursue thousands of New York City Web sites listed online at Yahoo.com.

## Top Ten NYC Titles for Early Readers

1. *Amy Elizabeth Explores Bloomingdale's,* by E. L. Konigsburg

2. *Tar Beach,* by Faith Ringgold

3. *Abuela,* by Arthur Dorros

4. *Nothing Ever Happens on 90th Street,* by Roni Schotter

5. *Music Over Manhattan,* by Mark Karlins

6. *Journey to Ellis Island,* by Carol Bierman

7. *The Brooklyn Bridge,* by Elizabeth Mann

8. *The Little Red Lighthouse and the Great Gray Bridge,* by Hildegarde H. Swift, illustrated by Lynd Ward

9. *The Adventures of Taxi Dog,* by Debra Barracca (see also *Maxi, The Star* and *Maxi, The Hero*)

10. *Eloise,* by Kay Thompson

And a few extra for good measure . . .

*You Can't Take a Balloon into the Metropolitan Museum,* by Jacquiline Preiss Weitzman and Robin Preiss Glasser

*The House on 88th Street,* by Bernard Waber

*My New York,* by Kathy Jakobson

*Next Stop, Grand Central,* by Maira Kalman

# Getting the Best Deals

To get good deals for New York City, you've got to be savvy. Following is a list of hotel and airline discounters (many of whom discount both). But remember, just because you get an air or hotel quote from a Web site or a discounter, it doesn't

*Fountains at the Metropolitan Museum of Art*

mean it's the best price going, so be sure to learn your prices and shop around.

## Airline Ticket Discounters

Travelocity
www.travelocity.com
*Best for airline discounts, but you can book hotels here too.*

Microsoft Expedia
www.expedia.com
*Air and hotel discounts.*

Cheap Tickets
800-377-1000
www.cheaptickets.com

Fly Cheap
800-FLY-CHEAP
www.flycheap.com

Fly 4 Less
800-FLY-4-LESS
www.lowairfare.com

## Hotel Discounters

Accommodations Express
800-444-7666
www.roomconnection.com

## Helpful Hint

The best thing to do is plan your vacation far
ahead—book plane tickets and hotel reservations
and call it quits. You're sure to get the best ad-
vance-purchase plane ticket fares available (the only
way you'd do better would be by last-minute booking; not only is that a gamble, it's also highly inadvis-
able for families). Because hotel rates are often
based on availability, you'll get reasonable rates, if
not rock bottom. After you book, call the hotel once
every month and inquire about room rates. Don't
tell them you already have a reservation, just ask
about rates to find out if you can re-book if rates
have dropped. (See chapter 4 for more advice.)

Central Reservations Service
800-950-0232

Express Reservations
800-356-1123
www.express.com

Hotres.com
www.hotres.com

Hotel Reservations Network
800-964-6835
www.hoteldiscount.com

Quickbook
800-789-9887
www.quickbook.com

Room Finders USA
800-473-7829

800-USA-HOTEL
800-872-4683
www.1800usahotels.com

Travelscape
888-335-0101
www.travelscape.com

## Money-Saving Tip

Read the travel section in your local paper, pick up a copy of the Sunday *New York Times,* and check other big city papers for travel deals (usually in the Sunday papers). Air–hotel travel packages are often a great way to save money, and, if the timing works out, you can save hundreds of dollars. Find out as much as you can about the hotel, because the last thing you need is for you and your family to have sleepless nights.

## What to Pack

Packing for a vacation to New York City shouldn't be that much different from packing for a vacation anywhere else, and the one reassuring thing is that if you forget it—whatever *it* might be—you can always find it in New York City, maybe even for less. A few important things to remember:

New York City is a walking town, so bring comfortable shoes. Sneakers (or whatever shoes your kids find comfortable, although open shoes like sandals aren't advisable on account of the traffic dangers and the dirt) are acceptable attire for everyone in all but the dressy restaurants and perhaps the opera and symphony. Even if your transportation is primarily by taxi, inevitably, you'll find that will end up being easier to get to certain destinations by bus or subway, which also means at least a short walk on either end. And the best way (if at all possible) to see New York is really on foot, so why not be comfortable? At the same time, New York City can also be a formal city (in this town, you can *never* be overdressed), and it's nice, on occasion, to dress up. Therefore, it's good to throw in a pair of slacks and a button-down shirt for boys and a skirt or dress for girls. You'll be sure to impress the locals with your spiffy family.

For carting things around, you and the kids will each be best off with a backpack. Moms can pack something a little more stylish for going out on the town, but for general city exploration, with all that you'll probably end up carrying (snacks, extra clothes, water, sightseeing materials, etc.), it's the most efficient and painless (literally) way of carting the load. And by the way, carry the backpack as it was intended—on your back. Tourists who insist on carrying their backpacks on their fronts are a dead giveaway—it's like wearing a sign.

Strollers are a mixed blessing in New York City. It's generally easy to navigate the streets, but things get tricky on public transportation and in taxis. The bothersome part is getting into and out of and onto and off of whatever. Subways are worst of all because of all the stairs (virtually no elevator access). If you're traveling as a couple, at least you have enough hands to get the job done, but it's also difficult to keep your eyes on the children. Bus travel is a bit easier; you only have to navigate a couple of stairs. No matter what, it's best to avoid rush hour—especially on the subway. With taxis, you're best off with a quick-folding stroller that's easily tossed into the trunk. Consider a soft carrier like a Snugli for infants, and a backpack carrier for toddlers, as alternatives to a stroller. That way, everyone will need naps at the same time!

Winter in New York can be cold and windy, so it's best to pack a good coat, hats, gloves, and scarves. If you forget any of these items, all but the coats can be bought on the street for around $5. It's also good to have a pair of boots—if it snows; even though the plowing is extremely efficient, New York gets pretty messy.

Summer, especially during July and August, is often hot and, worst of all, humid. As everyone is always saying, "It's not the heat, it's the humidity." Unfortunately, New York often gets hit with both, so keep that in mind if you're visiting during this time of year. Neat shorts and tee shirts are acceptable virtually everywhere, and hats (and sunglasses) are advisable for all. Do keep in mind that all commercial enterprises (including public transportation, restaurants, and hotels) are well air conditioned, so it's a good idea to keep a sweatshirt or long-sleeved shirt handy for each of the kids.

Spring and fall in New York are magnificent, but the seasons are often fraught with variable weather—snow or rain in April and Indian summer in November. Usually, things start to warm up in mid-April, with temperatures climbing toward the end of the month and into early May. September and October usually promise sunny and similar temperatures to May, with the mornings and evenings crisp and cool—perfect autumnal weather to go with the changing leaves. It's best to have a range of clothes for these seasons. Layering is an efficient way to keep warm—and cool—and it's also a good strategy for avoiding over-packing.

# Information for International Travelers

## National Holidays

Even on national holidays, you'll find that many shops and restaurants in New York City remain open, and public transportation functions 365 days a year, 24 hours a day. However, most banks, government offices, and many other businesses will be closed on most holidays.

New Year's Day: January 1

Martin Luther King Jr. Day: 3rd Monday in January

Presidents' Day: 3rd Monday in February

Memorial Day: Last Monday in May

Independence Day: July 4

Labor Day: 1st Monday in September

Columbus Day: 2nd Monday in October

Veterans Day: November 11

Thanksgiving: 4th Thursday in November

Christmas: December 25

New Year's Eve: December 31

## Smoking and Drinking Laws

International travelers may be unfamiliar with various laws—nothing that will get you into extreme trouble, but it's good to be aware. New York City has very strict smoking laws, and if you break them, countless people will be quick to tell you. For the most part, smoking is not allowed in any indoor area, including restaurants, and virtually all establishments abide by this rule (although a few don't). Fortunately for smokers, most bars do allow smoking. Which brings us to alcohol. The national legal drinking age is 21 (though in restaurants, if you're looking to give a taste of wine to a teen, it isn't strictly enforced).

## Health Insurance

It is absolutely crucial to purchase a travel insurance plan that includes health insurance. The United States does not have a

## Top Ten NYC Titles for Pre-Teens

1. *From the Mixed-Up Files of Mrs. Basil E. Frankweiler,* by E. L. Konigsburg
2. *The Cricket in Times Square,* by George Selden
3. *Stuart Little,* by E. B. White
4. *Harriet the Spy,* by Louise Fitzhugh
5. *The Pushcart War,* by Jean Merrill
6. *Brooklyn Doesn't Rhyme,* by Joan W. Blos
7. *All-of-a-Kind Family,* by Sydney Taylor
8. *The Adventures of Ali Baba Bernstein,* by Johanna Hurwitz
9. *Maria Tallchief, American Ballerina,* by Adele De Leeuw
10. *The Chosen,* by Chaim Potok

nationalized medical program, and so anyone needing medical attention is responsible for any medical expenses incurred. Obviously, we hope you'll never need it, but health care in this country, and especially New York City, is *extremely* expensive for the uninsured, so I urge you to purchase a reliable plan before you depart from home.

## Visas, Passports, Immigration, and Customs

Currently the United States has a reciprocity entry arrangement called the Visa Waiver Pilot Program (VWPP). This enables citizens of the following countries to enter for a period of 90 days or less without obtaining a U.S. visa: Andorra, Argentina, Australia, Austria, Belgium, Brunei, Denmark,

Finland, France, Germany, Iceland, Ireland, Italy, Japan, Liechtenstein, Luxembourg, Monaco, the Netherlands, New Zealand, Norway, San Marino, Slovenia, Spain, Sweden, Switzerland, and the United Kingdom. The only requirements are: Travelers cannot extend the visa, they must have a nonrefundable round-trip ticket, and passports must be valid for six months from the return date.

For those traveling from countries not included on the VWPP list (or those needing extensions), you must obtain a visa from the U.S. embassy or consulate in your country (or from a nearby country if there isn't one in yours) by filling out the required paperwork and providing a 1½-by-1½ inch passport photo (37-by-37 mm). There is no charge for the visa.

Because laws do change, to avoid any problems or confusion, it's best to check online for the most up-to-date information. Go to www.travel.state.gov and click on VISAS at the U.S. State Department Web site. For information on the Immigration and Naturalization Services (INS) go to www.ins.usdoj.gov.

Customs allotments entitle each person over the age of 21 to enter the country with 1 liter of alcohol and 200 cigarettes (1 carton), 50 cigars (non-Cuban), or 1 kilogram (4.4 pounds) of chewing tobacco. You may carry up to $10,000 undeclared in cash, traveler's checks, money orders, etc. If you carry more than that, you must declare it.

## Embassies and Consulates

Embassies are located in Washington, D.C., though most countries have consulates and/or missions in New York (because the United Nations is here). If your country isn't listed below, check the phone book for local listings or go to www.embassy.org/embassies.

Consulate Contact Information for New York City:

Australia
630 Fifth Avenue
212-351-6500

Canada
1251 Avenue of the Americas
212-596-1600

Ireland
345 Park Avenue
212-319-2555

New Zealand
780 Third Avenue
212-832-4938

United Kingdom
845 Third Avenue
212-745-0202

## Banking

You're best off using credit cards (you'll not only get favorable exchange rates, but you'll also have an itemized list of your purchases upon your return home, and you won't have to carry so
much cash) and ATM machines (you draw your cash in U.S. dollars [USD] to avoid the hassles of banks and costly surcharges,
though many ATMs do charge a $1 to $4 service fee, depending
on your bank at home). Visa, American Express, MasterCard,
Discover Card, and Diners Club are all widely accepted. You
should probably have at least one credit card with you for big-
ticket items like hotel bills and any unexpected expenses.

Banks are open Monday through Friday, usually from
9 A.M.–4 P.M. Many banks are also open half-days on Saturday

(9 A.M.–1 P.M.). In Chinatown, both Chase Manhattan and Citibank have branches that are open seven days a week (with limited hours on Saturday and Sunday). The Chase Manhattan Bank at Liberty and William Streets does not charge a commission fee for changing international currencies into USD.

## Currency

U.S. currency is pretty straightforward. Bills come in $1, $5, $10, $20, $50, and $100. $50s and $100s will be nearly impossible to use in taxis (cabbies don't carry much cash). If you need change for big bills, it's best to break them at your hotel or at any bank.

Coins come in 1-cent (a penny, $0.01), 5-cent (a nickel, $0.05), 10-cent (a dime, $0.10), 25-cent (a quarter, $0.25), and $1 pieces (though the $1.00 coins aren't very popular).

## Postage

International postage for postcards is 50 cents (40 cents to Canada). A letter of up to ½ ounce to an international destination is 60 cents (46 cents to Canada). Aerogrammes (single-sheet foldover lettergrams) are 50 cents each.

## Electricity

U.S. electricity runs on 110V to 120V (60 cycles)—so if you're coming from abroad with anything that runs on 220–240V (like a baby monitor), you'll need an adapter—something that's easiest to bring from home (though you can find one at any Radio Shack or at J&R downtown).

## Phoning Home

To call home, dial 011, the country code, and the telephone number. To find the country code, check the front of the phone book in your hotel room, ask the concierge, or dial 00 for the international operator (though don't allow the operator to put the call through because there will be a hefty surcharge for any call placed by an operator).

# Arrival and Departure

There are countless ways to get into and around New York City, some of which cost no more than a ride on public transportation ($1.50). Others cost hundreds of dollars (helicopter), but, for the most part, taxis are your best bet, at least upon arrival, when you'll be laden with bags and tired (and possibly cranky) kids. Taxis and car services in New York City aren't as costly as you might think, and when you're traveling in a group, sometimes it's actually cheaper to travel in comfort than on a shuttle or private bus (because you pay one fee for the whole taxi, as opposed to paying per person for a shuttle). So before you run yourself through the wringer trying to save a few bucks, do the math. You may find that you're saving no money at all, and you're actually paying more—and suffering the inconvenience.

## Money-Saving Tip

To save on international phone calls, purchase a prepaid international calling card and place calls to home from a pay phone in the hotel lobby. You'll save big bucks by avoiding the hotel's significant surcharges and inflated phone charges. Read the fine print on the card carefully before buying, though—many advertise low per-minute rates but actually levy a big surcharge on each call, effectively raising the price.

## Airports

There are three major international airports that service the New York metropolitan area. In New York City, they are La

Guardia Airport (LGA) and JFK International Airport (both are in Queens), and, in Newark, New Jersey, Newark International Airport (EWR).

Each airport has multiple transportation options to get into Manhattan: taxi, bus, shuttle, car service, helicopter, ferry, and even a bus/subway combo. But for ease and comfort (especially for those traveling with young children), I would strongly advise a taxi or car service or, to save a little money, a shuttle.

### By Taxi

*La Guardia:* Taxi fares will vary depending upon your destination within New York (uptown Manhattan will be substantially less than downtown). For to/from destinations within Manhattan, fares will run around $15 to $29 plus tolls ($3.50) and tip and take 15 to 40 minutes (with light traffic).

*JFK:* From JFK there is a $30 flat rate to any destination within Manhattan (plus tolls, $3.50, and tip). From Manhattan the fare is $2.00 for the first $\frac{1}{5}$ mile and 30 cents each additional $\frac{1}{5}$ mile (plus tolls and tip). There is a 50-cent surcharge after 8 P.M. Expect the trip to be 30 to 60 minutes (with light traffic) depending upon your final destination.

*Newark:* The taxi fare to/from Newark airport is the most expensive at about $34 to $38 plus tolls ($10) and tip. Expect the trip to take anywhere from 25 to 45 minutes (with light traffic).

### By Bus/Shuttle

| *Olympia Trails Airport Express* | 212-964-6233 |
| --- | --- |

Olympia offers roundtrip bus service for Newark airport. It takes approximately 35 to 50 minutes (more during rush hours) to get into the City depending upon which drop-off destination you select (Grand Central Station, Penn Station, Port Authority, or World Trade Center). The cost is $11 one way or $20 round trip.

| | |
|---|---|
| ***Gray Line Air Shuttle*** | **800-451-0455** |
| ***(Express Shuttle USA)*** | **212-315-3006** |
| **www.graylinenewyork.com** | |

Gray Line offers service for La Guardia, JFK, and Newark airports. It takes approximately 35 to 45 minutes to get into Manhattan from La Guardia and 45 to 60 minutes from JFK and Newark (more during rush hours and for travel below Midtown). The cost (one way) from La Guardia is $16; from JFK and Newark it's $19. Round-trip tickets purchased at the airport are $26 from/to La Guardia and $28 from/to JFK and Newark. Children under 5 ride free. The best thing about Gray Line is that they'll drop you off and pick you up at your hotel—door-to-door service in New York City without a full taxi fare is rare!

| | |
|---|---|
| ***Super Shuttle*** | **212-BLUE-VAN (258-3826)** |
| **www.supershuttle.com** | **800-BLUE-VAN** |
| | **(for out-of-town reservations)** |

Super Shuttle services La Guardia, JFK, and Newark airports. They say the cost is variable from different points within the City to each of the airports, but as far as I can tell, travel from all airports to any neighborhood within Manhattan costs the same: $19 each way. Sounds expensive, but each additional person (after the initial $19) costs only $9 and children under 3 ride free. Once again, the driver will pick you up or drop you off anywhere within the City at no extra charge. It's best to book at least 24 hours in advance when you are returning to the airport.

## By Car Service

There are dozens of car service companies in the City, and using one is a great way to get a little peace of mind. The fare is predetermined (most companies charge $22 to La Guardia, $32 to JFK, and $29 to Newark, plus tolls and tip), so you don't have to worry about meters, directions, or hailing a cab. Call a day or more in advance for a reservation, and a car will pick you up at the terminal (or upon return, at your hotel). Note: If you're calling for an airport pickup and you have a lot of stuff, you can request that your driver meet you near the luggage area—but usually you just meet outside so the driver doesn't have to park.

Accord Car & Limo Service
212-321-1212
800-801-3330

American Dream Car and Limo Service
212-426-1010
888-546-6484

Carmel Car and Limousine Service
212-666-6666
www.carmelcarservice.com

London Towncars
212-988-9700
800-221-4009

Sabra Travel Inc.
212-777-7171
800-722-7122
www.sabratravel.com

Skyline
212-741-3711
800-533-6325

Tel Aviv Car and Limousine Service
212-777-7777
800-222-9888
www.telavivlimo.com

## *By Ferry*

| *Delta Water Shuttle* | 800-543-3779 |
|---|---|

The Delta Water Shuttle runs between the Marine Air Terminal (part of La Guardia) and 34th Street, 62nd Street (both on the East Side), and Wall Street (Pier 11). The fare one way is $15, and the trip takes approximately 25 to 35 minutes. It's fun, if not entirely efficient, and advisable only if you're traveling *extremely light* and you know the kids will *love* it (you can always ride the Staten Island Ferry for free later in your visit—after you've settled in). You'll most likely have to catch a taxi from the ferry to your hotel.

## *By Helicopter*

| *National Helicopter* | 516-756-9355 |
|---|---|

National Helicopter services all three airports to and from heliports within Manhattan. The fare is a flat rate of $389 per helicopter, and each helicopter carries up to five people. You'll need a taxi from the heliport to your hotel, and unless you're traveling light, you might want to save the helicopter ride for a special treat after you're all settled in.

## Public Transportation

There is no direct route from any of the airports into the City on public transportation. But it can be done—if you're up for the challenge. **But I'd strongly advise you, especially if**

**you're carrying lots of luggage and you have young kids in tow, to spring for a cab or car service.** Still, if you're determined to give public transportation a whirl, here are the details.

*From/to La Guardia:* For the shockingly low fare of $1.50 (with a MetroCard, you get a free bus-to-subway transfer, but not with a token or coins), you can take the M-60 bus to 116th Street and Broadway (Columbia University) and transfer to the 1 or 9 subway for locations on the West Side. You can also take the Q33 bus to the Roosevelt Avenue station (in Jackson Heights) and transfer to the E or F train (subway), or take the Q33 to 74th Street/Broadway station and transfer to the 7 train, which will bring you into Grand Central where you can transfer to the 4, 5, or 6 trains (East Side). To go to La Guardia, follow the directions in reverse. Expect 90 minutes of travel time for the trip.

*From/to JFK:* Catch the Long-Term Parking Lot Bus (free) to the A train (subway) station. Take the A train into Manhattan and transfer within the City to get to your specific destination (in reverse, it's the A train marked for "Far Rockaway" and then the shuttle bus).

For further New York City bus and subway information contact:

New York City Transit (MTA)
718-330-1234

*From/to Newark Airport:* Take New Jersey Transit's Airlink bus #302 ($4) to Penn Station *in Newark* (there are, confusingly, Penn Stations in both New York and New Jersey). From there, you take the PATH train to Manhattan ($1) stopping at the World Trade Center, Christopher Street, 9th Street, 14th

Street, 23rd Street, and 33rd Street. To go to Newark, follow the directions in reverse.

For more information on New Jersey public transportation, contact:

New Jersey Transit (NJT)
973-762-5100

## Bus

Long-distance buses (Greyhound, Trailways, Peter Pan, Vermont Transit, etc.) arrive into the City at the Port Authority Bus Terminal, which is located between 40th and 42nd Streets from Eighth Avenue to Ninth Avenue. Catch a taxi to your hotel. It's by far the easiest and, with three or more people, will hardly cost any more than the subway or bus (unless you're going to one of the boroughs).

## Train

Amtrak trains arrive at Penn Station (31st St. to 33rd St., between Seventh Ave. and Eighth Ave.).

## Car

It could take you a decade and a Ph.D. to learn all of the different ways to drive into Manhattan—the best routes are a frequent source of discussion and debate, particularly among suburban commuters. What you need to know, at the most basic level, is that I-95 from the north and south and I-80 from the west will all lead you to Manhattan. If you're a member of AAA, get a triptik tailored to your exact itinerary; if not, see the map of New York City provided at the front of this book or get online and check out one of the following (or a few to cross-reference) Web sites for directions that will be best suited to your travel plans.

## Top Ten NYC Titles for Teens

1. *Time and Again,* by Jack Finney

2. *Old New York,* by Edith Wharton

3. *A Tree Grows in Brooklyn,* by Betty Smith

4. *The Blacker the Berry,* by Wallace Thurman

5. *The Age of Innocence,* by Edith Wharton

6. *Babe Ruth Slept Here: The Baseball Landmarks of New York City,* by Jim Reisler (for baseball fans of all ages)

7. *My Name is Asher Lev,* by Chaim Potok

8. *Bodega Dreams,* by Ernesto Quiñonez

9. *The Great Bridge,* by David McCullough

10. *Here Is New York,* by E. B. White

**And a few extra for good measure . . .**

*New York City Ghost Stories,* by Charles J. Adams III

*722 Miles, The Building of the Subways and How They Transformed New York,* by Clifton Hood

*It Happened in New York,* by Fran Capo and Frank Borzellieri

*Life at the Dakota,* by Stephen Birmingham

Yahoo
www.yahoo.com
*Go to the MAPS section*

Excite
www.excite.com
*Go to MAPS and DIRECTIONS section*

Mapblast
www.mapblast.com

# CHAPTER 2

# Taking Charge of NYC

## Contingency Plans

To ensure that you'll have a wonderful New York vacation, take a cue from the Boy Scouts: Be prepared. Here are a few tips to help keep your trip on track.

### Emergencies

It's every parent's nightmare to become separated from a child, but in New York City, because of the sheer magnitude and population, the mere thought of it is overwhelming and devastating. Take the following steps to avoid this scenario altogether:

- Talk to your children before you arrive and again upon settling into the hotel to emphasize the importance of sticking close to either parent. Tell young children to hold onto the stroller of a younger sibling, a parent's hand, or the hand of an older sibling.

- Be sure that each child has the name, address, and telephone number of the hotel in his or her pocket or backpack every day before setting out for your adventures, as well as your cellular phone number (but we'll get to that later).

ℰ With older children, if you are separating in a museum, zoo, or other attraction, pick a meeting place and time and confirm both before setting off in different directions.

ℰ Have a plan and discuss it with your children in the event that you do get separated.

ℰ Consider bringing a cellular phone. Having a cellular phone along (or even two, one with the older kids and one with the parents or one for each parent if you plan to separate at all) can raise your level of comfort and security. And if anyone gets separated, you can always be in touch for an easy reunion. Because cellular phone service is currently so reasonably priced (and most plans even include nationwide coverage), I strongly suggest that you consider it for the trip.

ℰ In closed areas, such as museums, pick a place to meet "just in case," like the information booth. As soon as anyone realizes that someone is missing, go to the designated place. As a backup, tell children to find the nearest security guard (easily recognizable by the uniform), who will help the family re-unite (this happens all the time).

ℰ Outside of the hotel, be sure that the cellular phone is on as soon as you realize that someone is missing (or charge the phone each night and keep it on all day). Advise the kids to call you or, if they're the keepers of the phone, call them. Call the hotel and advise the kids to do the same. If the children are older, you can have a plan (write it down for them in case they're not quite old enough): After a given amount of time has passed, hail a taxi (show the driver the paper with the name and address), and go to the hotel (be sure each child has a small stash of emergency money, $10 or so—enough for a cab to the hotel). Also, tell children to ask a grownup for help (you can discuss who might be an appropriate person to ask— police, other people with children, well-dressed adults in business suits, etc.).

❧ In case of a medical emergency, call 911. No money is needed to make this call from public pay phones. Often though, if the emergency is not life threatening, you're best off hailing a cab and telling the cabbie to take you to the nearest hospital emergency room.

## Avoiding Crime

It's no secret that in the past New York City had its share of crime, but the City gets safer every year—in fact, it's now the safest large city in America. But it's still a major metropolitan area, which means that you must take steps to be sure your family is as safe as possible.

❧ Listen to your gut instincts—if you feel unsafe or uncomfortable, you're likely right, and the worst that can happen is that you've erred on the side of caution.

❧ Do not enter Central Park (or any other park, for that matter) after dark unless you're going to an event that hundreds or thousands of other people are also attending.

❧ Keep a watchful eye on your belongings, though there's no need to be paranoid. On subways and buses, keep bags in front of you or on your lap.

e Keep your money in front pockets and split the wealth and credit cards between the adults so that no one person has everything.

e Be unobtrusive with your money, jewelry, and belongings. It's okay to pay cash, but don't walk down the street with your wallet open or bills in your hand. Leave your best jewelry at home if you can, but if you can't live without it, tuck fancy necklaces and gemstones out of view if you're in a questionable area.

e In restaurants and theaters, *do not drape your bags across the back of your chair*—hold your belongings in your lap or on the floor in front of you where you can see them. You may even want to hook the strap of your purse or bag around your ankle.

e Don't be afraid to ask for directions. If you're lost, just stop someone who's "safe looking" and ask for help. New Yorkers might appear rushed and harried (we are), but only a scant few wouldn't stop to help out—even if they're late for a very important meeting.

e Use common sense. New York is a city like any other, so follow the same rules you would anywhere else to avoid being a crime target.

### Common Scams to Avoid
Ah, yes. The old shell game. It looks so simple and yet you can *never* win. Familiar with the saying, "There's a sucker born every minute"? Well, don't be the one to prove it true—here are some common scams to avoid.

e As a general rule, never give *anyone* any money unless you're paying for something. Plenty of people will ask you for money during your visit to New York City, and, though it may sound cold, you're best off giving none of yours to anyone. Panhandling is against the law in New York. If you want to give money to the homeless, make it a family project, and write a check to a reputable organization that you've researched (or learned about while in town) after you get home.

@ Don't fall for the well-dressed person with the sob story— "I lost my wallet and I need money for the train ticket to Westchester" or "I found this wallet with lots of money in it, and if you give me $50 to pay a lawyer to put it in escrow, we can split it" scam. Just because the person is well dressed, it doesn't mean he or she isn't trying to rip you off. Don't let anyone talk you into going to an ATM or lending money ("I promise I'll pay you back! What's your address, I'll mail you a check") or anything else. Just say no and walk away.

@ Avoid the shell game scam (a guy on the street set up with a cardboard box–like table, three shells, and the little red ball—if you pick the shell with the ball under it, you win). Same goes for three-card Monte (similar setup only you're looking for the jack, king, or whatever). You can *never* win—because it's a scam.

@ Avoid riding in unlicensed cabs (livery-service cars). They'll pull over or honk. Most are sedans. Stick to taxis, licensed car services, and public transportation. Be sure the taxi driver uses the meter.

@ When buying things on the street, always agree to a price in advance—before you take out your money. Don't falter on the agreement. If the seller doesn't have change, get your money back and buy the item elsewhere or get change yourself and pay the agreed-upon amount.

## Weather

If your plan for the day was to be outside and you wake up to find that it's raining cats and dogs, head for one of the many indoor attractions (theater, museum, stock exchange, etc.) to keep everyone happy and engaged. Even in the snow, the buses continue to run, as do the sub-ways—usually without a hitch (though it's best to avoid taxis in the snow because the drivers are usually unaccustomed to driving in such conditions).

*The Statue of Liberty*

If it does snow, be sure to head for Central Park. It's a magical place when blanketed in white, and it's one of the few places where the pristine snow stays white for more than a few hours.

# Important Telephone Contacts

- @ Police and Fire Departments: Dial 911 (Note: For non-emergency police calls, dial 212-374-5000.)
- @ Animal Bites: 212-566-2068

@ Doctors on Call: 718-745-5900

@ Poison Control Center: 212-764-7667

**For Animal Emergencies**
Animal Medical Center
510 East 62nd Street
212-838-8100
*Emergency animal hospital, 24 hours, 7 days a week.*

**For Emergency Prescriptions (24-Hour Pharmacies)**
Duane Reade
224 West 57th Street (at Broadway)
212-541-9708

Duane Reade
2465 Broadway (at 91st St.)
212-799-3172

Duane Reade
1279 Third Avenue (at 74th St.)
212-744-2668
*For a complete listing of Duane Reade locations and store hours, go to www.duanereade.com.*

Rite Aid
303 West 50th Street (at Eighth Ave.)
212-247-8384
212-247-8736

Rite Aid
542 Second Avenue (at 30th St.)
212-213-5284 (main number)
212-213-9887 (pharmacy number)
*For a complete listing of Rite Aid locations and store hours, go to www.riteaid.com.*

*Passport Information*
212-399-5290

*General Information*
New York Convention and Visitors Bureau
810 Seventh Avenue (at 53rd St.)
New York, NY 10019
212-484-1200
www.nycvb.com

## Money-Saving Tip

Bring all basic supplies with you. New York City is a bargain-hunter's paradise, but it's also very expensive to buy bulky staples like diapers and formula—especially at the mini-marts in the major hotel neighborhoods. If you're driving and have the luxury of a trunk, you wouldn't be crazy to bring cans of soda, bottles of water, and nonperishable snacks—each item you bring could save you a dollar or more.

# What Things Cost

New York can be one of the most expensive cities on earth, but it's also home to many of the world's best bargains. Though the basics, like a can of soda or a package of Pampers, are often more expensive than they would be in the rest of the country, prices for many other items may be just the opposite—you'll find substantial discounts on clothes, cameras, and all manner of consumer electronics.

Here's a rough idea of what everyday things typically cost in New York City:

- Can of soda from a street vendor or mini-mart: $1.00

- McDonald's Happy Meal: $2.99 with hamburger; $3.09 with cheeseburger; $3.59 with McNuggets; Big Mac Extra Value Meal: $4.69

- Slice of pizza at a typical pizzeria: $1.75

- Bagel (plain): $0.75; $1.25 with a "schmear" (cream cheese)

- Bus or subway ride anywhere in the system: $1.50

- Roll of Kodak Gold 24-exposure 35mm color-print film: $2.09 at a discount camera-and-electronics store; $6.00 in a neighborhood mini-mart

- Taxi from the Upper East Side to the Theater District: $8.00; from Midtown hotels to Greenwich Village: $7.00; from Times Square to the World Trade Center: $14.00

- Local call from a payphone: $0.25

- Movie ticket: $6.00 child; $9.50 adult

- Bayer Aspirin: $3.39 (24 tablets); generic aspirin: $3.99 (250 tablets)

- Tylenol pain reliever: $3.99 (24 tablets); generic acetaminophen: $3.99 (100 tablets)

- Digital thermometer: $9.99

- Spill-proof cup: $5.09

- Huggies diapers: $7.49 (24 count)

- AA batteries: $4.49 (4-pack)

- Enfamil infant formula: $3.15 (13 ounces)

- Similac ready-to-feed infant formula: $4.50 (1 quart)

## Helpful Hint

Always carry enough cash—about $100—to pay for a meal or get you back to your hotel in a taxi; but never carry too much. New York has ATMs by the thousands, and most establishments accept credit cards (the best way to pay for anything, in case there's a dispute later). Traveler's checks can be useful (and are widely accepted), but they often slow things down. If you have an account at a major bank, you're much better off just getting your cash at ATMs. Most hotels cash personal checks (for guests) for up to a few hundred dollars.

# Tipping

Tipping in New York tends to be a little more generous than the national average, but not by much. Of course, the size of the tip is a personal decision and should be influenced by the quality of service rendered, but please remember that many service-industry people make nearly their entire incomes from tips, and you should only withhold a tip under extraordinary circumstances. The following are basic customary guidelines for good service:

- Restaurants: 16.5 percent of the bill (just double the tax, which is 8.25 percent) in a standard restaurant and 18–20 percent in a luxury restaurant

- Bartenders: 15 percent of the tab

- Taxis: 15–20 percent of the fare on the meter, plus an extra couple of dollars if the driver helps you with luggage or packages

- Car service: Same as for taxis

- Hotel doorman: $1–$2 for helping you in or out of a taxi or car with your luggage or packages

- Hotel bellhop: $1–$2 per bag

- Hotel housekeeper: $1 per day per room

- Coat-check attendants: $1 per item

- Parking-lot attendants: $1

- Hairdressers: 15–20 percent

You are not expected to tip at self-service or fast-food restaurants, nor do theater ushers or gas-station attendants expect tips.

### Helpful Hint

Some restaurants have taken to adding an automatic service charge for large parties (five or more), so be sure to read your bill carefully. You're not expected to tip over and above this charge.

## Sales Tax

New York sales tax is 8.25 percent. This applies to just about every purchase you make, including restaurant meals, though there are a few exceptions: Certain "necessities" are not taxed, such as most grocery items, shoes, and clothes costing under $110 per item.

## Area Codes

Four area codes cover New York City: 212, 718, 917, and 646. Calls within and between these area codes are considered

## Top Ten Free Activities and Attractions

1. Staten Island Ferry cruise (p. 57)
2. New York Stock Exchange tour (p. 181)
3. Sony World of Wonder (p. 427)
4. Big Apple Greeter tours (p. 61)
5. Stroll over the Brooklyn Bridge (p. 175)
6. Thanksgiving Day Parade (p. 12)
7. Christmas windows at department stores and Christmas tree at Rockefeller Center (p. 15)
8. Visit to FAO Schwarz (p. 452)
9. Pay-what-you-wish days at museums (p. 190)
10. Fourth of July fireworks (p. 9)

*local* calls (25 cents from pay phones). Most telephone numbers in Manhattan are 212, but due to a recent shortage of the 212 exchange, new Manhattan telephones are being assigned 646 and 917 numbers. In addition, most New York-based cellular phones and pagers are 917 or 646. The boroughs (other than Manhattan) are 718.

# Getting Around New York City

The primary modes of transportation for New Yorkers, and the ones I strongly encourage you to use, are walking and public transportation. New York is one of the most walkable cities in the world—walking around New York is an activity in and of itself—and the best way to plan a day's itinerary is to include as much walking as you and your kids can handle. This means clustering your events together so that you can take, for example, a subway in the morning to cover your long-haul travel (say, the trip from your Midtown hotel to the Financial District) and then walk from nearby place to nearby place (from the Stock Exchange to the World Trade Center to the Statue of Liberty ferry) before taking public transportation to the next far-away attraction.

## Public Transportation

The New York City transit system is one of the most extensive and complex public transportation systems in the world, operating 24-hour-a-day bus and subway service throughout the five boroughs. New York City Transit has more buses than any other public agency in North America and the largest subway car fleet on the planet. Each day, more that six million people use New York City Transit—almost two billion customers annually.

### City Fact

New York City's subway system is the world's largest—714 miles of track, 469 stations, 6,089 subway cars. Subways run 24 hours a day and carry 1.2 billion passengers a year. If you added the number of stations in all other subway systems in America, it would total only 35 more than in New York City alone. The NYC public bus system has 300 routes and carries 600 million people a year (the most in the nation) on 4,200 buses.

Children under 6 years of age ride for free on the public buses and subways. Otherwise, full fare is $1.50, paid with a MetroCard, transit token, or $1.50 in exact change—coins only, no bills (exact change can be used on buses but not subways). This is the fare no matter how long or short your trip is (you could ride the A train 31 miles for that fare!).

*In the boroughs, some subways are still elevated.*

MetroCards are available on a pay-per-ride basis (with one free ride for every 10 purchased), or as unlimited-ride cards, in one-, seven-, or thirty-day denominations. Current prices are $4 for the unlimited ride, one-day "FunPass;" $17 for the seven-day unlimited pass; and $63 for the thirty-day unlimited pass. Unlimited MetroCards are valid for one person's use on all MTA buses and subways (though not on privately run express buses—you need a special MetroCard for that, which, as a visitor, you're not likely to want).

You can purchase MetroCards and tokens at all subway station booths, and many stations have installed automated MetroCard machines where you can purchase or refill Metro-Cards using cash, credit cards, or debit cards. There are also more than 3,500 MetroCard merchants (many newsstands, check-cashing centers, and currency-exchange bureaus sell them), so finding one will never be a problem. Note, however, that the one-day fun pass is not available at subway station booths—you can only get it from an outside vendor or from the machines. The pass is activated the first time you use it and is valid until 3:00 A.M. the next day.

Kids love riding in the first car of the train and looking out the front window as the underground tracks go flying by;

if you ride a bus, kids can look out the window at the passing pageant of New York City life. The subways and buses are safe, clean, and graffiti-free. Transfers are free between buses and (only if you use a MetroCard) between buses and subways. Ask for a transfer (you'll get a slip of paper with transfer points listed on the back) *when you get on the bus* if you're planning to switch to another bus en route. No transfer slip is needed (or given) for a transfer if you use a MetroCard; subway stations do not give out transfers.

You can get a free copy of a transit map at any subway station booth or at many hotels or visitor's centers. For further information, visit the Transit Authority on the Web at www.mta .nyc.ny.us/ or call the following numbers:

> The Transit Authority's Passenger Information Line:
> 718-330-1234 for people who speak English
> 718-330-4847 for people who do not speak English
>
> Long Island Rail Road
> 718-217-5477
>
> Metro-North Railroad
> 800-METRO-INFO outside NYC
> 212-532-4900 in NYC
>
> MTA Long Island Bus
> 516-766-6722

## Taxis

New York's cabs let everyone ride together for one price—the fare is per cab, not per person (up to a maximum of four adult passengers per cab, plus one small child in a lap). Taxis are widely available around Manhattan south of 96th Street (they're harder to come by north of 96th St. on the East Side and north

## Learning Tips

The New York City public transportation system is a wonderful topic for a school report. Did you know that:

ℚ The reason New York City buses don't accept paper money is because coins and tokens are removed from fare boxes by giant vacuum hoses. This process would shred bills.

ℚ By tradition New York's bus and subway fares have always been identical, but they strayed apart for 2 years (between 1948 and 1950) when the bus fare was 7 cents and the subway fare was 10.

ℚ The first woman subway-train conductor was I. A. Lilly, who began work on Brooklyn Rapid Transit Company cars on December 28, 1917.

ℚ Coin-operated subway turnstiles were first used on May 10, 1920. Before that, subway customers bought fare tickets. Since turnstiles could not handle two coins, tokens were introduced in 1953 when the fare went from a dime to 15 cents.

ℚ Bus maintenance involves more than 7,000 separate parts.

ℚ The subway uses enough power annually to light up the city of Buffalo for a year.

ℚ Jackie Gleason played a New York City bus operator on *The Honeymooners* TV series. In real life, his mother worked as a railroad clerk for 15 years. The Jackie Gleason Depot was once an elevated railcar inspection shop.

of 118th St.—Columbia University—on the West Side). All you have to do is stick out your hand and hail one (kids love hailing cabs since it gives them a good reason to jump up and down and yell). Outside of Manhattan it's a bit trickier, but you can usually hail a cab on the major thoroughfares in Queens and Brooklyn. Otherwise, north of 96th Street in Manhattan, and around Queens, Brooklyn, and the Bronx, there are other certified taxi services besides the yellow cabs for transportation, and you can usually hail one that is cruising.

How do you tell if a taxi is available for a pickup? If the *light on the roof is illuminated,* the cab is available. If it's dark, the cab is full. If the "off duty" sign is illuminated, it's not available for service.

Taxi fares are regulated, and drivers stick to the meter (rates are posted on the doors and inside every cab). The fare is $2.00 for the first ⅕ mile and 30 cents each additional ⅕ mile. There is a 50-cent surcharge after 8:00 P.M. (until 6:00 A.M.) and a rate of 20 cents per minute if standing. It is customary to tip 15–20 percent of the fare. If for some reason the driver doesn't start the meter, ask him to do so after he begins to drive.

**Be sure to buckle up! Everyone—kids and adults—should wear a seatbelt at all times!**

## Car-for-Hire Services

In the Arrival and Departure section in chapter 1, I listed several private car services. You can use these services not only for airport transportation, but also as an alternative to yellow cabs. Although you lose the convenience of being able to flag down a cab any time you want and the car-service cars are more expensive for short rides, the car-service cars do have their advantages: They tend to be larger and more comfortable than taxis; they will appear at a preset time and location (especially important during rush hour, when taxis are hard to come by); and they can be hired by the hour.

This last benefit is one that I encourage families to explore, especially if they're in New York to do a lot of shopping. You can hire a car from any of the major car services for approximately $25 per hour. Thus, for about $150, you can have the equivalent of a chauffeur for six hours—a full day of shopping or sightseeing. To be sure, this is a significant expense, but it's probably cheaper than the sum of all the taxis you'd have to take between 20 different stores, and you can leave all your packages in the trunk of the car while you shop, or even do a drop at your hotel.

## Driving and Parking

Driving around the congested arteries of New York City is difficult enough for a seasoned native, and it's something I strongly recommend that visitors not even try. If you come to New York City by car, I suggest you leave your car in your hotel's parking lot for the duration and rely on public transportation for your local motorized transit needs. Not only is driving around the City a hassle, it's also very difficult to park on the street, very expensive to park in a lot (even for a short time), and very expensive to pay for parking tickets (at least $35 a pop). Many cities have parking lots costing 50 cents an hour; in a New York parking lot you'll likely pay $20 or more for the same privilege.

If you do drive in New York City, remember that *right-turn-on-red is forbidden everywhere*, that you must be on extra careful lookout for pedestrians crossing against the traffic signals, and that failure to keep pace with the flow of traffic can be just as hazardous as driving at the typically fast pace favored by New York City drivers. Most streets, with the exception of a few avenues and major cross streets, are one way. Typically, in Manhattan, odd numbered streets run west, while even numbered streets run east, although there are some exceptions.

In most neighborhoods of Manhattan, there are on-street parking meters. Most cost 25 cents per 15 minutes. It's important, however, that you *read not only the meter instructions but also the posted signs nearby.* It may be that a certain meter is only valid during certain hours, so that the mere acceptance of your quarters is not a guarantee that you're complying with the parking laws.

In addition to parking lots and meters, there is free on-the-street parking in most of New York City's residential neighborhoods. Provided you leave no visible possessions in your car, it will likely be safe (auto theft and burglary are no longer major problems in New York's better neighborhoods). Still, you can't just find a parking space and leave your car there for a week. All of New York City engages in what is called alternate-side-of-the-street parking. To allow street cleaning machines to pass, each side of each block must be vacated at certain hours during the week. A given block might require that the left side be vacated from 8:00 A.M. until 11:00 A.M. on Tuesday and Thursday, and the right side during the same hours on Monday and Friday. Thus, you will have to observe and learn the parking signs no matter where you choose to park. And, of course, you may not park in front of a fire hydrant or in any other restricted space (indicated by signs or yellow lines painted on the curb).

## Transit Fun (Transportation as Activity)

I'm always amazed, and admittedly somewhat surprised, by how much kids enjoy transportation, something that so many of us adults view as mundane or even dread—a necessary evil of getting from one place to another. But when you think about it, it's really not surprising at all, and perhaps it's the adults who need the attitude adjustment. After all, what isn't great about whooshing through New York's maze of underground tunnels on the subway or riding high above the city streets on the Roosevelt Island Tramway? Listed below are favorites of city kids and visitors from around the globe.

*Trams and Ferries*

### *Roosevelt Island Tramway*  212-832-4543
### Second Avenue (at 60th St.)
### www.rioc.com

Unobtrusively situated on Second Avenue is the Tramway to Roosevelt Island. You could miss it if you aren't looking up or don't hear the clanking as the tram reaches the Manhattan platform. It's a great ride from one side to the other and well worth the cost of the fare (same as riding the bus or subway). You'll glide above Manhattan briefly before you slide high over the East River (parallel to the 59th Street Bridge) and dock on the other side. The views of the City are great, especially if you catch a clear day. There isn't much to do on the other side. Roosevelt Island is a small residential island that's officially part of Manhattan, though its slow pace and lack of vehicles create an environment that's worlds apart. You may want to take a stroll, but you won't be missing much if you just jump back onto the next tram and ride back to the City. Teens may want to check out the Sylvester Stallone movie *Nighthawks*, in which terrorists highjack the Tramway.

### *Staten Island Ferry*  718-815-BOAT
### www.si.web.com/transportation/dot.htm

It used to be that the ferry to Staten Island ("the boat" as commuters call it) cost 25 cents, but it is now free. That's right, it's

*The Staten
Island Ferry*

absolutely free, and
it's unequivocally one
of the best—and
most enjoyable—deals
going. You can ride the ferry any time, day or night, and there
are merits to both times. A daytime cruise affords views of the
Statue of Liberty and Ellis Island, the Manhattan skyline,
Governor's Island, the Brooklyn Bridge, the Verrazano Nar-
rows Bridge, cargo ships, tugboats, sailboats, and even the occasional river kayaker. At night, millions of twinkling stars
illuminate the skyline of Manhattan, the City That Never
Sleeps. Either way, try to spend at least part of the trip outside
on the deck (deck access is on the older ferries only) and keep
careful watch for Lady Liberty on the way out, because that's
when you'll get the best view. The ride takes about 30 minutes, and although you have to disembark at St. George, you
can line up nearby to get right back onto the return ferry. As
long as you've made the trip, though, you may also want to
consider some of the many wonderful activities that Staten Island has to offer (see chapter 5).

### Subway

The New York City subway system is an intricate maze of 714
miles of track, conveniently connecting the neighborhoods of
Manhattan and the boroughs of Brooklyn, Queens, and the
Bronx to one another (Staten Island has a similar system,
called Staten Island Rapid Transit). Within central Manhattan

and much of the boroughs, the trains run underground, while outside the more high-rise, urban areas of the City (yes, there are some), the trains run above the street on elevated tracks, as they do in Chicago. But beyond being an extremely convenient, efficient, and economical mode of transportation, the subway is also a great ride. Get on an express train during off-peak hours to get a feel for how fast the trains really move. You get the best of all rides at the helm of the train—head for the front car where the kids can stand at the window and watch the train barrel through the subway tunnel. The D, B, and Q trains even go across the East River on the Manhattan Bridge. I've never known a kid (or adult) who does not love this experience, and you may find that it takes more than one ride to exhaust the impulse! Be sure to hold on, though, because when those trains get going, they really move fast.

## Tours

Many people don't like the idea of a tour—they associate it with tour buses and large, impersonal groups following around a bored leader. But the fact of the matter is that New York City can be a lot more manageable when you explore with an experienced guide. And I think you'll find, with most of the operators below (I've only listed the best established of the bunch), that your tour is much more informative, distinctive, and interesting than you might have imagined.

### Walking Tours

Walking tours are a great way to familiarize yourself with New York City. It's important to remember, however, that most walking tours are inappropriate for children under the age of 10 because they last 90 minutes to 2 hours (and up to 4

## Top Ten New York City Movies

1. *Miracle on 34th Street*
2. *Stuart Little*
3. *Home Alone II*
4. *King Kong*
5. *Big*
6. *Superman*
7. *You've Got Mail*
8. *Splash*
9. *Working Girl*
10. *Crossing Delancey*

hours). During that time you will either be walking or standing on the street listening to history, stories, and details about the area. So unless you have a real trouper with a very good disposition and hearty attention span, you'll likely be better served by a hop-on, hop-off bus tour, a cruise, or some public transportation fun. In all instances, it's important to call in advance to confirm the schedule and book your spot.

### *Adventure on a Shoestring*    212-265-2663

Tours run all year round. Tours of neighborhoods and theme tours, mostly in Manhattan but a few in the boroughs too (Astoria, Little Odessa). Ask for the haunted tours and the Lights, Action, Camera tour (go to sites of filming). Guides request that only children 10 and older participate. "$5 for 37 years and will never run any higher," Howard Goldberg, owner and founder.

## Big Apple Greeter                  212-669-2896
www.bigapplegreeter.org

Tour New York City with a local. Volunteers, known as "Greeters," introduce you to New York City by taking you around the city on a tour in any of the five boroughs. You're matched up with a Greeter, who is chosen based on various factors—interests of the group, age group, neighborhood, and the like (it's you and the Greeter; no more than six total, please), and your tour will last two to four hours. These tours are completely free—it's our way of saying, "Welcome to New York!"

## Big Onion Walking Tours          212-439-1090
www.bigonion.com

Big Onion tours focus primarily on New York's ethnic neighborhoods and historic districts. All guides hold advanced degrees in American history and are licensed by the City of New York. Call or check the Web site for fees.

## Central Park Conservancy          212-397-3809
Trolley Tours of Central Park

A nice way to get an overview of Central Park before you hoof it, these trolley tours last 1½ hours and are offered end of April through end of October (no weekends or holidays). Free.

## Central Park Walking Tours        212-860-1370

Walking tours of Central Park with an emphasis on the historical aspects of the upper and lower regions of the park, flora, and fauna. Call for a schedule and fees.

## Joyce Gold History Tours of New York  212-242-5762
www.nyctours.com

A variety of walking tours offered all over the City. The fee is $12 per person, and children ages 9 and up are welcome. Check the Web site for the schedule of tours.

## Lower East Side                    888-VALUES 4
## Discount Shopping Tour

Every Sunday morning (April–December) at 11 A.M. the LES discount shopping tour departs from Katz's Deli (at the corner of Ludlow and East Houston Sts.). For decades the LES has been a destination for discount shoppers; now you too can get the inside scoop on this free tour. Most appropriate for teens.

## Rockefeller Center                 212-698-2950
## 30 Rockefeller Center

Grab a map in the lobby of 30 Rockefeller Center for a self-guided tour around the plaza and, while you're at it, don't forget to stop by the *Today* show, which films weekday mornings and often has special guests, like rock stars, who set up outside in the street.

*A bicycle built for four, Central Park*

| *Small Journeys, Inc.* | 212-874-7300 |

Custom tours ranging from four hours to six days. These tours are not for the budget conscious—the four-hour tours start at $240 (walking tour), and the coach tours (small, well-appointed vans) have the added cost of the vehicle (starts at about $260). The guides are all seasoned veterans.

## Sightseeing Bus Tours

You have many options for sightseeing tours in New York City, and I highly recommend a double-decker bus tour *upon arrival.* It's a good way to familiarize yourself and the family immediately with the City (if you don't do it right away, you'll likely find that you've already covered some of the same ground, and the kids may get bored). At the same time, kids will get a kick out of riding around on the top of a double-decker. Seemingly straight out of London, the buses tour throughout Manhattan, stopping at all of the favorite tourist attractions. You can stay on for the full ride, or hop on and off to see the sights. Be sure to call in advance for reservations and updated schedules.

| *Gray Line New York Tours* | 212-397-2600 |
| **Port Authority, Eighth Avenue** |
| **(at 42nd St.)** |
| **www.graylinenewyork.com** |

Double-decker sightseeing tours feature outside seating on the top deck. Narration is available in different languages—just ask.

*Harlem Spirituals*                          212-391-0900
Gospel and Jazz Tours
www.harlemspirituals.com

Tours range from Manhattan City tours (New York, New York) to multicultural tours of the boroughs (the Bronx, Brooklyn, A Full Day City Tour, Triboro Tour) and, perhaps the favorite of all, the Gospel and Jazz tours (Harlem on Sunday with Gospel Brunch). Call or check the Web site for details and prices.

*New York Apple Tours*                          212-944-9200
Eighth Avenue (at 53rd St.)

Tours of the boroughs and Harlem—in many languages. But be advised, these guys have recently been criticized in the press for violating safety regulations.

*New York Double Decker Tours/*                          212-967-6008
*Gateway Bus Tours*
Empire State Building (at Fifth Ave. and 34th St.)
www.nydecker.com

These buses run a two-hour narrated circuit (starting at the Empire State) and are of the hop-on, hop-off variety. Tickets are $12/$18 (downtown/full-city tour) for kids, $20/$30 for adults.

## Flightseeing and Cruises

Flightseeing and cruise tours are a great way to get a feel for the overall-island aspect of New York, and they're also loads of fun. Remember to book in advance and call for an updated schedule.

*Circle Line Sightseeing Cruises*　　212-563-3200
Pier 83 (West 42nd St. at Twelfth Ave.)
South Street Seaport Pier 16 (at Water St.)
www.circleline.com

Cruise the waters around Manhattan with trips lasting 30 minutes to 3 hours. Live music is offered seasonally on many cruises. Beast Speedboat rides are especially popular, and narration is available in many languages.

*Helicopter Flight Services*　　212-355-0801
Downtown Heliport (at Pier 6 and the East River)
www.heliny.com

Manhattan flightseeing tours and charters.

*Liberty Helicopters, Inc.*　　212-967-6464
www.libertyhelicopters.com

Flightseeing tours around Manhattan (departing from different locations).

*New York Waterway*　　800-533-3779
www.nywaterway.com

New York harbor sightseeing cruises. Free bus service between terminals and many Manhattan locations.

*The Spirit of New York*　　212-727-2789
Pier 61, Chelsea Piers
(at West 23rd St. and West Side Hwy.)
www.spiritcruises.com

Lunch, dinner, and jazz cruises around Manhattan departing from Manhattan and New Jersey. Cruising throughout the year.

| *Pioneer* | 212-748-8786 |
| --- | --- |
| Pier 16 (at Fulton and South Sts.) | |

Historical sailing cruises around New York harbor (through the South Street Seaport Museum). Cruising daily, May through September.

| *World Yacht Cruises* | 212-630-8100 |
| --- | --- |
| Pier 81 (West 41st St. | 800-498-4270 |
| at the Hudson River) | www.worldyacht.com |

Dinner and Sunday brunch on year-round cruises.

## Making the Trip Educational

Simply setting foot in New York City can be tremendously educational. Throughout this book you'll find highlighted Learning Tips, which are designed to make your children's trip as educational as possible—without the classroom and without the books (hey, learning can be fun!). I've selected subjects that will excite and engage kids of various ages. And if your children are taking time off from school for their trip to New York City, I've included plenty of subject ideas for reports and class presentations. Also, don't overlook the timeline in the introduction and all of the potential for learning in the museums. I guarantee you that New York City will engage your children and get their creative juices flowing.

## Babysitting

Just because you're taking a family vacation doesn't mean you can't have a night (or two) out on the town without your kids. After all, New York is a great town for adults, too. So, what's the best way to enjoy an evening out without having to worry that you're leaving your kids in bad company? You have two options: Bring a babysitter along with you, or find one in the City.

Obviously, if you have the means to go with the former, the extra hands will come in handy, not just for nights when you want to go out without the tykes, but also during the day when one child wants to do one thing, another wants to do something completely different, and your third child is in desperate need of a nap. Of course, even if you don't have three kids, the extra help can be a godsend, if only to have an extra pair of eyes to watch wandering kids, wait in line for tickets, help squelch tantrum uprisings—all the same things you deal with at home, only multiplied because you're on vacation, and there's so much stimulation. It's hard to keep up with it all.

But not everyone can or wants to have someone who isn't a family member along on the family vacation, so your other option is to go with the latter: Hire a babysitter in the City. This is surprisingly simple and safe. Countless agencies around town offer babysitting services. They're happy to send a sitter to your hotel while you enjoy an evening out or to lend an extra pair of hands during the day while you're exploring the town. I've selected the five most reputable companies, many of which have been in business for decades. Each of the following agencies does background checks on the sitters, and most retain their employees for years on end. And if you're feeling a little anxious, rest assured—not only are you selecting from the best of the best with this list, but also no babysitting business would last more than five minutes in New York City if it weren't offering reliable and safe sitters. It's not just tourists who use these services either— plenty of City residents use them too (my sister-in-law in Brooklyn included).

A word about cost: Though it may seem like the hourly wage of babysitters in New York is astronomical (it is), surprisingly, these agencies don't charge much above the going rate (which, in Manhattan, would be $10 per hour, even to the high-school kid down the block). In fact, some of them don't charge any more at all. It's also standard procedure to pay for the babysitter's transportation.

### A Choice Nanny                              212-246-KIDS

A Choice is an excellent resource not only for "grown-up" evenings out but also if you need an extra pair of hands while touring. Or, if you decide that the teens will be bored at the Children's Museum, you can split your group for an afternoon, sending the teens off with a nanny/companion (with or without one parent) while you enjoy the museum with the young ones. All of the personnel are fully screened with a thorough background investigation, and A Choice uses only highly qualified people with whom they are very familiar. Rates are $10 per hour and up.

### The Baby Sitters Guild, Inc.          212-682-0227
www.babysittersguild.com

Established in 1940, the Guild has been providing babysitters to New York's high-end hotels (like the Four Seasons and the Carlyle) for years. The staff is made up of professionals, including women with baby-nursing backgrounds, teachers, and history and art specialists, some of whom have been working for the Guild for as many as 30 years. Rates begin at $15 per hour, with a minimum of four hours (plus transportation). The Guild is licensed and bonded and is a member of the Better Business Bureau, the NY Chamber of Commerce, and NYCVB.

## Best Domestic 212-685-0351
www.bestdomestic.com

Recommended by 25 major publications (including the *New York Times, Daily News,* and *Town & Country*), Best Domestic offers 24-hour babysitting service. Within Manhattan, rates are $12 per hour (including transportation), with a 4-hour minimum. Office hours are 9 A.M.–4 P.M., Monday through Friday, so book in advance.

## Pinch Sitters 212-260-6005

If you need a weekend sitter, call a week in advance. Pinch Sitters provides service in Manhattan and "Brownstone Brooklyn" (the areas of Brooklyn near Manhattan). Office hours are 7 A.M.–5 P.M., Monday through Friday (summer hours are 9 A.M.–5 P.M.). Rates are $14 per hour with a four-hour minimum, and after 9 P.M. there is an additional charge for transportation.

## Town and Country 212-245-8400

Babysitters are available for daytime and evening support. T&C does thorough checks on all babysitters, all of whom must have long-term and recent references. For concerned parents, be assured that most of the nighttime sitters have been with T&C for many years. Rates are $12 and up, with a four-hour minimum (plus transportation, $3 during the day, $8 after 8 P.M.). Office hours are Monday through Friday, 9 A.M.–5 P.M. during the school year (so you have to plan ahead for weekends) and Monday through Thursday 9 A.M.–5 P.M., Friday 9 A.M.–1 P.M. during the summer.

# Getting to Know NYC Through Its
# Neighborhoods

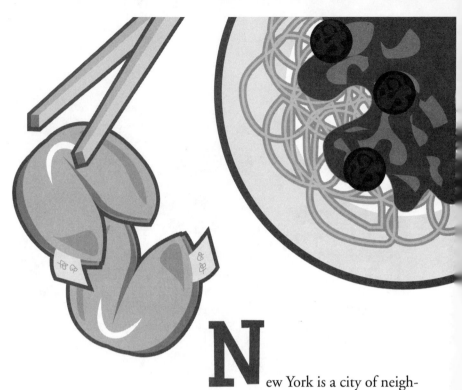

**N**ew York is a city of neighborhoods—fascinating, unique neighborhoods unequaled anywhere in the world for their diversity. Yet sadly, most tourists spend most of their time in New York's least interesting neighborhood: Midtown.

Yes, Midtown is home to the theaters and the theme restaurants, but nobody actually lives there. It's a place where New Yorkers go to work, and tourists come to visit, and therefore it has little to offer beyond the commercial. But if you walk just a few of blocks out of the Midtown core or, even better, ride the subway a bit, you'll be where New Yorkers actually live; where the restaurants are more diverse, the sights are more authentic, and the mere act of walking around is both educational and fun.

The first part of this chapter is an overview of the major ethnic neighborhoods in New York City, which are wonderful instructional and (for the majority of us who descend from immigrants) genealogical tools—if your kids are working on

*Street
performers at
Union Square*

term papers, here's
their topic. The sec-
ond part is a general
discussion of Manhat-
tan neighborhoods,
which will help you
navigate the many wonder-
ful, nontouristy neighborhoods of New York City.

In both instances, I encourage you to make the exploration of these neighborhoods the core around which you
build your New York vacation. If you use a neighborhood-
based approach to mastering New York City, your kids will
come away from the trip with a coherent set of memories
rather than a disjointed set of images. Not to mention that exploring the neighborhoods is free.

*Note:* Though the bulk of information on attractions
(chapter 5), dining (chapter 6), and shopping (chapter 7) is
elsewhere in this book, I have listed points of interest in each
neighborhood to enhance the experience of strolling through
them. But please use this chapter with the others, because
space constraints allow me to list only highlights here.

## Ethnic New York

We're a nation of immigrants. Unless you're a Native American, your family came here from somewhere else. An amazing

40 percent of people in the United States today can trace their ancestry to the 12 million immigrants who landed at Ellis Island, in New York harbor, between 1892 and 1954.

Today, New York remains a major world center of immigration. More than half the City's population was born in another country. This explains why New York's ethnic neighborhoods are such an important part of the City's fabric.

In this section, I've had to strike a balance: Hundreds of ethnicities are represented in New York, and I had to leave many out. I've chosen the neighborhoods that I think are most educational (whether or not you descend from that particular group), accessible, and vibrant. Consider this a starting point. If you come from an interesting background, you may want to hit the library and find your particular enclave—I assure you, it's here somewhere. For example, if you hop on the #7 train (nicknamed "The Orient Express" for the diversity of neighborhoods it serves) in Midtown Manhattan and head out to Queens, you'll pass through neighborhoods populated by Indians, Ecuadorians, Peruvians, Jamaicans, and Chinese—not to mention Shea Stadium, home of the Mets.

Looking at the neighborhood descriptions that follow, you'll discover I've emphasized food. This is because cuisine is the great diplomat—you need no special language skills or historical knowledge to appreciate good food. Children, especially the adventuresome ones, respond wonderfully to the infinite delights of ethnic food markets and restaurants. But remember, feeding your kids on unfamiliar cuisine can be stressful—so it never hurts to pack a few familiar snacks on these journeys.

## Chinatown

If you visit only one ethnic neighborhood during your New York vacation, it should be Chinatown. This is by far Manhat-

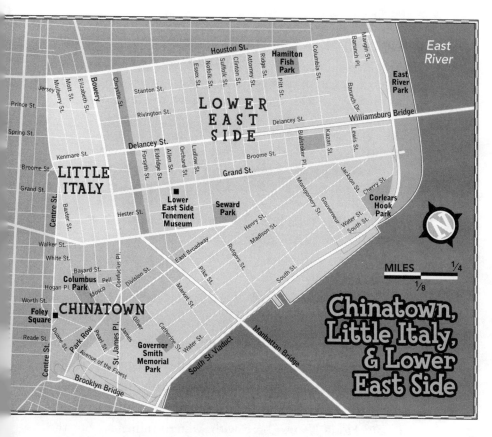

Chinatown, Little Italy, & Lower East Side

tan's most vibrant ethnic community. In most others, such as
Little Italy and the old Jewish Lower East Side, the immigrants arrived "fresh off the boat." Most started off poor, got
jobs, or started businesses and, as they worked their way out
of poverty, moved out of the old neighborhood to other parts
of the City or to nearby suburbs. As a result, their former
neighborhoods—once thriving cultural centers—are today
only shadows of their former selves. Not so in Chinatown,
where fresh waves of immigrants arrive daily, and the neighborhood's borders keep expanding.

Chinatown is getting cleaner, brighter, and admittedly a
bit more westernized. But don't fear, Manhattan's Chinatown

## Helpful Hint

Chinatown is *extremely* crowded and busy *all* the time, so keep an eye on your kids and tell them, before you arrive, that it's important to stay close. Pick a meeting place and write down the name and address for each child to keep in his or her pocket. If you do get separated, everyone will know where to meet. A good meeting place is the Chinatown Ice Cream Factory; it's right in the heart of Chinatown, and everyone will know it. It has a big banner hanging that is visible to anyone who can read (it also has a huge dragon on it for those who can't).

still has an excess of character, and the westernization of the establishments in the neighborhood comes from a blend of cultures East and West. For example, the new tea stores and pastry shops that are springing up around the neighborhood are similar to what you would find if you were to visit Singapore and Hong Kong—both with western influence, but the offspring of local Chinese (or Chinese investors from abroad).

Take the time to stroll through this neighborhood—you should allocate at least half a day. It's quite large, so don't expect to cover the whole area. I've suggested some places to visit (in the form of directions), but you don't have to do the whole route (especially if you're with small children) and, if you're feeling ambitious or adventuresome, deviate from the directions and strike out down side streets and explore a bit. There's something interesting around every corner.

Starting from the Canal Street subway station (#6 train), walk east along Canal crossing over Centre. On the far right corner of Centre, have a look outside at **Kong Kee Food.** If your children are interested, point out the extensive variety of tofu (fried, pressed, wet, strips), bean sprouts, and wet rice cakes. Are those rice cakes like the ones you see in the supermarket? These items are mainstays of the Chinese diet; an entire store is dedicated to selling them, and yet most westerners don't eat them regularly—unless they're eating in a Chinese restaurant.

As you walk across Canal, you'll see countless little shops, stalls, and outposts. This is a good place to pick up cheap tee shirts (usually three for $10), hats, watches, handbags, umbrellas, traditional Chinese-style clothing, trinkets, and souvenirs. Remember, here every price is negotiable.

Cross over the triangle at Walker Street (staying on Canal) and note the change from dry goods to fish vendors, fruit stalls, apothecaries, and restaurants. Observe the different kinds of fish (some children will enjoy this and will linger, others won't like it at all and will want to move on, but every child seems to be fascinated, one way or another, by the fish vendors).

### Learning Tip
Discuss how different cultures incorporate various foods into their diets and rituals. Throughout this chapter, we'll be examining shops where you can observe these distinctive cultural practices yourself.

At 200 Canal, walk into the **Kam Man Food** store (I'll point out another similar store later if you want to bypass this one). Take some time to wander around. Quite different from the Grand Union, Shop Rite, and Price Club at home, isn't it? How many kinds of dried scallops are there in the big glass jars? How many oysters and shrimp? Look at all of the hot, soy, and hoisin sauces. Imagine if you were Chinese and went to an American grocery store to pick out ketchup, how would you choose?

Just past Kam Man is the **Tai Pan Bakery.** This is a new addition to the Chinatown scene. It's extremely popular with locals and tourists and is a good place to cool down (or warm up) with a drink and a snack if the troops need a break.

*Educational note:* Have you noticed all of the people selling fruits, vegetables, and foods from carts and stalls? This, again, is a cultural difference and is the way many people sell their wares in China, rather than in stores. Where do people take all of their wares when the day is over? It's a different way of doing things.

Continue along Canal, turning right on Mott Street. This is the main drag in Chinatown. **Ten Ren Tea and Ginseng** (75 Mott St.) is an authentic Chinese tea and herb shop and is definitely worth a browse. Check out the giant teapot (in the corner behind the door) with the dragon etched into its side. How many cups of tea do you think that would hold?

In Chinatown, many of the stores don't have names in English or even street numbers, so it's up to you and your kids to pick and choose and discover great things on your own— you can't look them up in advance.

At Häagen Dazs, go left on Bayard Street. Have a peek at the **Chinatown Ice Cream Factory** (65 Bayard St., 212-

*Chinatown's very own McDonald's*

608-4170). Look at the flavors. A little different from Baskin-Robbins, isn't it? Lychee, green tea, and red bean are a few of the selections. Those feeling less bold may choose from some of the classics, too.

Continue along Bayard, going right on Bowery (or "the Bowery," as we say here). Check out the Chinese pagodalike **McDonald's,** with Ronald sitting out front on the bench. Everyone seems to love to have a picture taken with Ronald. This is a good place to use the bathroom if anyone needs it. Bathrooms in Chinatown are somewhat hard to come by.

*Side step:* If everyone is holding up well and doesn't mind a few extra blocks of walking, cross over the Bowery at the crosswalk at Doyers. You have just crossed into what is currently the most authentic part of Chinatown, where the locals shop and live, and where few tourists tread. This section is like an outpost of the neighborhood through which you've just been wandering. As Chinese immigrants flooded into Chinatown over the years, the supply of space could not meet demand, so little by little, the area has expanded to include parts of other shrinking downtown neighborhoods (like Little Italy and the Lower East Side). Take the right fork down Catherine Street, walking on the left. Cross East Broadway. This is a good place to buy fruit for snacks and veggies if you have cooking facilities.

Go right on Henry. Note how peaceful it is here in this residential area, compared with the hustle and bustle of the neighborhood. Turn right on Oliver; can you hear the birds chirping as you walk up the block? Cross over the big expanse of the Bowery to Citibank and turn right onto Mott. You are now at the opposite end of the street from which you started. If you didn't go into Kam Man (or your kids loved it), step into **Kam Kuo Food Corp.** This is where I like to stock up on

## Learning Tip

Look at the different kinds of fruits and vegetables. Chinese eggplant is actually a different shape and color than the kind you're probably used to buying. Do you think it tastes different? Chinese cucumbers are lighter green, have a different texture, and have ridges. Bok choy, Chinese apples, lychees, water chestnuts—look at the different produce. How do you think it tastes? Do you think it's eaten raw or cooked, or perhaps both?

my Chinese cooking ingredients. Hundreds of items are packed into the space, and if it's imported from the East (other than Japan), you'll likely find it here. Here again, you'll find little shops with souvenirs and trinkets. Kids love to browse through these stores, which are brimming with all sorts of interesting little items.

Take your first left down the hill onto Mosco. If there's no street sign, you'll know it by the long line: This corner is where the **"egg cake lady"** works her magic with two waffle iron–like contraptions. On this corner of Mosco and Mott, if you arrive after hours (whenever the batter runs out), all you'll see is a rust-colored, metal box with an accordionlike metal sheet that covers the "window." This nondescript outpost, which you would otherwise walk by without a second glance, is a hive of activity during business hours. When she's in action, the egg cake lady rolls up the accordion covering, heats up the irons, and ladles scoops of a secret batter into the contraptions. What, you wonder, could be so great that all of these people, from every walk of life, every race, religion, and country from around the globe, line up in the summer heat and the winter cold to get? Are they giving something away? No, what everyone is waiting for is a bag (or ten) of the hot-off-the-press egg cakes made from a secret family recipe. An egg cake is a sweet dessert (probably the only Chinese dessert item that I like—and I like all sweets) that is a cross between a cake, a cookie, and a waffle. Each egg cake is about the size of a quarter, and each order has ten cakes.

If you're with small kids, you might think twice before waiting on a long line. Then again, you could send them down the hill to **Columbus Park** and playground with one parent, while the other stands on line. It's a neat treat and also an interesting chance to talk to the other people—you'll find locals and other tourists alike line up for the unique treat. Would you believe the egg cake lady put several kids through college selling these confections at $1 per bag?

Walk to the bottom of the hill and turn right on Mulberry. If anyone needs a break, the playground across the street is a good place for it. There are plenty of benches, some swings, and lots of room to run around. At the corner of Bayard and Mulberry, in front of the building that houses the **Museum of Chinese in the Americas** (MoCA, 70 Mulberry St.), are a handful of old Chinese fortune tellers. I've never had my fortune read here (because I've never had it read anywhere), but if your kids are into that sort of thing, this is a great place to do it. Talk about authentic! To visit the tiny museum, step inside the old stone building, climb to the second floor, and go around the corner—there's MoCA. Though it is small, it is the "first full-time, professionally staffed museum dedicated to reclaiming, preserving, and interpreting the history and culture of Chinese and their descendants in the Western Hemisphere." The museum is free to children under 12; there is a $1 charge for students and $3 for adults.

Continue along Mulberry. Along the way, tell the kids to keep their eyes peeled for stacks of food items, like fifty-pound bags of rice, that are being unloaded and delivered around the neighborhood.

Finish up your walk around Chinatown at the intersection with Canal.

*Note:* Chinatown has grown so much in recent years that a second Chinatown has emerged in Flushing, Queens. It's also a fascinating neighborhood, but it's far less tourist-friendly than Manhattan's Chinatown (and correspondingly even more authentic). But if you're committed to studying New York Chinese culture to the fullest extent possible, you'll definitely want to check out Flushing's Chinatown, at the end of the #7 subway line.

## Little Italy

Italians started emigrating to America as early as the 1700s, but these weren't the Italians who settled in Little Italy—the early arrivals were aristocrats from northern Italy. It wasn't until the late 1800s that the big waves of Italians, mostly peasants from southern Italy, arrived and settled into what we now call Little Italy. Life was hard. The newcomers spoke no English, the area was crowded, and disease was rampant. As with many immigrant enclaves, new arrivals moved in with family members and friends from "the old country," and they worked hard to send money back home to Italy and to bring themselves out of poverty. These later Italian immigrants built, with their physical labor, muscle, and sweat, New York's highways and byways—they are largely responsible for digging the subway tunnels and the streets that we still use today.

As they worked and saved, the Italians of Little Italy wanted what all parents want: a better life for their children.

They started to move out of the neighborhood that was like an Italian village to the boroughs and the suburbs. What you see as you walk along Mulberry Street is really a shell of what the community once was. By the way, your kids may be familiar with Mulberry Street from Dr. Seuss's *And to Think I Saw It on Mulberry Street*. You may want to read that book with your family before or while visiting Little Italy. Now, only the elderly still live on these streets. And though some of the old businesses remain, it's mostly the restaurants and cafes that cater to the tourists and to the generations of Italian Americans looking for a weekend outing (from Staten Island, New Jersey, or Long Island) or a little nostalgia (but not nearly as good as Mama used to make).

Starting from the Canal Street subway station (#6), walk east along Canal to Mulberry Street, where you turn left. Or, from the Spring Street subway station (#6), walk east along Spring until you hit Mulberry; turn right onto Mulberry.

From either end of Mulberry Street, make your way up and down the street (or right down the middle on summer weekends, when they close the street to vehicular traffic). Mostly you'll see cafes and restaurants, some of which are more than one hundred years old (although the businesses may no longer be in their original locations). The waiters and maîtres d's will call out to you, inviting you to try their restaurant. There's a friendly air to the whole thing. No one is really being pushy, and it's all sort of like a game—you look at the menu; do you want to eat here or check out the next place? It's great, they'll tell you, and perfect for the kids. You walk on, and they go back to their conversation in Italian until the next group walks by.

All of the restaurants along Mulberry have very good lunch specials, often multiple courses for $5.95–$8.95. They also often offer early bird–type dinners—not fashionable, but perfect for kids (and very economical).

Some of my favorite stops on Mulberry are:

**Casa Bella,** on the corner of Mulberry and Hester (see chapter 6 for a full description).

**Café Roma** (385 Broome St.), where the Italians take their coffee. It's especially nice during the summer when the tables overflow out onto the sidewalk, and the atmosphere is so international you could almost swear you were sitting in . . . well, Italy might be a slight stretch, but you'd be surprised how close this comes.

**Ferrara's** (195 Grand St., follow the signboard) is an old neighborhood favorite. The prices are a bit steep, and the pastry is no better than anywhere else in the neighborhood (but that's still better than most other places—especially once you leave New York), but the people are friendly and eating a cannoli there is sort of like eating a piece of history.

**Italian Food Center** (186 Grand St.) is by far the best place in the city to get an Italian deli sandwich. If you step in here at lunchtime, you'll find the place packed to the gills. Many of the customers are daily regulars and walk almost half a mile from the courthouses to get a bite of the action. The benches out front are perfect for an impromptu picnic if the weather is good, and they also sell drinks so you can make it a one-stop shop.

**Alleva Ricotta and Mozzarella** (188 Grand St.), established 1 July 1896, is across the street. Stepping into this place is like stepping back in time. The mozzarella here is *so* good that I've been known to devour large hunks of the stuff shortly after exiting the store. If you have an adventurous bunch, a great meal is some "mozz" from Alleva and some fresh bread from (and a seat out front of) the Food Center. Those not in the mood for something new can always go with a sandwich while the others try the heavenly cheese.

If you're lucky enough to be visiting in September, you can catch the annual **San Gennaro Festival.** People from all over the tri-state area converge on Little Italy; Mulberry Street is closed to traffic; and the neighborhood is alive with lights, colorful decorations, food stands, games, and vendors. It's a real happening scene, but it does get extremely crowded, so if you're with young children, it's best to go before the biggest crowds arrive in the evening—try during the day or late afternoon.

## The Old Jewish Lower East Side (LES)

To see the old Jewish Lower East Side as it was back in its heyday will take a strong imagination. A little history will help to set the stage for this neighborhood that was once the heart of Jewish life and activity for poor Jewish immigrants during the second half of the nineteenth century. The first Jews settled en masse in this neighborhood in the 1850s, though interestingly enough, these were not the Jews who imparted their religious and cultural imprint upon this area. These Jews were of German ancestry and shared their tenements with the Irish and other Germans.

It was in the 1880s, when brutal pogroms broke out in Russia and Poland, that the religious Jews of Eastern Europe, fleeing for their lives, settled into life on the LES. This influx eventually established much of what remains of the neighborhood as we know it today. But at the time, the population was swelling by the thousands and the neighborhood was rife with disease. The streets were strewn with garbage, and large extended families of ten or more people would often share a single room to make their home. It was a difficult life for these newcomers. A few Jewish social aid groups were established by their brethren to help ease them into life in New York. People peddled and sold from pushcarts—everything from vegetables to rags—and made a living working long, backbreaking hours to better their lives. Just after the turn of the century, with more persecution in other countries, immigrant Jews again flooded into the LES. These Jews came from around the globe—more Russian Jews, Turkish Jews, and Greek Jews.

The LES was full of cultural life and activity, not to mention busting at the seams. By the 1920s, as people worked themselves out of poverty and made their fortunes, they looked to move out of the neighborhood to improved lives. The Jewish population has dwindled ever since, but some thriving businesses remain, established by these Jewish immigrants, that are still at the heart and soul of the neighborhood.

Take the F train to Delancey Street. When you exit, you'll be on one of the corners of Essex and Delancey. Walk west (away from the bridge) along Delancey until you reach Orchard Street. Turn right on Orchard.

The main artery of the LES is Orchard Street. This is where the action is and where, on weekends, the street is closed to vehicular traffic (from Delancey to East Houston). At one time, Jews from the neighborhood owned every storefront along this street, but times have changed and now only the most determined remain. What follows are my favorite LES destinations, which can be strung together in a walking tour of sorts—or you can stroll along Orchard Street and pick a few others to throw in too.

**Sosinsky & Sons** (143 Orchard St., between Delancey and Rivington) is a secret my husband begged me not to divulge. He always looks as though he's wearing a $100 shirt, but he actually pays $25 at Sosinsky's. This is one of the best places in the world to stock up on men's and teens' dress and casual shirts, bathrobes, and occasionally trousers and even shorts. In Old World fashion, you tell them your size (or they'll measure you) and out come boxes with shirts from which you can choose. The prices are incredible, and the stock often includes shirts from Burberry's, Gitman Brothers, and other top name brands. The best deals are on factory seconds. Shopping here is a blast—the mother-and-son sales team behind the counter is a great repository of LES oral history.

**Katz's Delicatessen** (205 East Houston St., corner of Orchard) has what some argue is the best pastrami and corned beef in the world. This is the only place in the City where they still carve the meat by hand. It's a real scene. Don't be intimidated by the shouting or the curt countermen. The hot dogs are also great (they make them themselves), as are the knishes and turkey sandwiches. The sandwich prices might seem steep, but each sandwich is easily big enough for two kids to share. Here you can go with waiter service or counter service. These days, with most of the old-time waiters gone (they used to tell great jokes), you're better off lining up at the counter. Don't be afraid to ask for what you want—nothing shocks them around here, but also don't be surprised if they say no.

**Russ & Daughters** (179 East Houston St.) is down the block from Katz's and well worth a browse, even if you're not interested in buying. What you'll find here is all of the best culinary representatives from your cousin's (or friend's) bar mitzvah, only done well—whitefish, pickled herring, and so many varieties of smoked salmon that it's actually an education. The dried fruit here is also excellent.

Back along Orchard, turn left onto Rivington to the newly sandblasted and renovated **Shaarey Shimoyim** (89 Rivington St.), the first American Rumanian Jewish Congregation. This building is absolutely exquisite. If you step inside

(Saturday is the Sabbath, so don't tour then), the *shamis* (the guardian of the synagogue) will happily answer your questions and show you around. Donations are welcome, and, as when touring any religious site, it's polite to make at least a token gesture.

**Economy Candy** (108 Rivington St.) is sure to be a hit with everyone. It is one of my all-time favorites, and I never get out of here without buying something, even if I'm there on the pretext of showing someone around. The candy selection is eye-popping, with standard favorites as well as more exotics both stocked.

**Essex Street Market** (120 Essex St., entrances at Delancey and just south of Rivington) is an interesting conglomeration of dry goods and foodstuffs. Mayor Fiorello La Guardia created this market in 1939 to keep the neighborhood's pushcart vendors from overwhelming the nearby streets. It's more a place to walk around than to buy, unless of course you're in the market for a carp. A good children's book (age 4–7) to read before departure is *The Carp in the Bathtub.* Everyone in the family will get a kick out of the story, and, when you're wandering through the market, you can look for the carp that often are kept in giant rubber "tubs." It always makes my day.

**Kossar's Bialys** (367 Grand St., just in from Essex) is across Delancey and left at Baskin-Robbins. This place is well worth a peek, even if you don't intend to buy anything, because there's a lot of activity with the dough and the ovens, and it's great to watch the bread come fresh out of the oven on the long wooden sticks (though if you've never had a bialy, it would be a grave mistake to miss the opportunity because they're by far the best in the City, and therefore most likely the best in the country).

People line up and down the block to buy **Guss's Pickles** (35 Essex St.). And if you've ever seen *Crossing Delancey* (a perfect movie for teen girls who are into love stories—with no skin whatsoever and great illustrations of the strains between the traditional and the modern lifestyles), you've seen Guss's. The pickles and other pickled stuff (tomatoes, sauerkraut, etc.) do not get better than this.

Several Judaica stores line Essex Street. At 19 Essex you'll find **Weinfeld's Skull Caps,** where I got the monogrammed yarmulkes for my wedding (they also sell bar mitzvah sets). The **Israel Gift Center** (23 Essex St.) is full of gift items that are expressive of Judaism, with religious items like yarmulkes and talises and adornments like jewelry. At 41 Essex is **Rabbi Eisenbach,** who carries everything from marriage contracts to eclectic menorahs and antique Judaica.

The **Lower East Side Tenement Museum** (97 Orchard St., tickets at 90 Orchard) is a great place to go to get a really good feel for what life was like on the LES decades ago. The museum is a recreation of tenement life. Special exhibits, tours, and children's programs are also offered.

The **Eldridge Street Synagogue** (12 Eldridge St.), one of many synagogues that used to line the streets of this neighborhood, is a reminder of the rich Jewish life that once characterized these streets. A National Historic Landmark, the synagogue was erected in 1886 and is undergoing a renovation to restore it to its former splendor.

## Brighton Beach (Little Odessa) and Coney Island

For Brighton Beach, take the D or Q train to Brighton Beach Avenue (BBA).

For Coney Island, take the D or F train to West 8th Street.

*Note:* These neighborhoods are in Brooklyn, and take about an hour to reach from Manhattan by subway.

Situated on the Atlantic Ocean, the seaside town of Brighton Beach (named for England's seaside resort of the same name) was, before the turn of the nineteenth century, a high-falutin' resort area for the wealthy. The neighborhood has since changed many times over. In its current incarnation, since the late 1980s, the neighborhood is locally referred to as "Little Odessa" on account of the first wave of Russian immigrants to settle in the area who were from . . . Odessa. Since then, other waves have included Russian immigrants from Kiev, Moscow, and elsewhere.

One of the most noticeable things about stepping down off the elevated train and onto the streets of Little Odessa is that no one is speaking English, and all of the signs are in English *and* Cyrillic. It's almost like taking a trip to old Russia, except that here, the food is bountiful and fresh. The main drag is Brighton Beach Avenue—this is where all of the action is: shopping, restaurants, and fruit stands. To get to the boardwalk, pick any side street and walk east, or just ask—everyone knows where it is.

To fill empty stomachs, the best destinations are **Primorski** (282 BBA, near 3rd, 718-891-3111), **Odessa** (1113 BBA, between 13th and 14th, 718-332-3223), and **National Restaurant** (273 BBA, between 2nd and 3rd, 718-646-1225). During the day, these large empty halls seem somewhat drab and tame, but the food is still good, prices are reasonable, and you'll get an authentic Brighton Beach dining experience. At night, they are transformed into nightclub restaurants where the meals are fixed price, the food comes piled on platters, the vodka flows, and the crowd, Russians of *all* ages and from all walks of life, comes to catch the entertainment and get down on the dance floor. The nightlife scene is great, but best for parents traveling with older teens (and if you do decide to hit one of these places at night, it's a good idea to arrange car service for your ride home).

**Caffe Cappuccino** (290 BBA, near 3rd St., 718-646-6297) is another good lunch spot. Far less cavernous and over-the-top than the aforementioned restaurants, Caffe Cappuccino serves Russian food (the blinis are great) and desserts, while Russian music videos run (at a reasonable, inoffensive volume) nonstop. This is a good place to try the Russian-style tea and sit with the locals (when it's crowded, people share tables).

The best Russian food market is **M & I International** (249 BBA, between 2nd and 3rd). It's always bustling, and you'll find that most of the shoppers are conversing with one another in Russian, but you'll have no problem if you want to order something or ask a question because the counter staff speaks English. All sorts of deli items are stocked in this two-level store, plus prepared takeout foods, breads, candies, kebabs, and canned goods. I like to come here just to browse and people-watch, but there's also plenty to buy if you need some snacks or food for a picnic on the beach.

After you've wandered and window-shopped past the stores selling thigh-high red leather boots and Russian videos, take a stroll on the boardwalk, which on a nice day is one of the most pleasant places to be. At one end (the end you're at in Brighton Beach), you'll find Russian boardwalk cafes, old folks sitting out on benches, families playing on the beach. On the other end is Coney Island and the New York Aquarium.

The walk down the boardwalk toward Coney Island is an interesting study in the varied cultures of the area. In Brighton Beach, you'll see mostly Russians and people of European descent. As you get farther away from Little Odessa and closer to the activity of Coney Island, you'll see more people of Hispanic descent.

If you're all the way out here anyway, you certainly should check out the **New York Aquarium** (Surf Ave. at 8th St. West, or enter from the boardwalk, 212-265-FISH) and the old **Coney Island Amusement Park.** The amusement park is a bit seedy by modern standards, but it's superauthentic, and your kids will gawk at the now-defunct hulk of the old Cyclone wooden roller coaster. Be sure to grab a frankfurter at the world-famous original **Nathan's** (Surf Ave., corner of Stillwell) and wander over to the wonderful **Philip's Candy** (1237 Surf Ave., next door to Nathan's).

For a break, stop by the huge playground (with foam rubber in appropriate places to avoid injuries) just up from the boardwalk restaurants, where neighborhood children play, basketball and handball games coexist side by side, and the older generation sits on nearby benches and watches the world go by. The beach here gets crowded, but the sand is clean (though I wouldn't recommend swimming in the ocean), and it's a nice place to take a break. There are also a few play areas set up on the beach by the boardwalk, perfect for injury-free play.

## Greek Astoria

N train to Ditmars Boulevard.

At the tail end of the 1920s, the Greeks started settling in Astoria, Queens, a neighborhood just across the East River from Manhattan that's also known locally as Little Athens. The Greek population in the neighborhood grew as families who were already settled brought relatives to America and labor bosses would arrange and pay for passage for those willing to work off their ticket. This neighborhood, like the others, has been through ebbs and flows, but unlike many of the others (except Chinatown), Astoria is still growing.

Astoria is full of Greek fish restaurants (the best around), cafes, and pastry shops—the likes of which you've probably never seen anywhere else. Take a stroll through the neighborhood, whose main drags are 31st Street (under the elevated subway) and Ditmars Boulevard. Walking here is like taking a walk through Athens (though a little less polluted and crowded). Don't be surprised if you hear more Greek spoken than English.

As in many ethnic neighborhoods, eating is a favorite pastime here. I've enjoyed many a meal and stroll followed by dessert in this neighborhood—it's truly a lovely way to spend an afternoon or evening. Even better, though, for children who are not up to an extended meal, these same restaurants, where some patrons linger, are extremely welcoming of families and will get the food on the table quickly. Noise and energy are already plentiful, lest you are worried that your crowd might offend anyone.

**Elias Corner** (24-02 31st St. at 24th Ave., 718-932-1510) is where I send people for fish, and **Telly's Taverna** (28-13 23rd Ave., between 28th and 29th Sts., 718-728-9056) is great for its wide-ranging Greek menu. In summer they have a nice "garden" café out back. **Christos Hasapo-Taverna** (41-08 23rd Ave., between 41st and 42nd Sts., 718-726-5195) is the traditional combination of Greek restaurant (steak) and butcher that rivals Manhattan steakhouses—and with better prices to boot. **Lefkos Pyrgos** (22-85 31st St.) and **Galaxy** (3722 Ditmars Blvd.) are my picks for dessert and coffee.

Along with eating your way through the neighborhood, you should stop to have a look at **Saint Demetrios Church**

(31st St. and 31st Dr.). Saint Demetrios has the largest Greek Orthodox congregation outside of Athens. The building itself is an extremely impressive edifice and well worth the visit.

## Arthur Avenue—Little Italy in the Bronx

Take the C, D, or #4 subway to Fordham Road, then transfer to the eastbound BX12 bus across the street from the station; get off at the Arthur Avenue stop. Be sure to use a MetroCard, so the transfer will be free.

Manhattanites hate to admit it, but today the most authentic Italian neighborhood in America is up north—in the Bronx, where Arthur Avenue meets East 187th Street. This Italian-American enclave is home to scores of the nation's finest and most authentic Italian shops.

I wouldn't necessarily advocate a pilgrimage to Arthur Avenue on its own merits (it's quite a haul from Manhattan), but the neighborhood happens to be just a hop, skip, and a jump from two of New York's absolute best tourist attractions: The Bronx Zoo and the New York Botanical Gardens (see chapter 5 for details). So if you're planning a day around these two locations, you definitely owe yourself a jaunt to Arthur Avenue.

At **Teitel Brothers Wholesale Grocery** (2372 Arthur Ave., 718-733-9400), you'll find an incredible selection of artisanal Italian food products: gallon jugs of olive oil from Italy's Lucca region (the best in the world), whole wheels of three-year-aged Parmigiano Reggiano cheese (they'll cut you a smaller piece, don't worry), and all the dry goods you'd need to open an Italian restaurant, with discounts that put Balducci's high Manhattan prices to shame.

As you open the door to the tiny **Calabria Pork Store** (2338 Arthur Ave., 718-367-5145), the pungent smell of cured meat and spices smacks you in the face. It's dark inside because the thousands of handmade sausages hanging from the ceiling (each tagged with a code to indicate its age) obscure the light fixtures. Once you've tasted Calabria's silken sopressata, you'll never be satisfied with mass-produced versions.

Like rubbernecking motorists gaping at a wreck, even herbivores can't resist checking out **Biancardi's** (2350 Arthur Ave., 718-733-4058) provocative window display. Poor little bunny, poor little lamb, strung up in the window, fur and all. But this is perhaps the best place in town to purchase impeccably fresh game, beef, lamb, and pork. Call ahead and they can get you just about anything. If you're with young children who might be upset by this display, you might want to walk past quickly—or take this opportunity to explain to them about the food chain.

For a quick pick-me-up, stop by **Madonia Brothers** (2348 Arthur Ave., 718-295-5573) for a hand-filled cannoli. Once you've chosen a hollow pastry shell from the display case, the teenage girl behind the counter will expertly squeeze the sweet ricotta filling into it. This is how cannolis were meant to be. Then wander right across the street to **Enzo's Café** (2239 Arthur Ave., no phone), where the standard for espresso is just as high—it's never bitter and always with a paper-thin layer of foamy crema on top.

The first time you visit the **Terranova Bakery** (691 East 187th St., 718-367-6985), Mr. Terranova himself might give you a tour of the enormous coal-fired ovens. On your second visit, you're a regular, and on your third, you'll likely be greeted with kisses. The specialty of the house is a totally addictive, ring-shaped sausage bread. You can get regular Italian loaves, too, and I slightly prefer Terranova's crust to that of the very similar, competing **Addeo Bakers** (Addeo Bakers, 535 East 187th St., no phone) around the corner.

Perhaps the warmest welcome on Arthur Avenue is at **Borgatti's Ravioli and Egg Noodles** (632 East 187th St., 718-367-3799), one of the nation's last remaining manufacturers of fresh, handmade pasta. The salespeople (all family members) cut sheets of pasta to order on the hand-turned press; you can specify whatever width you want for the noodles. Large, fresh ravioli, bursting with excellent ricotta cheese, are the house specialty, and Uncle Larry or one of his nieces will gladly spend all day discussing the finer points of boiling water.

A special treat for wine-aficionado parents: **Mount Carmel Wines & Spirits** (612 East 187th St., 718-367-7833, www.mountcarmelwine.com) is one of America's best-kept wine secrets. This veritable museum of wine has, without question, the best and most comprehensive selection of Italian wines in America. The 1990 Brunello di Montalcinos are all but gone from Manhattan stores, but here you'll find eight of them. The sales help is phenomenal—everybody in the store is fanatical about Italian wine.

After all that shopping and schlepping, your biggest decision of the day remains: Where to have lunch? For something portable, my favorite is **Mike's Deli** (2344 Arthur Ave., 718-295-5033, www.arthuravenue.com) in the Arthur Avenue Retail Market (the retail market is also where you'll find fresh produce and interesting vendors). It's hard to choose between the hot sausage-and-pepper hero and the Big Mike Combo (with mortadella, ham, salami, capicollo, and provolone), so you may as well get both. Another good bet is **Full Moon Pizzeria** (602 East 187th St., 718-584-3451), for a traditional New York slice. But for a sit-down meal, the clear choice is **Dominick's** (2335 Arthur Ave., 718-733-2807), where you'll get a hearty, family-style, no-menu, eat-what-they-cook-that-day, sit-down-at-the-big-long-table-with-strangers feast.

*A word to the wise:* If at all possible, visit Arthur Avenue midweek, when proprietors are far less harried.

# Guide to Manhattan Neighborhoods

The following are brief descriptions of the most important residential areas of Manhattan, which will help orient your family in your travels around the City. For each neighborhood, I've included a list of points of interest that I think characterize the area. Whether you're visiting a neighborhood for a grand tour or just for one specific attraction, store, or restaurant, it's nice to get a general feel for the area before you set out.

## Upper East Side

The Upper East Side is one of the two major uptown residential areas of interest to tourists (the other one is the Upper West Side). It's a huge swath of land and contains many sub-neighborhoods.

I live in Carnegie Hill, a small slice of the Upper East Side that runs from 86th to 96th Streets, and from Fifth to Lexington Avenues. It's an area characterized by sidewalk cafes (you'll see my neighbors Paul Newman and Joanne Woodward, as well as Ralph Lauren, Calvin Klein, and Michael J. Fox, at the nearby restaurants), a family atmosphere, and proximity to Central Park.

The rest of the Upper East Side is also quiet and houses some of the wealthiest people in America. Moving east from Carnegie Hill, there's Yorkville, which used to be a German neighborhood (you'll still find a few German shops along First Ave., near 86th St.) but is now home to numerous high-rise apartment buildings where a growing number of young professionals live. This is one of the best areas for purchasing kids' clothing and finding an economical family meal.

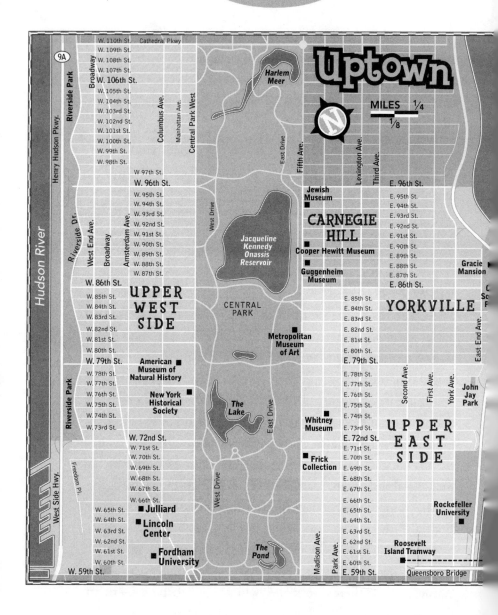

South of 86th Street lies the Upper East Side proper, where you'll find many of New York's wealthiest families along Park Avenue, Fifth Avenue, and East End Avenue. The Upper East Side is very safe and is therefore perfect for wandering around with your family, even at night.

Finally, across the river from the Upper East Side is the unusual area of Roosevelt Island. An island in the middle of the East River, Roosevelt Island is reached by the famed Roosevelt Island Tramway (a cable car running from Manhattan), which kids absolutely love to ride.

*Points of Interest*

@ Madison Avenue Shopping District (Barney's, Polo, and most designer boutiques)

@ Central Park (Conservatory Garden, Reservoir, Metropolitan Museum, Zoo)

@ Museum Mile (Metropolitan Museum of Art, Guggenheim, Cooper-Hewitt, Jewish Museum, International Center of Photography, and others)

@ Gracie Mansion (Mayor's residence)

@ Numerous distinguished private clubs (Harmonie Club, Metropolitan Club, Lotus Club)

@ Temple Emanu-El (largest—bigger than St. Patrick's Cathedral—and oldest Reform Jewish congregation) 1 East 65th Street at Fifth Avenue (212-744-1400)

@ Asia Society (art collection assembled by John D. Rockefeller), 725 Park Avenue at 70th Street (212-288-6400)

@ Frank E. Campbell Funeral Chapel (most prestigious in the world; James Cagney, John Lennon, Mae West, and Tennessee Williams as "customers"), 1076 Madison Avenue at 81st Street (212-288-3500)

@ 92nd Street Y (major Jewish cultural and community center), 1395 Lexington Avenue at 92nd Street (212-427-6000)

@ Synod of Bishops of the Russian Orthodox Church Outside Russia (dramatic 1917 Georgian mansion, now a cathedral), 75 East 93rd Street, between Park and Madison Avenues (212-534-1601)

@ Islamic Center of New York (New York's first major mosque, designed by Skidmore, Owings & Merrill), 1711 Third Avenue at 96th Street (212-722-5234)

## Upper West Side

If you stood at the corner of 68th Street and Columbus Avenue (near where my husband grew up) in 1970 and then traveled via time machine to the same corner in the year 2000, you'd assume your time machine had taken you to the wrong place. What was basically a slum in 1970 is now the site of one of New York's most luxurious new apartment buildings (which also house the exclusive Reebok Sports Club and the Sony IMAX theater). The transformation of the Upper West Side, triggered by the construction of Lincoln Center in the 1960s and bolstered by frantic luxury high-rise construction in the 1980s and 1990s, has made this neighborhood one of the world's great urban reclamation stories.

The Lincoln Square area is the southernmost part of the Upper West Side and has most of the more obvious tourist attractions (Lincoln Center, including the ballet). The rest of the Upper West Side is very residential and, as a result, has wonderful shops, family restaurants, and food markets.

The neighborhood is also home to many young modern Orthodox Jews who are attracted by the Lincoln Square Synagogue and an abundance of kosher restaurants in the West 70s and 90s and the presence of many other members of their faith.

### Points of Interest

@ Central Park (Reservoir, Strawberry Fields, Sheep Meadow, Tavern on the Green)

@ Lincoln Center (New York's major center of the performing arts, including the Metropolitan Opera House, Avery
Fisher Hall, and New York State Theater)

@ Christ and St. Stephen's Church (uncharacteristically
rural church in the middle of a developed city block),
120 West 69th Street at Columbus Avenue and Broadway (212-787-2755)

@ Lincoln Square Synagogue (1970 Hausman and Rosen-
berg building, now a leader of the Modern Orthodox
movement), 200 Amsterdam Avenue at 69th Street (212-
874-6100)

@ Beacon Theater (gorgeous old 2,700-seat theater used for
a variety of performances), 2124 Broadway at 75th Street
(212-496-7070)

@ New-York Historical Society (spelled with a hyphen, it's
one of the best American collections around), 170 Central Park West at 76th and 77th Streets (212-873-3400)

@ American Museum of Natural History (the premier natural history museum and research institute, now with a
dramatic new planetarium), Central Park West at 79th
Street (212-769-5000)

## West of Midtown: Clinton and Chelsea

Chelsea is in many ways like other young, affluent areas of
New York. You'll see attractive couples out for the evening or
just walking hand-in-hand down the street. But in Chelsea,
the couples are often men.

New York has a very substantial gay population, and the
City is historically very tolerant of gays—it would be exceptionally poor form to speak homophobically in Manhattan. And although Chelsea is probably the most visibly gay neighborhood

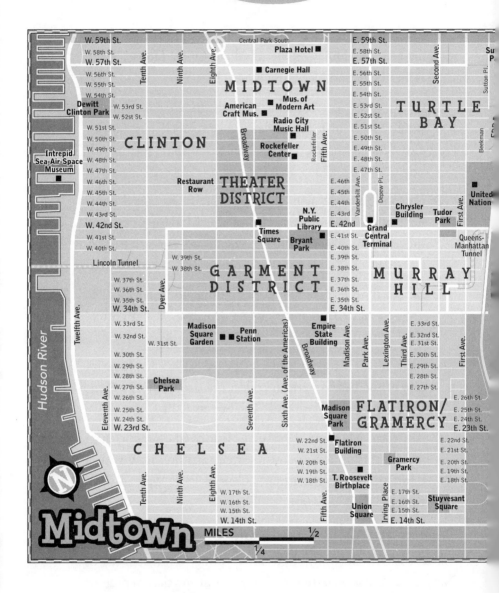

in New York right now, it is also home to many, many happily coexisting people of all stripes and preferences.

Chelsea is near the Garment Center and encompasses the Flower District. The streets feel open, and there are few high-rise buildings. An array of new stores has opened along Sixth Avenue in recent years; restaurants and shops now line Eighth

Avenue; and the western part of Chelsea contains several up-and-coming art galleries. The Chelsea Piers athletic and recreation complex has completed the neighborhood, providing a facility unlike any other in the world.

North of Chelsea is what is now called Clinton—and used to be called Hell's Kitchen. In the early 1990s, a few prestigious corporations and law firms, tired of paying Midtown rents, struck out into Midtown West and relocated their corporate headquarters into this neighborhood, which was formerly made up of porn shops, slums, and some artists' residences (mostly actors and dancers). The presence of these large companies spurred economic growth, and in just the past three or four years this neighborhood has really turned the corner. It's now one of the best places to dine in all New York, especially given its proximity to Midtown and the theaters.

### Points of Interest

- Broadway Theater District (most of the major theaters are here)

- Flower district (wholesale and retail), Avenue of the Americas from 27th to 30th Streets

- Antiques (this is a major center of antiques in New York City), Ninth Avenue from 20th to 22nd Streets

- Chelsea Piers (gigantic sports and recreation complex), West Street from 17th to 23rd Streets (212-336-6666)

- Javits Center (New York's largest convention center), 655 West 34th Street at Eleventh and Twelfth Avenues (212-216-2000)

- Port Authority (the main bus terminal for New York), Eighth and Ninth Avenues from 40th to 42nd Streets (212-564-8484)

@ Intrepid Sea-Air-Space Museum (beautifully preserved World War II aircraft carrier), 46th Street and Twelfth Avenue (212-245-0072)

## East of Midtown: Turtle Bay, Murray Hill, Gramercy

To the east and south of Midtown Manhattan you'll find a mixed bag of neighborhoods, each with its own personality and evocative name like Turtle Bay, Murray Hill, and Gramercy.

Murray Hill and Turtle Bay are genteel and affluent and are very near the United Nations. Thus, many consulates are nearby, and an international flavor is in the air.

The focal point of Gramercy Park is a beautiful private park (the only one in the City) open only to residents of buildings in the neighborhood (and those staying in the Gramercy Park Hotel, or lucky enough to have friends living on the park). It's a quiet neighborhood because the park cuts up the streets and prevents most through-traffic. The park is surrounded by nineteenth-century townhouses, and there are many great places to eat in this area.

### Points of Interest

@ Union Square Park (including the Union Square Green-market), from 14th to 17th Streets bounded by Union Square East and Union Square West

@ Theodore Roosevelt Birthplace (one of New York's most charming attractions), 28 East 20th Street (212-260-1616)

@ Flatiron Building (called "flatiron" for its shape; this was New York's first self-sufficient skyscraper), 175 Fifth Avenue at 22nd and 23rd Streets

@ Pierpont Morgan Library (America's finest collection of medieval and renaissance manuscripts, and then some),

29 East 36th Street at Park and Madison Avenues (212-685-0610)

## Greenwich Village and SoHo

The areas of Greenwich Village (pronounced "greh-nitch")
and SoHo (an abbreviation for South of Houston St.) are two
of the City's most perpetually hip neighborhoods.

The center of Greenwich Village (called the West Village
by some), physically and spiritually, is New York University and
nearby Washington Square Park. The residential streets in the

*Hanging out in Washington Square Park*

center of the Village are elegant and full of attractive old brick townhouses, plus some apartment buildings. If you're thinking funky and unusual, you've got the wrong image—many of the streets in the Village are as dignified as they come.

SoHo, home to the greatest concentration of galleries in the City, is another artists' neighborhood that has undergone extensive gentrification. SoHo is a great and fun area, with incredible restaurants and a bustling nightlife.

The gentrification of SoHo has, as is often the case, caused an outward push. Now, the nearby areas of NoHo (North of Houston), Little Italy (which is no longer home to many Italians), and Nolita (a relatively new designation meaning North of Little Italy) are fast becoming shopping and dining destinations as well.

### Points of Interest

- Numerous playhouses, music venues, galleries, and boutiques

- Washington Square Park (largest public space downtown, the focal point being the large Memorial Arch), from West 4th Street to Waverly Place and University Place to MacDougal Street

@ New York University (major institution of higher learning and a defining voice in the neighborhood), from West 3rd Street to Waverly Place and Mercer Street to La Guardia Place (212-998-4636)

@ Film Forum (New York's premier art house movie theater), 209 West Houston Street at Sixth Avenue and Varick Street (212-627-2035)

## East Village

The designation "East Village" was created to bestow some legitimacy on this formerly run-down part of the Lower East Side. And it worked. The neighborhood is now safe and fun, with bargain stores and restaurants galore and a funky, antiestablishment population. As you walk south from the East Village, you'll enter Chinatown and the Lower East Side—discussed earlier.

### Points of Interest

@ Major center of alternative culture, including music and boutiques

@ Saint Mark's Place (the most visible representation of East Village culture), from Avenue A to Third Avenue

@ Cooper Union (famous private college that is the oldest steel-beam building in America), 7 East 7th Street at Fourth Avenue (212-353-4100)

## TriBeCa and Lower Manhattan

TriBeCa (an abbreviation for Triangle below Canal Street), with its large-windowed cast-iron buildings, now looks more like SoHo than like the industrial neighborhood it once was. The warehouses and small factories are being reborn as residential

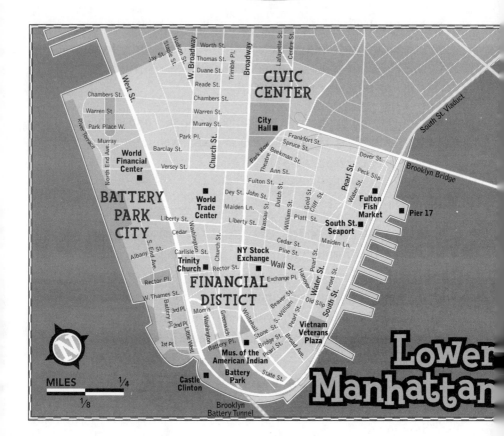

apartments—expensive ones. The restaurant situation is excellent, spurred by low rent in the 1980s and now sustained by a desirable clientele despite climbing rents. Not as artsy as SoHo, TriBeCa nonetheless is exceptionally active at all hours, boasts an attractive park (Duane Park), a bike path along the Hudson River, a fair number of clothing and design shops, plus great galleries.

    South and east of TriBeCa is lower Manhattan, where you'll find Wall Street and all the other downtown and Financial District attractions.

*The World Trade
Center Plaza*

### Points of Interest

- Many artsy and ethnic attractions in TriBeCa

- Center of the nation's financial markets (New York Stock Exchange, World Trade Center, World Financial Center, etc.)

- Site of many historic landmarks (Brooklyn Bridge, Trinity Church, Woolworth Building)

- Headquarters of government (City Hall, Municipal Building, Federal Building) and courts (State and Federal)

- Departure point for ferries to Statue of Liberty and Ellis Island

- Fraunces Tavern (where Washington said farewell to his officers), 54 Pearl Street at Broad Street

- South Street Seaport and Pier 17 (shopping, dining, and outdoor events)

CHAPTER

4

Where to Stay

# Hotels

Map shows highlights only. See chapter text for more listings.

Theres no nice way to say it: Hotels in New York City are expensive.

When visiting New York, your accommodations will most likely consume the bulk of your vacation budget. In most of America, you can expect to find a clean, spacious, modern hotel room for between $50 and $100 per night. In New York, such a room is virtually unheard of—it would constitute the off-season bargain *par excellence*. The price range for New York hotel rooms begins at expensive (for very basic rooms in out-of-the-way locations, for which you can expect to pay in excess of $100 a night) and climbs to mind-boggling (at the better Midtown hotels, where $400 might buy you the cheapest room on a slow night). What is considered cheap for a hotel room by New York standards might buy you one of the finest rooms in any other city in the country.

New York hotel rooms, like New York apartments, are also often quite small—a particular challenge for families. This should come as no surprise: Manhattan is a tiny island encompassing some of the most expensive real estate in the world, and almost every inch of it is covered either with buildings or planned parkland. But if you think hotel prices per square foot are bad, you should see what most of us New Yorkers pay per month in rent!

Thankfully, although accommodations in New York City are still outrageously expensive by national standards, recent years have brought a hotel renaissance of sorts. Rising tourism has spurred new construction as well as renovation, thus improving availability of quality hotel rooms across the price spectrum. And with safety rapidly improving all over town, it's now possible for a family to stay worry-free in neighborhoods that, just a few years ago, I wouldn't have been able to recommend with a clear conscience.

In preparing the listings in this chapter, I've inspected literally hundreds of New York City hotels to ferret out the winners in every price category. I've also sought out alternative forms of accommodation, such as short-term apartment stays, which are discussed at the end of this chapter. As with all aspects of city life, there truly is something for everyone.

# Getting the Most from New York City's Hotels

If I could offer just one piece of advice to travelers in search of hotel accommodations in New York City it would be: Flexibility is key. Once you've locked yourself in to a particular location or species of accommodation, your options rapidly diminish. Instead, don't be afraid to play outside the box. This is especially true when considering neighborhoods. All too often tourists think they want to stay in Midtown, because that's where the Broadway theaters and theme restaurants are.

## Helpful Hints

How to get the most out of your New York hotel dollar:

- Look for a room configuration that suits your needs. For example, if you're traveling with one or two kids, you can go with a junior suite (with a double pull out couch) instead of two rooms—a move that could save you hundreds of dollars over the course of a few days.

- Pick places where kids stay free. Many hotels will even add a rollaway bed to your room for a nominal charge.

- Look for included breakfast. The value of a free breakfast cannot be overstated: It saves you not only money but also time. And be sure to fill up before you set out for the day.

- Newer is better. Though old hotels can be charming, your best bets when traveling with kids tend to be hotels that are either new (larger rooms; better floor plans) or newly renovated (bright and clean).

- Look for package deals. Many hotels offer theater packages and other incentives, especially at slow times of year. But be sure you carefully evaluate such packages—there's no point in paying for what you don't want or need.

- Inquire about discounts. Many New York hotels accept AAA, corporate rates, and discounts in connection with professional associations or credit card companies. Be sure you ask when you reserve (don't hesitate just to ask outright, "Do you offer any discounts?"), because even a 5 to 10 percent discount can add up.

- Ask lots of questions. Before you book, establish with great specificity what a hotel does and doesn't offer. Don't just take "free breakfast" for an answer—ask what exactly the breakfast includes. If a hotel says it's "kid-friendly," ask what that specifically means. Make sure you get every last bit of information about the hotel's telephone billing procedures—phone calls at outrageous hotel rates can really add up. The more you know, the better your stay will ultimately be.

But it's also where you'll pay the most for a room. Remember, Manhattan is tiny. Even if you stay all the way downtown in the Financial District (perhaps the City's most underutilized hotel neighborhood, especially on weekends when the business travelers disappear), you'll only be twenty minutes from Midtown by subway.

Flexibility in your choice of dates is also a big help. Sometimes, it's the seemingly random events (especially business conventions) that throw the hotel rates out of whack. Sometimes, shifting your vacation by just a couple of days on either end can slash your room rates. And remember, New York City hotels are almost always cheaper on weekends.

## How to Use This Chapter

I've arranged this chapter according to the following price ranges for one night in a standard room:

$     $150 and under
$$     $150–$275
$$$     $275–$400
$$$$     More than $400

I've also indicated the neighborhood, using the following abbreviations:

BR: Brooklyn        BX: Bronx
CH: Chelsea        CT: Chinatown
EV: East Village        FD: Financial District
GD: Garment District        GP: Gramercy Park/Flatiron
GV: Greenwich Village        LES: Lower East Side
LI: Little Italy        MT: Midtown
MTE: Midtown East        MTW: Midtown West
Q: Queens        SH: SoHo

| SI: Staten Island | TBC: TriBeCa |
| TD: Theater District | TS: Times Square |
| UES: Upper East Side | US: Union Square |
| UWS: Upper West Side | WV: West Village |

A ★ indicates a particularly noteworthy hotel within its price range in that it is more kid-friendly or provides better value than its similarly priced competitors.

I've organized this chapter by price range rather than by neighborhood, because price is probably going to be your first and foremost consideration when you select a hotel. Within the price ranges, however, you'll find each hotel designated by its neighborhood.

Although every neighborhood has rooms in every price category, you'll find that you have the most flexibility if you operate in the range of $175 to $300. Anything less will be a squeeze; if you can afford more, you'll have an even wider selection with fewer restrictions, but you'll receive diminishing returns in terms of value.

Where I've indicated "under 12 free" or a similar designation, this pertains to the age of children entitled to free accommodation in a hotel room *with* their parents. *Don't forget: this age limit is often negotiable, especially at the high-end hotels.* Many hotel managers have confessed to me that this is a guideline and often can be changed at the discretion of the person at the desk. So smile, be nice, and maybe you'll get a few dollars knocked off your bill.

Where the price for a rollaway bed is indicated, that is the charge per night unless otherwise noted.

The price ranges I've indicated begin with a lower number indicating the price of rooms during off-peak dates and range up to a higher number representing room rates for peak-season accommodation (though extraordinary dates, like New Year's Eve, will fall outside the range). I've only considered rooms that can accommodate families. If, for example, a hotel's basic room simply can't accommodate more than two people, the lowest price I've listed is for a suite that will accommodate at least one child.

In general, winter is peak season for most New York City hotels, and summer is low season. But it really varies from hotel to hotel, and I can't lay down any hard-and-fast rules in this regard. Many guidebooks attempt this, but most such information is questionable at best. It's very difficult to generalize about the flow of guests at New York's hotels, because so many factors affect it, and they vary by neighborhood and type of hotel. Even veteran hotel managers have told me that they've been blindsided by demand on many occasions.

Finally, please understand that the ranges of room rates I've provided here are only guidelines. Hotels are notoriously cagey when it comes to releasing their room rates, because most engage in "yield management," a practice where rates adapt to supply and demand—just like the airlines. If a hotel anticipates being full on a given night, it will set a very high

### Money-Saving Tip

Unless a hotel is quite full, the first room rate that the reservationist quotes is really just the opening salvo in a negotiation. Ask repeatedly, "Is that the best you can do?" Also try to negotiate for free local phone calls, included breakfast, waivers of kid-related fees (cribs, etc.), airport transportation (depending on the airport, this alone can save you a hundred bucks), and anything else you can think of. They may say no, but it never hurts to ask!

rate, perhaps higher than what I've indicated here. Likewise, if it's looking as though there will be empty rooms, you'll see the rates plummet (I've witnessed some last-minute bookings at New York's top hotels for a third of the listed price). Thus, even though it's always wise to make your reservations as far in advance as possible, it's also wise to call the hotel repeatedly (and anonymously) as the date of your vacation approaches to see if rates have come down at all.

## "$" Hotels: $150 and Under

All of the hotels I've listed here are safe and clean, but they really are budget accommodations. Don't expect concierge service, doormen, swimming pools, or lots of amenities. Some children will be oblivious to this, but others simply won't be happy in most hotels at this level—only you can judge what will work for your family. Still, even in New York, budget hotels offer some benefits. Many have mini-fridges and microwaves in the rooms, and some even offer free Continental breakfast. I've included that information below, but be sure to ask when you make your reservation because policies change constantly, and it's always better to be safe than sorry.

| | |
|---|---|
| **Carlton Arms** | **$84–$106** |
| **160 East 25th Street** | **212-684-8337** |
| **(at Third Ave.), GP** | **212-679-0680** |

This former welfare hotel, now catering primarily to artsy types, is an incredible value by city standards. Doubles with private baths go for a mere $84, triples are $101, and quads are $106. Prices include free rollaways. They usually don't charge for kids (and don't have a firm policy on age), so you're likely to get away with paying for a double (there seems to be no rhyme or reason to this—what can I say, they're artists!). The rooms are very basic, so don't expect many amenities—there are no phones and no air conditioning. But the staff is friendly, the value is tremendous, the hotel is very safe, and the neighborhood is extremely pleasant. Be sure to book rooms with private baths (there are twenty such rooms available) at least a month in advance because they're the first to go. And let the staff know that you're coming with kids so that you get a room with cheerful art (all walls of the hotel are covered in murals, and each room has a theme—the kids might get a kick out of the Holstein room). As one staff member put it: "We get a lot of Europeans in here—it's sort of like camping."

| *Comfort Inn Midtown* | $89–$209 double |
|---|---|
| 129 West 46th Street (between | 212-221-2600 |
| Sixth Ave. and Broadway), MTW | 800-228-5150 |
| www.applecorehotels.com | (central number) |
| www.comfortinn.com (to check for online discounts) | |

Renovated in 1998, this small hotel (80 rooms), boasts an incredible location (a stone's throw from Times Square and the Theater District) and surprisingly reasonable rates. *Cribs (free), rollaways ($20); kids under 15 free; Continental breakfast (free), in-room coffeemaker*

| *Cosmopolitan Hotel* | $119–$149 |
|---|---|
| 95 West Broadway | 212-566-1900 |
| (at Chambers St.), TBC | 888-895-9400 |
| www.cosmohotel.com | |

Don't let the prices scare you away from this modest but clean hotel. All rooms have air-conditioning, cable TV, alarm clocks, and small but tidy bathrooms. Cribs are available for

free. Don't expect gigantic rooms or concierge service, but for the price it's hard to do better.

| ★*Habitat Hotel* | $79–$115 (shared bath), |
| 130 East 57th Street | $99–$155 (private bath), |
| (at Lexington Ave.), UES | $350 (suites) |
| | 212-753-8841 |

Renovated in 1998, this European-style hotel is relatively new on the scene. It's part of the City Life Hotel group, which aims to feature "tourist class, budget hotels that are very affordable but still classy." The hotel is in the heart of Midtown, and 70 percent of the rooms have shared baths, but you can get two adjoining rooms that share a bath that is therefore effectively private. The rooms are small (about 12 feet by 12 feet) but comfortable and clean and include either a queen-size bed or trundle bed. The atmosphere is cheery; the lobby was freshly renovated in 2000, and the restaurant was added in that year. The grand plan is for all rooms to have private baths by the end of 2001. *Concierge, restaurant, complimentary Continental breakfast, suites come with mini-fridges*

## City Fact

New York City has more than 62,500 hotel rooms. At an average occupancy rate of 83.9 percent, that means that out of towners spend 18,547,000 nights in New York City hotels each year.

*Herald Square Hotel*    $130 (two double beds)
19 West 31st Street (between    212-279-4017
Fifth Ave. and Broadway), MTW    800-727-1888

After a facelift in early 2000, rooms have firm new mattresses, fresh coats of paint, in-room safes, TVs, and telephones with voicemail. You get a cheerful greeting at the desk. *Cribs (free); kids under 12 free*

*Hotel Newton*    $105–$170 suite
2528 Broadway (between    212-678-6500
94th and 95th Sts.), UWS    888-HOTEL58
www.newyorkhotel.com/newton

This AAA-approved hotel is a great value for the money. Located on the desirable Upper West Side, it puts you a block from the 1, 2, and 3 subway lines and just a short distance to the heart of the UWS's best shopping and attractions. The real values here are the suites (costing less than most double rooms in the City), which come with a microwave and mini-fridge, plus the option for two double or queen-size beds (request these when you make your reservation). *Kids under 17 free*

The Upper West
Side skyline, from
Central Park's
reservoir

| *Portland Square Hotel* | $125 double, $150 triple, |
|---|---|
| 132 West 47th Street (between | $160 quad |
| Sixth and Seventh Aves.), MTW | 212-382-0600 |
| | 800-388-8988 |

Legend has it that James Cagney lived in this building (as did a few Radio City Rockettes). A family sharing a quad reaps the obvious rewards of the value. *Cribs/rollaways (free)*

| *Washington Square Hotel* | $142–$174 double-quad |
|---|---|
| 103 Waverly Place | 212-777-9515 |
| (at MacDougal St.), WV | 800-222-0418 |

Renovated in 1999, and with regular updates since, this small hotel doesn't have lots of amenities, but the staff is kind and the rooms are clean. Located in a hip neighborhood, this is especially good for pre-teens and teens who will be interested in the goings-on in the Village and nearby Washington Square Park. A word to the wise: Not all of the rooms have windows, so request one that does. *Cribs/rollaways (free)*

## Helpful Hint

You may be tempted to beat the system and save a few dollars by seeking accommodations outside the City. Forget about it. The economics just don't work out once you factor in the cost of transportation and the extreme time commitment over and above staying in Manhattan.

## Top Ten Family-Friendly Hotel Deals

1. Best Western Seaport Inn (p. 127)

2. The Milburn Hotel (p. 136)

3. Gracie Inn (p. 142)

4. Holiday Inn Downtown (p. 133)

5. Habitat Hotel (p. 122)

6. Belvedere Hotel (p. 126)

7. Clarion Hotel Fifth Avenue (p. 129)

8. Excelsior (p. 131)

9. Novotel New York (p. 137)

10. Hotel Newton (p. 123)

| *Wolcott Hotel* | $130 double, $190 suite |
|---|---|
| 4 West 31st Street | 212-268-2900 |
| (at Fifth Ave.), CH | www.wolcott.com |

The value here is in the suites. Though the Wolcott doesn't have an official kids-stay-free policy, the charge is overlooked for the suites, which can accommodate two adults and two kids. All of the rooms were renovated in 1998 or 1999, and the exterior of the building was given a face-lift in the spring of 2000. All suites have mini-fridges, as do some of the queen rooms—request a fridge in advance if you need one, and they'll do their best to accommodate. *Cribs/rollaways (free)*

## Insider's Tip

"Always have snacks and drinks on hand in your hotel room. Never, ever, under any circumstances should you allow hungry, cranky kids to force you to resort against your will to room service or the mini-bar, where you'll pay at least a 300-percent markup on all items. Whereas, if you have your own drinks, even if there's no fridge, you can always get ice for free!" —*Dave, father of two*

## "$$" Hotels: $150–$275

This is the price range, albeit high, in which you'll maximize the value of New York hotels. This is also where you'll have the most competition for rooms during busy times, so reserve early.

| | |
|---|---|
| ***Belvedere Hotel*** | **$140–$200 (up to four people)** |
| **319 West 48th Street (between** | **212-245-7000** |
| **Eighth and Ninth Aves.), MTW** | **888-HOTEL58** |
| **www.newyorkhotel.com/belvedere** | |

Renovated in 1998, it's hard to believe that this modern boutique hotel charges so modestly for its rooms. Located smack-dab in the Theater District and only two blocks from great cheap eats on Ninth Avenue, the Belvedere is a New York gem. The kitchenettes—in every room—are a great bonus, and the full breakfast buffet ($8) is a good value if you have hearty eaters in tow. *Cribs (free), rollaways ($20); kitchenette (mini-fridge, microwave), concierge, full breakfast, Nintendo video games*

| ★*Best Western Seaport Inn* | $159–$195 |
|---|---|
| **33 Peck Slip (between** | **212-766-6600** |
| **Front and Water Sts.), FD** | **800-468-3569** |

This Seaport charmer is in an out-of-the-way corner, down a cobblestone street, which may explain why it has remained one of the City's better-kept hotel secrets. Great values for families at any time of year, every room is equipped with a VCR, adjoining rooms are available, and plenty of rooms have two queen-size beds. For an extra $20, you can get a room with a terrace (ask for one overlooking the Brooklyn Bridge) and/or a whirlpool. For $20, where else can you do that! And the location is not to be overlooked—you'll be right at the South Street Seaport and Pier 17; Chinatown is less than ten blocks away; and the Financial District and ferry to the Statue of Liberty are within an easy walk. *Cribs (free), rollaways ($25); kids under 18 free; complimentary breakfast*

| *Broadway Inn Bed & Breakfast* | $135–$170, |
|---|---|
| **264 West 46th Street (between** | **$195–$225 (suites)** |
| **Broadway and Eighth Aves.), MT** | **212-997-9200** |
| **www.broadwayinn.com** | **800-826-6300** |

The stated aim of this forty-one-room inn is to make you feel as if you're at your "home away from home." And, as at home, there is no elevator (there are only three floors), so be prepared to walk those stairs. In the heart of the Theater District, the intimate charm of the Broadway Inn is a welcome change from some of the chain hotel giants. Built in 1918, this historic building may not look like much from the outside, but the inn itself dates to 1996 and was completely renovated at that time. A fireplace and library welcome you in the lobby (where you can also enjoy the complimentary breakfast), and the rooms are modest, tidy, and comfortable. Each of the eleven suites (which have a pantry with microwave) can easily accommodate a family of four. And though the hotel doesn't have a restaurant (you're better off with the vast selection lining Ninth Avenue), when you check in you'll get discount vouchers for several good area dining spots.

| *Chelsea Inn* | $89–$129 guest room, |
|---|---|
| 46 West 17th Street (between | $169 studio, $199 suite |
| Sixth and Seventh Aves.), CH | 212-645-8989 |
| www.chelseainn.com | 800-640-6469 |

This country-style inn is housed in a classic turn-of-the-century brownstone. Accommodations range from the guest room with shared bath to the suite, each with a kitchenette (refrigerator, hotplate or stove, coffeemaker), TV, and voicemail. Unless you're traveling with toddlers, the best bets for families are the "guest rooms." Every pair has its own vestibule entry off the hall and shares a bathroom. There are 26 rooms, and you'll feel more as if you're in an Old World–style inn or European *pension* than in a Manhattan hotel.

| *Chelsea Savoy Hotel* | $125–$185 |
|---|---|
| 204 West 23rd Street | 212-929-9353 |
| (at Seventh Ave.), CH | www.chelseasavoy.citysearch.com |

Built in 1997, the Chelsea Savoy, unlike many hotels in this price range, was actually built to be a hotel. So you'll find that the rooms are practical, well laid out, and fairly roomy. The rates are per room, so if you get a room with two doubles, you can sleep four at no additional charge. The furnishings are a bit chain hotel–like, but everything is clean, new, and well looked after, plus the neighborhood is especially hip and trendy right now. *Cribs (free), rollaways ($50); restaurant, complimentary breakfast, mini-fridge*

| *Clarion Hotel Fifth Avenue* | $169–$379 double |
|---|---|
| 3 East 40th Street (between | 212-447-1500 |
| Fifth and Madison Aves.), MTE | 800-252-7466 |
| www.hotelchoice.com | |

Tucked away in Midtown, the Clarion is across the street from the City's grandest library, a few blocks from Grand Central Station, steps off Fifth Avenue, and only six blocks from the Empire State Building. Renovated in the fall of 1999, upgrades on technological equipment (like two-line phones and dataports) don't mean that corners were cut elsewhere—check out the bathrooms and towels, which are downright luxurious for a hotel in this price category. Rooms are configured with either a queen-size bed and a sleeper sofa or two doubles. Refrigerators are available upon request at no additional charge, and in-room coffeemakers will enable you to have a cup before setting out for the day. And as if that weren't enough, local calls (which can really add up) are free. *Cribs/rollaways (free); kids under 18 free; AAA, AARP, senior discounts; concierge, restaurant, Continental breakfast ($4 per person)*

| *Comfort Inn Manhattan* | $144–$244 |
|---|---|
| 42 West 35th Street (between | 212-947-0200 |
| Fifth and Sixth Aves.), GD | 800-228-5150 |
| www.comfortinnmanhattan.com | |
| www.comfortinn.com (check for online discounts) | |

If tourist sights are a high priority, this location is hard to beat—you'll be around the corner from the Empire State

## New York's Top Ten Most Family-Friendly Hotels

1. **Le Parker Meridien (p. 152)**

2. **The Peninsula (p. 154)**

3. **Best Western Seaport Inn (p. 127)**

4. **Millenium Hilton (p. 147)**

5. **Lyden Gardens (p. 144)**

6. **Surrey Hotel (p. 159)**

7. **Habitat Hotel (p. 122)**

8. **The Regency (p. 156)**

9. **The Pierre (p. 155)**

10. **Four Seasons (p. 150)**

Building and Macy's, a short walk to Fifth Avenue's best shopping, and close to the subway. To get an even better value, you can request a room with a microwave and/or mini-fridge (there are twenty such rooms) or book into a king room with double sleeper sofa (these cost extra, but it's still far cheaper than getting two rooms). And don't forget to ask about special rates and promos, as they are common here. *Kids under 18 free; complimentary Continental breakfast*

| *Days Hotel Midtown* | **$119–$349 (2 double beds)** |
| --- | --- |
| 790 Eighth Avenue | **212-581-7000** |
| (at 48th St.), MTW | **800-572-6232** |

In the heart of the Theater District and one block from Times Square, don't expect quiet when you step out of the lobby and onto the street because the City doesn't get much busier than this. The guestrooms, which are quite large by Manhattan standards, underwent a full makeover in 2000–2001. This property is no stranger to tour groups, so don't be surprised if you see busloads pulling up in front. *Cribs (free), rollaways ($20); concierge, restaurant, mini-fridge ($20/day)*

| *Empire Hotel* | $175–$1,000 |
|---|---|
| **Broadway (at 63rd St.), UWS** | **212-265-7400** |
| **www.empirehotel.com** | **888-822-3555** |

Directly across the street from Lincoln Center, the Empire is ideally located for jaunts into Central Park, the Upper West Side, and Times Square. The lobby of this hotel is grand by any standards, but rooms are a bit small. A deluxe room is big enough to accommodate a rollaway, and the junior suites (with a double bed and a pullout couch) and one-bedrooms are better for more space, if everyone needs to be in close proximity. Don't overlook connecting rooms as a (surprisingly) more economical option to the suites. VCRs and CD players as well as complimentary lending libraries for both are good extras, and renovations are planned for the rooms starting in early 2001. *Cribs (free), rollaways ($20); kids free (ages vary); concierge, restaurant, mini-fridge ($25 per stay)*

| ★ *Excelsior* | $149–$369 |
|---|---|
| **45 West 81st Street (between Central** | **212-362-9200** |
| **Park West and Columbus Ave.), UWS** | **800-368-4575** |

Many of us City residents would kill (and pay a lot) for this location—in the heart of the Upper West Side, less than a block from Central Park, and directly across the street from the new Rose Center (planetarium) at the Museum of Natural History. Surprisingly, the rates at this four-star hotel (converted from apartments) are not as high as one might think. A standard room with two queen-size beds is large enough to house a family comfortably. All one- and two-bedroom suites have pullout couches and computers, while junior suites have only the former. "Park" view rooms (overlooking the museum) cost just $10–$20 more than those without. *Cribs (free), rollaways ($25); kids under 15 free; mini-fridge ($10 per day)*

| *Gramercy Park Hotel* | **$180–$210 and up for suites** |
|---|---|
| **2 Lexington Avenue** | **212-475-4320** |
| **(between 21st and 22nd Sts.), GP** | **800-221-4083** |

"It's very European," the staff informed me, which I'll translate to mean smoky and somewhat campy in nature. Full of artists and rock stars, this hotel is in a great location and a good value if you can handle the smoky lobby and slightly tattered edges. Probably the best feature is that guests have access to the lovely, peaceful, beautifully kept, *and* private Gramercy Park, which is accessible only to those who reside on the park's boundaries (I've *always* wanted to go in there!). Some rooms have park views, for which there is no extra charge (just ask), and some also have kitchenettes. I would only advise this hotel for families comfortable with smoking, though. *Cribs (free), rollaways ($10); kids under 12 free; restaurant*

**Taking a break near Central Park**

*Helmsley Middletowne Hotel*  $170–$560 (two beds)
148 East 48th Street (between               212-755-3000
Lexington and Third Aves.), MTW       800-221-4982
www.helmsleyhotels.com

This converted apartment hotel offers many of the trappings of
a high-end property (multiple phone lines, data ports, plush
linens, and fine furniture) but really delivers on value, especially if you're looking to keep your kids close at hand (i.e., in
the same room). Two children under 12 can share a room with
their parents, and even the most modest rooms (read: the
cheapest) are quite spacious by New York standards and can be
requested with two double beds. Otherwise, one- and two-bedroom suites are also available, though in terms of value, you
might be best off with two doubles as an alternative. *Cribs
(free), rollaways ($20); kids under 12 free; concierge, mini-fridge*

★*Holiday Inn Downtown*                        $150–$300
138 Lafayette Street (at Canal St.), CT   212-966-8898
                                                        800-465-4329

If you want to be in the hustle and bustle of it all but Times
Square isn't your cup of tea, the Holiday Inn Downtown is a
great option. Room rates vary with the seasons, but doubles
can accommodate a family, as can the suites with pullout
couches. If you want a real New York experience, this neighborhood ensures it—and you'll be close to Little Italy, the
South Street Seaport, and the World Trade Center, too. *Hint:*
Though the Continental breakfast isn't technically included, if
you join the Holiday Inn's club (for which there is no charge),
you get the breakfast for free. *Cribs (free), rollaways ($25); kids
under 12 free; concierge, restaurant*

| *Holiday Inn Midtown* | $99–$289 |
|---|---|
| 440 West 57th Street (between | 212-581-8100 |
| Ninth and Tenth Aves.), MTW | 800-HOLIDAY |

If you take comfort in the familiarity of chain hotels, the Holiday Inn Midtown fits the bill just fine. Renovated in 1998, the rooms remain clean and tidy and are of a decent size. It's a bit of a hike to public transportation and attractions, but room rates are very attractive, and you'll surely appreciate the rooftop pool in summer. *Cribs (free), rollaways ($15); kids under 18 free; concierge, restaurant, mini-fridge ($10), rooftop pool (outdoor/seasonal)*

| *Hotel Beacon* | $195–$500 |
|---|---|
| 2130 Broadway (between | 212-787-1100 |
| 74th and 75th Sts.), UWS | 800-572-4969 |
| www.beaconhotel.com | |

Long one of the UWS's best bargains (though not as much of a secret as it used to be), the Beacon has many charms. A standard room comes with two double beds or a king, one-bedroom suites have a double pullout in the lounge area, and two-bedroom suites can comfortably sleep six. All of the rooms were renovated in 1999; each has a kitchenette with a range, mini-fridge, and coffeemaker; the bigger the room, the more extensive the kitchenette (bigger refrigerator and more accoutrements). The Beacon offers all sorts of discounts (it seems like everyone checking in has some sort of a special deal), so be sure to ask when you call—AAA, seasonal specials, corporate, whatever. *Cribs (free), rollaways ($15); kids under 12 free*

*Hotel Metro*          $165–$255 double, $200–$325 suite
45 West 35th Street (between                    212-947-2500
Fifth and Sixth Aves.), GD                      800-356-3870

The Metro is, for the price, an absolutely fab hotel. The decor
is playful and the rooms are sizeable, but the bathrooms,
though spotless, are a bit on the tight side. Perhaps one of the
best things about this hotel is the view from the rooftop
deck—it's got one of the best views of the Empire State Building I've ever seen. *Cribs (free); restaurant, complimentary Continental breakfast*

*Loews New York*  $179–$389 rooms, $199–$419 suites
569 Lexington Avenue                            212-752-7000
(at 51st St.), MTE                              800-836-6471

This Loews has a very central location, virtually across from the
Waldorf, a few blocks from Madison and Fifth Avenues (and
Sony World of Wonder). Renovated in the fall of 2000, the entire property has undergone a face-lift, smoothing the previously
tattered edges. Rooms with two double beds can comfortably accommodate a family, as can the junior suites, which have either
one king or two doubles and a pullout couch in the sleeping
area. Perched atop the #6 subway and with a good gourmet coffee shop (that is unrelated to the hotel), you can start your day
with a cup of java (the kids will have plenty of breakfast choices
with bagels and baked goods) and easy transportation via foot or
train to the best the City has to offer. *Cribs/rollaways (free); kids
under 18 free; mini-fridge, concierge, restaurant, children's amenities (pull-out couches, babysitting arrangements available, concierge
has lists of nearby children's activities)*

## Insider's Tip

"Most hotel concierges maintain a list of trusted babysitters who will come to your room and watch the kids for a few hours. It's not cheap, but it may be worth it for that one big night out on the town." —*Albert, hotel concierge*

| *The Mayflower Hotel* | $210–$330 |
| --- | --- |
| 15 Central Park West (between | 212-265-0060 |
| 61st and 62nd Sts.), UWS | 800-223-4164 |
| www.mayflowerhotel.com | |

Located directly across the street from Central Park, the Mayflower is a bit worn around the edges, but in what some would consider a comforting way. Formerly an apartment building, the hotel has cavernous rooms that are the primary benefit to guests (my first apartment in New York City wasn't as big as some of the doubles I saw), along with easy proximity to attractions. Double rooms (with two double beds) can comfortably accommodate a family, and suites (with a king or two queens and a pullout) are big enough for gymnastics and tumbling. All rooms come with mini-fridges, and continuous improvements and renovation keep the charming old building up to snuff. *Cribs (free), rollaways ($20); kids under 16 free*

| ★ *The Milburn Hotel* | $159–$205 |
| --- | --- |
| 242 West 76th Street (between | 212-362-1006 |
| Broadway and West End Aves.), UWS | 800-833-9622 |
| | Fax: 212-721-5476 |

Nestled in the heart of the Upper West Side, The Milburn is perfect for families looking for a good value. The prices are shockingly reasonable considering what you get—a continuously renovated hotel (and regularly undergoing improvements and upgrades), kitchenettes in every room (microwave, range, coffeemaker, mini-fridge), VCR, free video lending library, and Playstation video games upon request (free). A junior suite, with a king-size bed and a rollaway, is the smallest option for a family of three. For larger families or more space (though the rooms are generous by New York standards), one-bedrooms (with two twins, one king, or a queen with a pull-out couch) are the better bet. *Cribs (free), rollaways ($10); kids under 13 free; kitchenettes, Playstation video games (free)*

| ★*Novotel New York* | $159–$389 |
|---|---|
| 226 West 52nd Street | 212-315-0100 |
| (at Broadway), MT | 800-NOVOTEL |
| www.accor.com | |

While all other hotels seem to have vacancies, the Novotel is finding itself booked solid, even during anticipated seasonal lows—and it's obvious why. Fully renovated in 1999, all of the rooms are in top shape and noticeably large by City standards (12 feet by 12 feet or 10 feet by 14 feet). Rooms have either two doubles or a king and a pullout sleeper, as well as hardwood floors in the bathrooms (the only hotel in New York City that can make this claim), and the added bonus of free full buffet breakfast for the kids (summer rates often include breakfast for parents, too). Check out the outdoor "sky-lobby" that overlooks Broadway, outfitted with chairs for lingering and relaxing. There's free nightly entertainment in the lounge in the lobby, and the hotel welcomes small pets (the reservationist warns, "no horses"). *Cribs (free), rollaways ($20); kids under 17 free; concierge, restaurant; mini-fridge ($10)*

138

| San Carlos | $195–$265 junior suite, |
| --- | --- |
| 150 East 50th Street | $225–$310 one-bedroom suite |
| (between Lexington and | 212-755-1800 |
| Third Aves.), MTE | 800-722-2012 |
| www.sancarloshotel.com | |

The location speaks for itself at this welcoming, modest Midtown hotel. Busy even during the low season, the fair pricing and the convenience of in-room amenities like kitchenettes make the San Carlos a good bet for families. Junior suites can sleep three, and the one-bedroom suites sleep up to five.

| Travel Inn | $175–$200 |
| --- | --- |
| 515 West 42nd Street (between | 212-695-7171 |
| Tenth and Eleventh Aves.), MTW | 800-869-4630 |

The big attractions here are the free parking (wow!) and the large outdoor pool (which is seasonal). A family of up to four can easily stay in one room, with two double beds. For more space or privacy go for adjoining rooms. The Travel Inn is close to the Circle Line, the Intrepid, and the Javits Center, but not much else (it's even a hike to the subway from this far-west location). So if you have young children or aren't big walkers, you might be better off elsewhere. *Cribs (free), rollaways ($15); kids under 18 free; free parking*

# "$$$" Hotels: $275–$400

Hotels in this range are expensive, to be sure, but they often offer great comfort and convenience. Look especially for good deals on suites and adjoining rooms and for low-season specials (which can drop these hotels to the low end of the price range).

*Barbizon*
140 East 63rd Street
(at Lexington Ave.), MTE
www.thebarbizon.com

$205–$1,500 penthouse suites
212-838-5700
800-223-5652

More like a European boutique hotel than a Manhattan standard, the Barbizon once housed the likes of Joan Crawford, Grace Kelly, and Liza Minnelli when it was an all-women's residence. It went through a $40 million renovation in 1998, so you'll see no signs of the previously tattered edges or disrepair, but the hotel still maintains its original class and character. The standard rooms (superior/deluxe and up) are too small for rollaways (although they are available for $20), but rooms of all sizes can adjoin. *Cribs (free), rollaways ($20); concierge, minifridge (upon request)*

## Money-Saving Tip

Remember your frequent flier miles. Many frequent flier programs have tie-ins with the big national hotel chains, and in some cases the exact same number of miles that will buy you a room in Cleveland will also buy you one in New York City!

★*Beekman Tower*
3 Mitchell Place
(First Ave. at 49th St.), MTE
www.mesuite.com

$279–$418 one bedroom,
$517–$685 two bedroom
212-355-7300
800-637-8483

The Manhattan East Suite Hotels, of which this property is a part, are a real boon to traveling families. The rooms are all, as the name indicates, suites. Accommodations are unusually large for New York, and all have full kitchens. Located virtually on top of the UN, the Beekman Tower was last renovated in 1997 and is still holding up well despite its popularity. The one-bedroom suites range in size from 450 to 650 square feet and can accommodate up to four. The two-bedroom suites run from 700 to 900 square feet and can comfortably sleep six. Take a trip up to the rooftop lounge early one evening for great, unobstructed views of the City. *Cribs (free), rollaways ($20); kids under 12 free; concierge, restaurant*

| ★ *Crowne Plaza Manhattan* | $199–$469 |
|---|---|
| 1605 Broadway (between | 212-977-4000 |
| 48th and 49th Sts.), TS | 800-243-NYNY |
| www.crowneplaza.com | |

If it's bright lights, glitz, and glitter that you're after, this 46-story glass edifice in the heart of Times Square is the answer to your prayers. The hotel is centrally located near all of the City's attractions (you're pretty much in the middle) and within easy walking distance of Broadway favorites like *The Lion King.* The masterful "ticket and attractions" staff (i.e., the concierge) can help you get tickets even to sold-out shows (though you'll pay for the privilege). Renovated in 1999, the rooms are virtually new and the amenities are excellent—there's even a swimming pool (lap pool with restricted kids hours). Rooms sleep a maximum of four with children under 18 staying free, but better still is the program where children under 12 eat free—at all three meals! If this location is booked, or you're looking for a bit more peace and quiet, you can also try the Crowne Plaza at the United Nations (304 East 42nd St. at Second Ave., 212-986-8800, 800-243-NYNY). *Cribs (free), rollaways ($20); kids under 18 free; concierge, restaurant (kids under 12 eat free), mini-fridge ($10), small pets welcome (under 30 pounds), coffeemakers, pool*

**★Doubletree Guest Suites**  $239–$350
1568 Broadway (at 47th St.   212-719-1600
and Seventh Ave.), TS   800-222-TREE
www.doubletreehotels.com

If you want to be in Times Square, this is an extremely good option for families. All of the rooms are, you guessed it, suites—so you get more space for your money, and you can keep everyone together without worrying about what's going on in your kids' room next door. The rooms are fully equipped too, including not one but two TVs, a microwave, refrigerator, coffeemaker, pullout couch, and even hair dryers. This also happens to be an extremely kid-friendly hotel—there's a playroom with all sorts of activities sure to interest and engage children ages 3 to 12. *Cribs (free); kids under 18 free; concierge, restaurants*

**The Franklin**  $295 superior room
164 East 87th Street (between   212-369-1000
Lexington and Third Aves.), UES   877-847-4444
www.boutiquehg.com

The Franklin, like the other four New York hotels in the Boutique Hotel Group (The Shoreham, The Roger Williams, the Hotel Wales, and The Mansfield), has been transformed from a questionable property to a beautiful neighborhood hotel. Admittedly, the rooms are small—only the superior rooms can accommodate a crib or a rollaway—but everything is top-notch, from the in-room VCR and CD player to the complimentary "European" breakfast. The sitting room is perfect for breakfast, a snack, an afternoon story break, or a cappuccino (on the house, of course) pick-me-up for rundown parents. *Kids under 18 free*

## New York's Top Ten Hotel Swimming Pools

1. Le Parker Meridien (p. 152)

2. Millenium Hilton (p. 147)

3. The Peninsula (p. 154)

4. New York Marriott World Trade Center (p. 148)

5. Travel Inn (seasonal) (p. 138)

6. Regal UN Plaza (p. 156)

7. Days Hotel Midtown (p. 130)

8. Crowne Plaza Manhattan (p. 140)

9. New York Marriott Financial Center (p. 148)

10. Holiday Inn Midtown (seasonal) (p. 134)

★ *Gracie Inn*                  $279–$399
502 East 81st Street (between     212-628-1700
York and East End Aves.), UES

This hotel is more like a mom-and-pop bed and breakfast than an urban hotel. With only twelve rooms (all with efficiency kitchens), you'll quickly feel at home in the cozy, somewhat small accommodations. The four one-bedrooms and two duplex penthouses are the best bet for families. The duplexes sleep six, have a VCR and terraces, and one even has a glassed-in Jacuzzi. Continental breakfast is included, and it's delivered to your room. Long-stay discounts are offered (and encouraged) at a shocking rate of 10 percent off per week up to a whopping 40 percent for a four-week stay. *Cribs (free), rollaways ($25)*

★ *The Kimberly*      **$279–$449 one bedroom;**
**145 East 50th Street**    **$429–$689 two bedroom**
**(between Lexington and**       **212-755-0400**
**Third Aves.), MTE**          **800-683-0400**
**www.citysearch.com/nyc/kimberly**

A New York gem, The Kimberly has suites that are perfect for families and also happen to be well priced. The one bedrooms are 600 square feet, sleep four, and have a full kitchen (with dishwasher!) with all of the cookware and utensils you could need. Home improvements and sprucing-up (like new mattresses and carpets) were eagerly undertaken throughout 2000. And the rooms, already well outfitted with high tech accoutrements, have two-line phones, a fax machine, and data-port as well as two televisions and VCRs upon request. There is no pool; as a hotel guest, you're entitled to the great bonus of free passes to the NY Health & Racquet clubs (located around the City), which do have children's hours (so plan ahead to avoid disappointment). *Cribs/rollaways (free); kids under 18 free; concierge, restaurant, VCR (free)*

*The Lucerne*    **$160–$280 rooms, $250–$390 suites**
**201 West 79th Street**         **212-875-1000**
**(at Amsterdam Ave.), UWS**

A relative newcomer to the Upper West Side, the Lucerne opened in 1995 with a complete head-to-toe renovation. A beautiful brownstone landmark (built in 1903), don't let the age fool you. In your room you'll find the comforts of home with Internet access (via the TV), pay-per-view Nintendo ($5.95 for 24 hours), and kitchenettes in the queen and king suites. The location is great for visits to the Children's

Museum (four blocks away), the Museum of Natural History (two blocks), and loads of great kid-friendly restaurants like EJ's and the Columbus Bakery. *Cribs (free); kids under 17 free; concierge, restaurant*

| ★*Lyden Gardens* | $364–$639 |
|---|---|
| **215 East 64th Street (between** | **212-355-1230** |
| **Second and Third Aves.), UES** | **800-ME-SUITE** |

The size of these rooms alone makes the Lyden Gardens an incredible value, but add to that the full kitchenettes, complete with stove, microwave, coffeemaker, and all of the necessities for cooking and eating, and you've got yourself a perfect setup. On top of that, extended stays (7 to 29 days and 30 days or more) are substantially discounted (more than ⅓ off for 7 days or more). You'll need a junior suite ($364) if you want your kids in the same room (two queens and a pullout). Some nice extras include an in-house movie and grocery service (ask at the desk for details). The high level of repeat business (70 percent) and the near full occupancy level (98 percent) are telltale signs of satisfied customers. Call as far in advance for reservations as possible. *Cribs (free), rollaways ($20); kids under 18 free*

**Helpful Hint**

Be sure to tell the reservationist at the time of booking that you're traveling with kids. Many hotels offer free toys, trinkets, and kids' amenities, but they can only provide them if they know the kids are coming.

| *Marriott Marquis* | $319–$520 and up double, |
|---|---|
| 535 Broadway (between | $359 concierge floor |
| 145th and 46th Sts.), TS | 212-398-1900 |
| | 800-843-4898 |

Centrally located in the middle of Times Square and considered by many tourists to be one of the City's most luxurious hotels (on the level of a five-star), and certainly one of the favorites, this behemoth (1,946 rooms and 50 floors) won't disappoint those eager to be in the bustle of Times Square. Still, it's hard to forget that you're in a Marriott. Families can comfortably fit into the standard rooms, but depending upon the price variation at the time, you might consider an upgrade to the concierge level, where you get free Continental breakfast, evening appetizers (and an honor bar), and a quiet lounge outside of the rooms to sit or play games. *Cribs/rollaways (free); under 18 free; concierge, restaurant, movie theater*

| *The Michelangelo* | $295–$345 executive |
|---|---|
| 152 West 51st Street | 212-765-1900 |
| (at Seventh Ave.), MTW | 800-237-0990 |

Just off Seventh Avenue, this hotel is steps away from the activity of Times Square. But in spite of that, tranquility and quiet pervade the moment you step into the lobby. An "Italian" hotel, the decor is luxurious with grand oil paintings, gilded accessories, and large chandeliers. The rooms here are large, and it's the "executive" rooms (600 square feet) that have two beds that can accommodate families. The complimentary Continental breakfast (at the Michelangelo, it's called by its Italian name: *buondi*) is a nice way to start the day—coffee, tea, cappuccino (it's divine; I'd stay here for that alone), and a limited selection of pastries—but it's not a full meal. *Cribs/rollaways ($30); complimentary Continental breakfast*

| Millennium Broadway | $295–$495 |
|---|---|
| & The Premier | 212-768-4400 |
| 145 West 44th Street (between | 800-622-5569 |
| Sixth Ave. and Broadway), TS | |
| www.millenniumbroadway.com | |

This gigantic Times Square hotel is similar to the others. Though it doesn't actually overlook Times Square, it's just in from the corner of Broadway, so you're not at all removed from the action (which is what you want, otherwise you wouldn't be staying here). The rooms are fairly standard in a familiar and comforting way, and there's always a lot of activity here. *Cribs (free), rollaway ($20); kids under 15 free; concierge, restaurant, pet friendly (very small dogs/cats)*

### Insider's Tip

"Use the staff. You're paying not only for your room but also for the salaries of all those people working at the front desk, and often a concierge as well. Especially on longer stays, learn these people's names and utilize their expertise. Many of them are parents, too, and they'll steer you to their favorite local spots." —Annie, hotel desk staffer

Next door is the new Premier, which would really only be appropriate with older, well-behaved children (it's *really* a businessperson's hotel). This lush addition to the Millennium has its own entrance, which is in muted tones, and rather than standing at a desk while reception checks you in, you're invited to sit down for the proceedings. Everything about the Premier is premier, from the beds to the exquisite bathrooms with Aveda bath products. The extensive complimentary breakfast and evening drinks and appetizers in the lounge are very nice extras.

| ★*Millenium Hilton* | $139–$389 |
|---|---|
| 55 Church Street (between | 212-693-2001 |
| Courtland and Dey Sts.), FD | 800-HILTONS |
| www.newyorkmillenium.hilton.com | |

This Hilton, despite its strange spelling, is an all-around winner. It's a large hotel by all accounts (though considered midsized by Manhattan standards), but you'll never suffer for attention when you're staying here. An army of attendants is on hand for swift check in, and the concierge staff is doubled on weekends, in anticipation of the hotel guests' needs. The rooms are spacious and modern with up-to-date technology and most have excellent views of one of the two rivers, the World Trade Center, or other downtown sights. At the front desk, there are games and toys for children to borrow and play with; microwaves and mini-fridges are available free upon request; and the fifth-floor, 15-yard pool is glassed in all around and affords a spectacular view of Saint Paul's Church. Double rooms are suitable for two, and adjoining rooms are available. For junior suites (one king and a pullout couch) add $50 to the room rate on weekends, $75 during the week. *Cribs/rollaways (free); kids under 18 free; concierge, restaurant, pool, children's amenities (games, toys, etc.) available from concierge*

| *New York Marriott Financial Center* | $129–$399 |
|---|---|
| **85 West Street (between** | **212-385-4900** |
| **Albany and Carlisle Sts.), FD** | **800-228-9290** |
| **www.marriott.com** | |

Seemingly somewhat on the fringe (because it's just off the West Side Highway), this Marriott is actually close to many downtown attractions and only a few blocks from the World Trade Center. A good value, especially during summer months and weekends, the Marriott Financial Center has a modest swimming pool that welcomes kids and nice added touches like cold lemonade on a hot summer day and apples for guests in the lobby. The rooms, if somewhat cookie-cutter in style, are neat and clean—and you can request adjoining doubles for the kids. *Cribs/rollaways (free); kids stay free (ages vary); minifridge (free)*

| *New York Marriott* | $159–$399 **rooms,** |
|---|---|
| *World Trade Center* | $359–$1,750 **suites** |
| **3 World Trade Center** | **212-938-9100** |
| **(at Liberty and West Sts.), FD** | **800-550-2344** |

You wouldn't think that this would be the place for value, but the Financial District hotels actually offer worthy bargains on weekends and for summer stays. Located right next door to the World Trade Towers and within the World Trade Plaza, you're within comfortable walking distance of downtown attractions, and you can roll right out of bed to get on line for half-priced Broadway tickets at the downtown outpost of TKTS (at Two World Trade Center). Small it ain't, so don't expect the doorman to know your name, but only a hotel this size could support the twenty-second floor panoramic fitness center (worth a trip to the top for the view alone) and four-lane, fifty-foot pool (which welcomes kids). *Cribs/rollaways (free); kids stay free (ages vary); concierge, restaurant*

| *Omni Berkshire Place* | $222–$429 superior |
|---|---|
| 21 East 52nd Street (between | 212-753-5800 |
| Fifth and Madison Aves.), MTE | 800-843-6664 |

This very classy four-star and four-diamond rated hotel is a bit stuffy, but they're clearly trying to improve upon this because they've recently added an "Omni Kids Rule" program that offers special programs and amenities for children. Favorites include a special children's menu with surprisingly inexpensive children's sized portions of food, an amenities kids' pack given to children at check-in (coloring books, small toys, a listing of appropriate activities around the City), milk and cookies at turndown, and special backpacks with toys for use during the stay. The superior guestrooms, at 380 square feet, are probably the best option (the one category below superior would be a bit cramped) if you're sharing. *Cribs (free), rollaways ($30); concierge, restaurant*

| ★*Plaza Fifty* | $259–$425 one bedroom, |
|---|---|
| 55 East 50th Street | $537–$687 two bedroom |
| (at Third Ave.), MTE | 212-751-5710 |
| www.mesuite.com | |

The central location of this Manhattan East Suite Hotel (see Beekman Tower) in conjunction with the convenience and affordability of having a fully equipped kitchenette in your suite makes Plaza Fifty a great value for families. Check out the Web site for pictures and especially for the extremely helpful floor plans of the different rooms at the hotel. *Cribs (free), rollaway ($20); kids under 12 free; concierge*

Though I've listed only my two favorites of the proper-
ties, there is detailed information on all of the ten very respectable Manhattan East Suite Hotels on the Web site.

| *The Wyndham* | $340–$380 two-bedroom suite |
|---|---|
| 42 West 58th Street (between | 212-753-3500 |
| Fifth and Sixth Aves.), MTW | 800-257-1111 |

This hotel occupies a prime location in the heart of the hustle
and bustle of Midtown, around the corner from Central Park
and close to Fifth Avenue's best shopping, the Central Park Zoo,
and many museums. With an extremely reasonable price tag, the
two-bedroom suites are the best way to accommodate a family;
all other rooms can accommodate only two (fire safety regulations) and only the suites connect. The sole problem here is that
the staff is often rude, especially the brusque and dismissive
management, so if you have a problem you'll likely be on your
own. *Cribs/rollaways (free)*

## "$$$$" Hotels: More than $400

At these, the most luxurious of the City's hotels, you'll be
waited on hand and foot—and you'll pay for it. But if such accommodations are within your budget, these are some of the
finest hotels on the planet.

| *Four Seasons* | $475 and up |
|---|---|
| 57 East 57th Street (between | 212-758-5700 |
| Park and Madison Aves.), MTE | 800-332-3442 |
| www.fourseasons.com | |

As historical as the landmark Pierre is, the Four Seasons is modern. Punctuated with high ceilings and light-colored woods,

*One of the City's many monuments; a favorite for family snapshots*

nothing is overlooked at this contemporary sister property. In the heart of Midtown, the bulk of weekday guests at this classy favorite are business travelers. But if you're a fan of the Four Seasons' legendary service, this branch won't disappoint. Rooms are large by City standards (averaging around 600 square feet), and soundproofing goes a long way toward ensuring a good night's sleep. *Cribs (free), extra bed ($50); kids' amenities*

| | |
|---|---|
| **Hotel Wales** | **$440 and up suites** |
| **1295 Madison Avenue** | **212-876-6000** |
| **(between 92nd and 93rd Sts.), UES** | **877-847-4444** |
| **www.waleshotel.com** | |

You'll find this neighborhood, Carnegie Hill, to be among the quietest in the entire City. Only a block away from Central Park and Museum Mile, this century-old charmer includes a hearty Continental breakfast in the vast Madison Room, as well as 24-hour cappuccino, in-room VCRs and CD players, and a library of videos for guests to borrow free. The rooms are small, so only the suites (which have pullout couches) can

## Learning Tip

Many New York hotels have colorful histories. The Hotel Chelsea (222 West 23rd St., between Seventh and Eighth Aves., www.hotelchelsea.com) boasts a bustling lobby filled with museum-quality works by prominent current and former residents. Thomas Wolfe wrote *You Can't Go Home Again* at the Chelsea; Arthur Miller penned *After the Fall* in its welcoming arms; William Burroughs moved in to work on *Naked Lunch*; and in a defining moment of punk-rock history, Sid Vicious reportedly murdered girlfriend Nancy Spungeon here. Does your hotel have any interesting history? Even if it's a new hotel, what building was on the site before?

accommodate families. In addition to the beautiful decor, the rooftop garden, and the historic preservation (the hotel has been completely renovated in 1999–2000), the art that adorns the walls is magnificent, including the children's book pictures from *Puss and Boots*. *Cribs (free), rollaways ($20); mini-fridge (upon request)*

| | |
|---|---|
| ★*Le Parker Meridien* | $395–$575 |
| 118 West 57th Street (between | 212-245-5000 |
| Sixth and Seventh Aves.), MTW | 800-543-4300 |
| www.parkermeridien.com | |

If you can afford it, I think this is hands-down the best choice for families. From the enormous (the length of one entire city block), naturally lit atrium to the all-day breakfast restaurant, the rooftop swimming pool (where children are *always* welcome), and the team of super professional concierges (who can get you VIP passes to Mars 2112, Harley Davidson Café, and a few others), you and your children will feel welcome at this Midtown winner. On top of that, $60 million has been poured into renovating the rooms (which I thought were pretty nice already), completed in March 2001. Some nice extras include children's amenities like cookies and milk at turndown and licorice sticks in the rooms' penholders. But better still is the modified basketball court (by reservation to avoid disappointment) and special swimming classes like "mommy and me" that are open to hotel guests. If your children aren't the "joiner" types, there are plenty of pool toys and swim aides to keep them occupied. There is a lifeguard on duty, but children under 14 must be supervised by an adult. *Cribs (free), rollaways ($30, waived for kids under 12); kids under 12 free; concierge, restaurant*

| *The Lowell* | **$395 and up** |
|---|---|
| **28 East 63rd Street (between** | **212-838-1400** |
| **Madison and Park Aves.), UES** | **800-221-4444** |

The front desk attendants could not be friendlier or more helpful at this UES boutique hotel (though management is on the icy side). You'll be welcomed into the small lobby with smiles and salutations and whisked off to your room or suite (many of which have kitchenettes, balconies, even fireplaces or gardens) in no time. Kids will get a kick out of the fact that Madonna was in residence for a time but, before moving in, insisted upon having a private gym built in her suite. *Cribs/ rollaways (nominal charge)*

★ *The Mark*     $480 and up (specials from $299)
25 East 77th Street (between     212-744-4300
Fifth and Madison Aves.), UES     800-843-6275

Just steps off Madison Avenue, the second you enter The Mark, you'll feel the peace of the place settle over you. Part of the Small Luxury Hotels association, luxury is indeed the name of the game here. Rooms are variable in size, so specify if you intend to have a rollaway brought in (deluxe and up). And if you want a kitchenette, request that at booking too because many deluxe (and larger) rooms are fully equipped. Family options range from rollaways to suites and connecting rooms. *Cribs (free), rollaways ($30); kids under 17 free; concierge, restaurant/bar (children's menu)*

*The Peninsula*     $535 and up ($390 seasonal specials)
700 Fifth Avenue (at 55th St.), MTE     212-956-2888
www.peninsula.com     800-262-9467

Forty-five million dollars later, this landmark hotel is back in business (they closed the whole year of 1998 for the renovation) with renewed spirit (and everything else). Ideal for parents who are combining work with pleasure, the rooms at the Peninsula have all the trappings of the modern office (they say that each room is equipped with $17,000 of technology)—silent fax machine, double-line phones, modem, phone, and ISDN lines. But there's plenty for the kids too. Special gifts at check-in (the backpack with Velcro pull-off pouch is *sooo* cute) and amenities, like cookies and milk and stuffed animals at turndown, are always winners. The enclosed rooftop pool (with children's hours) and close proximity to Fifth Avenue favorites are also guaranteed to make the kids smile. *Cribs (free), rollaways ($50); kids under 12 free (flexible); concierge, restaurant*

| *The Pierre* | **$480 and up** |
|---|---|
| Fifth Avenue (at 61st St.), UES | **212-838-8000** |
| www.fourseasons.com | **800-743-7734** |

Ah, the Pierre! A Four Seasons landmark hotel, you'll be hard-pressed to find anything amiss at this exquisite historical favorite. Murals and tapestries adorn the walls, and equally impressive crystal chandeliers hang from the ceilings. Across the street from Central Park, and a stone's throw from FAO Schwarz and the best of Fifth and Madison Avenue shopping, the location couldn't be better, nor could the friendly and accommodating staff. As a special treat, especially for little (and grownup) girls, try afternoon tea in the Rotunda—I guarantee you, they won't forget it (and neither will you). *Cribs (free), extra beds ($50); kids under 18 free; kids' amenities (cookies and milk, coloring books, VCRs, video games, babysitting), pet friendly, mini-fridge and microwave (upon request)*

| *Plaza Athénée* | **$480 and up** |
|---|---|
| 37 East 64th Street (between | **212-734-9100** |
| Park and Madison Aves.), UES | **800-447-8800** |
| www.plaza-athenee.com | |

This peaceful Upper East Side hotel fits right in with the ritzy neighborhood. The staff is helpful, if a bit formal, and rooms are on the somewhat small side—but what each room provides is strictly top-notch. *Cribs (free), rollaway ($35); mini-fridge, VCR*

| *Regal UN Plaza* | $250–$300 rooms, |
| 1 United Nations Plaza | $379–550 junior suite |
| (at 44th St. and First Ave.), MTE | 212-758-1234 |
| | 800-222-8888 |

Perhaps one of the best things about the Regal UN is the "guaranteed view." Starting on the twenty-fourth floor (the lower floors are occupied by the United Nations), there are no buildings around that are as tall; therefore, every room at the Regal UN is assured a view of either the East River or the city skyline. Surely there is no other hotel in town that can promise that. The sizeable (remember, Manhattan-sized) pool is another great reason to stay here, as are the peace and quiet of the neighborhood. For theatergoers (or those who just want to get across town in ease and comfort) the hotel also offers free drop-offs in the Theater District. Double rooms can only accommodate two, but they can adjoin two rooms, and the junior suites can sleep four with a pullout couch. For larger families, or those looking for more space, there are also two-bedroom suites. *Cribs/rollaways (free); concierge, restaurant*

| ★ *The Regency* | $375–$650 and up |
| 540 Park Avenue (at 61st St.), UES | 212-759-4100 |
| www.loewshotel.com | 800-235-6397 |

This high-end hotel is part of the Loews chain. An extremely kid-friendly property, the Regency also welcomes pets—including dogs of any size (you might still want to leave the Great Dane at home, though). The rooms are well appointed and sizeable, and every effort is made to make your kids feel at home. Small toys are handed out at check-in (tell them you're bringing kids when you make your reservations), and some rooms, like the luxury kings (which come with either a king bed or two doubles), have the convenience of a kitchenette. Some of the larger rooms, like the $650 suite, have a king bed, a pullout couch, sitting and work area, two bathrooms, and plenty of extra space to tumble around in. *Cribs/rollaways (free); concierge, restaurant, toys, pet-friendly (even big dogs)*

| *Rihga Royal* | $299–$495, $345–$570, $455–$625 |
|---|---|
| 151 West 54th Street (between | 212-307-5000 |
| Sixth and Seventh Aves.), MTW | 800-937-5454 |

The great thing here is that all of the rooms are suites, and they're all pretty much the same size, regardless of what category level you spring for. There are three levels of suites, all of which are about 500 square feet and have a living room and bedroom separated by French doors and a bathroom with separate tub and shower. The pricing is pretty straightforward—the higher the floor, the more expensive the room. There are also some two-bedroom suites, which range from $600–$1,100. On weekends, every room receives vouchers for $25 or $50 (depending on your category) to spend on food and beverages anywhere in the hotel—including room service—and some of the room categories also include free car service to and from the airport, so be sure to ask when you book. *Cribs (free), rollaways/queen-size pullouts ($29); concierge, restaurant*

| ★ *The Stanhope* | $495 and up, ($295 summer |
|---|---|
| 995 Fifth Avenue | and weekend specials) |
| (at 81st St.), UES | 212-774-1234 |
| | 800-223-1234 |

The Stanhope is a classic, Old World, New York favorite. Located directly across from the Met and Central Park, and only

steps from other favorite museums and Madison Avenue boutiques, the Stanhope is a great property for families who enjoy
the lap of luxury in a quiet neighborhood. Part of the Hyatt
family, the Stanhope renovated rooms in 1999 and continues
to update and improve amenities in 2001. A great money-saving feature is the family plan: When parents book one room at
the standard rate, they get a second connecting room with two
beds at half price. Other options include suites with pullout
sleepers. Though there is no children's menu, the chef aims to
please, so requests for things like pb&j or macaroni and cheese
are met with pleasure. *Cribs/rollaways (free); kids under 18 free;
concierge, restaurant/bar, mini-fridge (free upon request), VCR
(upon request), children's amenities*

---

**★St. Regis**     **$580–$730 rooms; $990–$11,500 suites**
**2 East 55th Street (at Fifth Ave.), MTE     212-753-4500**
**www.stregis.com                             800-759-7550**

---

Widely considered one of the very best hotels in the world,
Elton John, Michael Jordan, and the Prince of Saudi Arabia, all
stay here when they're in town. So why not you? An exquisite
hotel with extremely attentive service, walking into the St.
Regis is like walking into a movie—it's just that nice. Marble
bathrooms, double sinks, and separate tub and shower are only
the beginning of what you get in these luxurious surroundings.
The way it works here is that your wish is their command—all
for a price, of course. Fabulous afternoon tea service, with a
live harpist and pastries by Chris Broberg, who many (me included) consider to be New York's best pastry chef. *Cribs (free),
rollaways ($90); children's amenities, babysitting*

★ *Surrey Hotel*                          $415–$725
20 East 76th Street                    212-320-8027
(at Madison Ave.), UES            800-ME-SUITE
www.mesuite.com

This all-suite hotel is sister to the Lyden Gardens and a bit more upscale. An equally great value, all rooms have a kitchenette and all of the accoutrements for cooking and eating. The larger suites have a full kitchen (some even have dishwashers, a feature many city residents live without). One- and two-bedroom suites are ideal for families, though connecting studios are also an option. The neighborhood is peaceful and quiet, only one block to Central Park and Museum Mile and close to all of the boutiques on Madison Avenue. Substantial discounts are offered for extended stays (it's no wonder so many guests are quasi-residents), and pets are welcome. *Cribs (free), rollaway ($20); kids under 18 free*

*Trump International Hotel and Towers*  $335–$1,500
1 Central Park West (between         212-299-1000
59th and 60th Sts.), UWS            888-448-7867

Perfectly centered between Midtown and the Upper West Side, the Trump Hotel is everything you'd expect of Donald Trump. No corners cut here. Virtually all of the rooms have fully equipped kitchens and in case your kids need a video break, the VCR can entertain them while you enjoy the stereo (or telescopes). The fitness center includes a two-lane (it is New York, after all) 55-foot pool, which welcomes children, and the close proximity (directly across the street) to Central Park is another great plus. *Cribs (free), rollaways (free most of the time; $50 during Thanksgiving and Christmas); concierge, restaurant, kitchenettes*

| *Waldorf-Astoria (Hilton)* | $229–$659 doubles, |
| 301 Park Avenue (between | $329 and up suites |
| 49th and 50th Sts.), MTE | 212-355-3000 |
| | 800-925-3673 |

The president stays at the Waldorf when he's in town, in part because there's a private concrete security bunker underneath and in part because the suites are among the best in the City. This old New York classic is as much of a tourist destination as a classy place to stay. Renovated in 1999, it's a real charmer, though for the money, unless you're feeling nostalgic or need to be in that specific location, you might want to, like me, look elsewhere. *Cribs (free), rollaways ($30); kids under 18 free; concierge, restaurant*

## Money-Saving Tip

Make all your phone calls from the pay phones in the lobby of your hotel. Many New York hotels charge as much as $2.00 for a local call, which can really add up, especially compared to 25 cents for the same service at the lobby payphones. And if you have a cell phone with an included-minutes plan, don't hesitate to use it, even when in your room.

## Apartment Stays

In addition to hotels, there's also the option of staying in a furnished apartment. There are obviously some advantages to this option, not least of which is that you'll feel like a local as you come and go from your place. But ironically, with that freedom also come some drawbacks: There is no concierge to advise you on attractions or make reservations, no maintenance to call when the toilet backs up, no maid service to come and clean up after you, nor any of the other conveniences that come with staying at a hotel (which you can have at the Lyden Gardens, the Surrey, and the Gracie, all of which offer substantial discounts for extended stays). Furthermore, traveling with kids, you might not save as much money as you might think because, with three or more people, the smallest rental you can secure is a one bedroom (usually a big jump up in price from a studio).

You might be getting the message that I don't necessarily recommend this form of accommodation. But then again many people really like the idea of staying in a real apartment in New York City, and that's a perfectly respectable view. Certainly, it's well worth researching this option if you think it's right for your family.

Listed here you'll find some of the City's best rental agencies, more of which are springing up every day. I've included only the most reliable, reputable, and long standing of the bunch. And don't forget, these apartments book up early, so be sure to call as far in advance as you possibly can.

| *Abode Ltd.* | $135–$400 (4-night minimum) |
|---|---|
| www.abodenyc.com | 212-472-2000 |
| | 800-835-8880 |

Abode has apartments ranging in size from studios to three bedrooms, all of which require a minimum four-night stay. Apartments include a full kitchen, TV, telephone, answering machine, hair dryer, iron, and clock radio and some have extras like a microwave, stereo, VCR, fax machine, balcony, whirlpool bath, fireplace, and health club. Apartments are located throughout the City.

### Bed, Breakfast, and Books — $125–$250
(2- to 3-night minimum)
212-865-8740

Studios and one-bedrooms and a few two-bedroom apartments are available for stays of two to three nights (depending upon the time of year) or longer. Sprinkled throughout the City, all of the apartments are near public transportation and are centrally located to areas of interest. Discounts are available for extended stays. With only thirty units, the stock here goes pretty fast.

### New York Habitat — $135–$500 (2- to 4-night minimum)
www.nyhabitat.com — 212-255-8018

A pioneer in the field, New York Habitat is one of the most highly regarded agencies—and its rates are very compelling. Prices vary according to location and many other factors, and some apartments are available on a bed-and-breakfast basis.

### Oxbridge — $140–$225 (4-night minimum)
www.oxbridgeny.com — 212-348-8100
800-550-7071

With apartments concentrated on 46th Street (between Fifth and Sixth Aves.) and the Upper East Side, Oxbridge has zeroed in on great locations. Some of the apartments are in blocks, so you could even rent adjoining apartments if they're available. If these neighborhoods aren't to your liking, ask about other locations because Oxbridge has other apartments here and there throughout the City. Like the others, these are self-catering apartments (no maid service) and require a minimum four-night stay.

| | |
|---|---|
| ***Urban Ventures*** | **$170–$700 (4-night minimum)** |
| **www.nyurbanventures.com** | **212-594-5650** |

Urban Ventures has apartments throughout the City ranging in size from studios to three bedrooms. Perhaps the largest of all of the apartment rental groups, Urban Ventures has more than 900 units in its repertoire, all of which require a minimum four-night stay. The units range in cost from $170 for a one bedroom up to $700 for the most expensive three bedrooms, but you can also get three bedrooms starting at $380—it all depends on the size, location, and swank-factor. Price adjustments are available on extended stays.

# INDEX TO HOTELS BY NEIGHBORHOOD AND PRICE

## GRAMERCY PARK/ FLATIRON

*"$" Hotels*
Carlton Arms (p. 120)

*"$$" Hotels*
Gramercy Park Hotel
(p. 132)

## MIDTOWN

*"$$" Hotels*
Broadway Inn Bed & Break-
fast (p. 127)
★Novotel New York
(p. 137)

## MIDTOWN EAST

*"$$" Hotels*
Clarion Hotel Fifth Avenue
(p. 129)
Loews New York (p. 135)
San Carlos (p. 138)

*"$$$" Hotels*
Barbizon (p. 139)
★Beekman Tower (p. 139)
★The Kimberly (p. 143)
Omni Berkshire Place
(p. 149)
★Plaza Fifty (p. 149)

*"$$$$" Hotels*
Four Seasons (p. 150)
The Peninsula (p. 154)
Regal UN Plaza (p. 156)
★St. Regis (p. 158)
Waldorf-Astoria (Hilton)
(p. 160)

## MIDTOWN WEST

*"$" Hotels*
Comfort Inn Midtown
(p. 121)

Herald Square Hotel
(p. 123)
Portland Square Hotel
(p. 124)

*"$$" Hotels*
Belvedere Hotel (p. 126)
Days Hotel Midtown
(p. 130)
Helmsley Middletowne
Hotel (p. 133)
Holiday Inn Midtown
(p. 134)
Travel Inn (p. 138)

*"$$$" Hotels*
The Michelangelo (p. 145)
The Wyndham (p. 150)

*"$$$$" Hotels*
★Le Parker Meridien
(p. 152)
Rihga Royal (p. 157)

## TIMES SQUARE

*"$$$" Hotels*
★Crowne Plaza Manhattan
(p. 140)
★Doubletree Guest Suites
(p. 141)
Marriott Marquis (p. 145)
Millennium Broadway &
The Premier (p. 146)

## TRIBECA

*"$" Hotels*
Cosmopolitan Hotel
(p. 121)

## UPPER EAST SIDE

*"$" Hotels*
★Habitat Hotel (p. 122)

CHAPTER

5

Attractions
& Activities

TICKET
TICKET
TICKET
TICKET

# Attractions

## City Sights

Map shows highlights only. See chapter text for more listings.

## s and Zoos

ican Museum of Natural History (p. 191)
ren's Museum of Manhattan (p. 207)
enheim Museum (p. 218)
id Sea-Air-Space Museum (p. 208)
East Side Tenement Museum (p. 212)
politan Museum of Art (p. 197)
um of the City of New York (p. 213)
um of Jewish Heritage (p. 214)
um of Modern Art (p. 215)

**14** Museum of Television & Radio (p. 216)
**28** New York City Fire Museum (p. 217)
**7** Whitney Museum of American Art (p. 219)
**10** Central Park Zoo (p. 245)

## Concert Halls

**12** Carnegie Hall (p. 278)
**11** Lincoln Center (p. 279)
**16** Radio City Music Hall (p. 280)

ow that you've decided to visit New York City, it's time to figure out what you're going to do with your time here. There are so many thousands of things to see and do in this ever-changing town that I can't stress enough the importance of advance planning. I've listed more activities and attractions here than a family could possibly do in a year (it's taken me a lifetime of living in and near New York to accumulate all this information), so it's up to you to figure out what your family will enjoy most. For 99 percent of families, a visit to one of the City's several zoos will be sufficient. If you come from a great zoo town like San Diego, though, you may be better off spending your time elsewhere. Or maybe your kids are zoo fanatics and want to visit all of New York's zoos, gardens, *and* the aquarium—so be it, you'll find the information you need here. Here are the two most valuable pieces of advice I have to offer:

1. **Always call ahead.** It is essential that you confirm the location and hours of any attraction you seek to visit. Even

the most reliable operations are occasionally forced to close or change their hours on a moment's notice. The last thing in the world you want to do is waste all that time and energy getting to a destination, only to find it closed or otherwise not up to your expectations. The old adage, an ounce of prevention is worth a pound of cure, certainly applies here.

2. **Always have a backup plan.** Sometimes, no matter how much planning you've put in, and even if you've called ahead, things fall through—or the lines turn out to be so long that you have to back out. Luckily, there's so much variety among New York's attractions that you should be able to fend off heartbreak and disappointment with some creative planning. If things aren't working out at the World Trade Center, try the Empire State Building. Or just be aware of the shops and restaurants near all your destinations, so you have efficient ways to use your extra time. Act confident, and your kids may never know you switched to Plan B.

In this chapter, I've listed the major venues for activities in New York City. I designed this book so it could be the only resource you'll need when it comes to planning a trip to New York and choosing your activities. But when it comes to what will be happening at specific places on the specific days you'll be in New York, you won't know until much closer to the actual date of your trip. Thus, when you start planning, you'll want to begin by making a list of desired activities. For some of those activities, like the most popular Broadway shows, you can purchase tickets months in advance. Other spots won't announce their activity schedules until weeks or days before the actual event. But whatever you do, please don't just show up in New York without at least the outline of a game plan—it's really too much of a city for you to wing it.

Here are some resources for planning your New York City activities schedule:

❧ For current listings, the most user-friendly sources are *New York Magazine* and *Time Out New York.* They're often available at large chain bookstores like Barnes & Noble, even outside the New York region. Listings run about two weeks in advance of the magazines' dates of newsstand release. Though the physical magazines are much easier to work with, both also maintain Web sites (www.timeoutny.com and www.nymag.com). For most needs, you probably won't need to go any farther in your research than *New York* and *Time Out.*

❧ Also very useful are the listings in the free *Village Voice* newspaper (www.villagevoice.com) and the Friday *New York Times* "Weekend" section (www.nytimes.com and www.nytoday.com).

❧ On the Web, CitySearch (www.newyork.citysearch.com) has the best listings, though I still favor the print sources.

❧ An excellent local monthly is *New York Family,* a magazine specifically targeted at families with kids (www.parenthoodweb.com). There's also the *Big Apple Parent* paper (www.parentsknow.com) and *ParentGuide* (www.parentguidenews.com). These publications are intended mostly for New Yorkers, but tourists can glean some useful information from them as well.

❧ *Where Magazine* (www.wheremagazine.com) also has good listings, and you'll probably get a free copy in your hotel room.

ℯ In addition, once you land in New York City, you'll be buried under free brochures that list all manner of family-appropriate events. Your hotel lobby and the lobbies of the main tourist attractions should have plentiful collections. Particularly useful are any publications from the NYCVB (Convention & Visitors Bureau).

ℯ If your kids have very specific interests, such as modern art, you'll want to look into specialty publications. I've listed the most important of these in the applicable sections that follow.

## Money-Saving Tip

Use combined attractions passes for big savings. The CityPass gets you into the Empire State Building Observatory, Top of the World Trade Center, Guggenheim Museum, American Museum of Natural History, Museum of Modern Art, and Intrepid Sea-Air-Space Museum at half the cost of purchasing separate tickets for each. Passes are $32.00 for adults, $21.75 for seniors, and $24.00 for kids 12 through 17 (not available to younger kids). You can buy CityPass at the main entrance of any of the attractions or online at www.citypass.net. Less of a savings, but still respectable, is the Best of New York package, available at the Empire State Building or online through www.skyride.com. It includes admission to the Empire State Building Observatory, New York Skyride, Madison Square Garden's "All Access Tour," and Radio City's "Stage Door Tour." It's $42.00 for adults and $30.00 for kids 5 through 12 (a savings of $8.50 and $4.50, respectively). Don't buy a combined attractions pass unless you really plan and want to visit enough of the included attractions.

@ But really, despite the wealth of resources available, there's no need to go into research overkill. This book plus a copy of the relevant issues of *New York* or *Time Out* should suffice for planning all but the most unusual trips.

# City Sights

This section includes a mixed bag of attractions, all of which have that "Only in New York!" quality. Ranging from the Brooklyn Bridge to the United Nations, here is where I've included New York's most unique buildings, monuments, and centers of activity. The really nice thing is that, with many of the listings in this section, there's little or no cost involved—it doesn't, in general, cost anything to look!

I've indicated the neighborhood, using the following abbreviations:

BR: Brooklyn
CH: Chelsea
EV: East Village
GD: Garment District
GV: Greenwich Vilage
LI: Little Italy
MTE: Midtown East
Q: Queens
SI: Staten Island
TD: Theater District
UES: Upper East Side
UWS: Upper West Side

BX: Bronx
CT: Chinatown
FD: Financial District
GP: Gramercy Park/Flatiron
LES: Lower East Side
MT: Midtown
MTW: Midtown West
SH: SoHo
TBC: TriBeCa
TS: Times Square
US: Union Square
WV: West Village

A ★ indicates an attraction that stands out, particularly in relation to the others in its category.

## ★Brooklyn Bridge
**Connecting the Manhattan and Brooklyn Civic Centers**
**Manhattan entrance near Park Row and Center Street**
**(close to the 4, 5, and 6 subways)**
**Brooklyn entrance near the High Street A and C train**
**station**

Something about the Brooklyn Bridge inspires awe in all who lay eyes upon it—Walt Whitman, Hart Crane, me, and everybody else in New York. It's not the world's largest suspension bridge (though it was for a while), and it's not the oldest of its kind (the Roebling Bridge in Cincinnati predates it by several years), but it nonetheless has a certain appeal that combines aesthetics, engineering, and tradition to create what many believe is history's most perfect bridge. Walking across the Brooklyn Bridge is an experience all but the smallest children should have—you can walk one way (allow about half an hour at an average walking pace) and take the subway back, or you can combine the walk with a visit to other Brooklyn attractions. Construction of the bridge began in 1867, and it was completed in 1883. Designed by John Roebling, the project was haunted by misfortune. Roebling was mortally wounded in 1869 when a ferry rammed a waterfront piling on which he was standing. Washington Roebling, his son who took over the project, was taken ill with the bends in 1872. When the Brooklyn Bridge opened, a dozen pedestrians were killed in a stampede started by someone who shouted that the bridge was collapsing. A year later, P. T. Barnum crossed the bridge with a herd of elephants to demonstrate its safety. The situation has improved steadily ever since.

★ *Cathedral of Saint John*  212-316-7540 general info
*the Divine*                   212-932-7347 tour info
1047 Amsterdam Avenue    212-662-2133 event info/
(at 112th St.), UWS                        tickets
www.stjohndivine.org

Saint John the Divine has been under construction since 1892, and it's still not finished! Even uncompleted, though, it's the world's largest Gothic cathedral, the size of two football fields, with seating for 5,000 worshipers. There are tours offered six days a week (no Mondays) at 11 A.M. (Sundays at 1 P.M.), plus there's a special tower tour (you climb an eleven-story spiral staircase to the top of the cathedral, where the views are fantastic) twice a month (the first and third Saturday of each month, at noon and 2 P.M.). A token admission fee is suggested. The free New Year's Eve concert is a New York favorite, as is the Blessing of the Animals each October.

*Chrysler Building*
405 Lexington Avenue (at 42nd St.), MTE

You can't actually ascend the Chrysler Building unless you work there, but chances are you'll pass by it at some point during your visit to New York. It's worth a look (from the outside, as well as inside from the Art Deco lobby that features African marble), because this—not the Empire State or World Trade—is probably New Yorkers' favorite building. Note the radiator-cap ornaments and gargoyles.

## ★ *Ellis Island*                    212-363-3200
New York Harbor
www.ellisisland.org

Between 1892 and 1954, 17 million immigrants passed through Ellis Island. More than 40 percent of Americans living today are the descendants of those immigrants. Renovated and reopened in 1990, Ellis Island is now an absolutely fascinating museum of immigration. The emphasis is on the personal experience of immigration. The "Through America's Gate" exhibit focuses on photographs and oral histories. The "Treasures from Home" exhibit displays family heirlooms, religious articles, rare clothing, and jewelry, all donated by descendants of immigrants. At the American Family Immigration History Center, you can research your family's history. For transportation information, see the Statue of Liberty—the same ferry services Ellis Island and the Statue of Liberty, and you'll likely want to visit both.

## ★ *Empire State Building*          212-736-3100
350 Fifth Avenue (at 34th St.), MTE
www.esbnyc.com

What a colorful history the Empire State Building has. At 102 stories and 1,454 feet, it stood for years as the world's tallest building. King Kong fictionally scaled it in 1933. A military aircraft really crashed into it in 1945. That funny structure at the top? It was intended as a mooring mast for blimps, but was only used once. Observation decks are on the 86th and 102nd floors, and, even though it's lower, you should give the 86th-floor deck your attention—many experienced New Yorkers say it's the better choice. You can see 80 miles from the observation decks on a clear day, and the best times to go are first thing in the morning or late at night (the largest crowds come in the late afternoon and early evening). Also within the building: New York Skyride (888-SKYRIDE or 212-279-9777, www.skyride.com), a flightseeing simulation that takes you on a virtual aerial tour of New York's major landmarks, but it's not nearly as fun as the real experience of the observation decks.

Take a look at the Empire State Building at night, and you'll see the top of the Empire State Building illuminated by thousands of colored floodlights. The colors change often, to commemorate important holidays and events. Some are easy to figure out: red, white, and blue for Independence Day; green for Saint Patrick's Day. But the building also glows red, black, and green for Martin Luther King Jr.'s birthday; purple, teal, and white for part of National Osteoporosis Month; red, yellow, and green for Portugal Day; blue and white for Hanukkah; green, white, and orange for India Independence Day; and lavender and white for Gay Pride Day. The building is unlit for AIDS Awareness Day. The Empire State Building's Web site (www.esbnyc.com) contains a lighting schedule along with a wealth of other building facts.

**Empire State Building hours:** Daily 9:30 A.M. to midnight (last chance to purchase tickets is 11:25 P.M.). *It's critical that you call ahead, as the observation decks can be closed in foul weather.*

**Observatory admission:** $9 adults, $7 seniors, $4 children under 12, children under 5 free

**Skyride hours:** Daily from 10 A.M. to 10 P.M.

**Skyride admission:** $11.50 for adults, $8.50 for kids and seniors

**Combined admission:** $17 adult, $10 child

## Helpful Hint

To build anticipation, study the Empire State Building's exterior and lobby first. The best places to view (and photograph) the outside are from the top floor (food court) of the Manhattan Mall (34th St.) and from the base of the Flatiron Building (23rd St.). When you enter the building, be sure to spend some time examining the beautiful details and the mural in the soaring lobby.

### Flatiron Building
**175 Fifth Avenue (at 23rd St.), GP**

One of New York's favorite landmarks, this triangular building (so named because it's shaped like an iron—as in laundry) dates back to 1902 and is only 6 feet across at its narrow end. It contains no specific attractions or events, but it's a great building to observe from the street—then you can turn around and get a phenomenal view of the Empire State Building up the avenue.

### Grand Central Terminal          212-935-3960 tour info
**42nd Street (at Park Ave.), MTE**
**www.grandcentralterminal.com**

Travelers returning from Europe invariably comment on the beauty of European train stations, but the truth is those stations have got nothing on Grand Central. Though the station, designed by Warren & Wetmore with Reed & Stem, fell into disrepair for many years, it has recently been the beneficiary of a $175-million renovation, and construction continues to this day. The terminal is now again one of the world's greatest public spaces, and many say it's better than it ever was. Observe Jules-Alexis Coutan's neoclassical sculpture, "Transportation," at the south entrance (the central character is Mercury, the Roman god of, among other things, travel). The sky ceiling shows the constellations, lit by fiber-optic cables. Particularly noteworthy and useful for families is the wealth of new restaurants and food stalls, particularly on the new downstairs dining concourse, which features absolutely no chain junk food—just authentic, local, New York fare, including Junior's cheesecake and the Grand Central Oyster bar with its famous, vaulted tile ceilings. There's a tour of Grand Central Station every Wednesday at 12:30 P.M.—meet in front of the main-concourse information booth (you can't miss it). The tour is free, but donations to the Municipal Art Society are accepted.

| *New York Public Library* | 212-869-8089 |
| **Fifth Avenue and 42nd Street, MTE** | 212-930-0800 |
| **www.nypl.org** | |

This Beaux Arts edifice was designed by Carrère & Hastings in 1911 and is made of white Vermont marble with Corinthian columns and, in front, the famous lion sculptures: Patience (left) and Fortitude (right). Mayor Fiorello La Guardia joked, "Read between the lions." The New York Public Library is one of the world's great libraries, with 6 million books, 12 million manuscripts, and 2.8 million photographs. The library also hosts numerous exhibitions and lectures throughout the year—call for details.

**Main Reading Room and exhibition hall hours:** Monday, Thursday, Friday, and Saturday 10 A.M.–6 P.M., Tuesday through Wednesday 11 A.M.–6 P.M. A free one-hour tour is available Monday through Saturday at 11 A.M. and 2 P.M. (departs from Astor Hall).

## Top Ten Public Spaces to Take a Break

One of the great new trends in construction in New York City is the abundance of public spaces carved out of mostly commercial office plazas. Some are indoors, others are outdoors, but all are open to the public for a rest, a snack, or even a low-key picnic.

1. World Financial Center—Hudson River at Vesey and Liberty Sts. (indoors)

2. Paley Park—53rd St., just east of Fifth Ave. (outdoors)

3. Sony Plaza—55th St., at Madison Ave. (indoors)

4. Rockefeller Center—47th to 50th Sts., between Fifth and Sixth Aves. (outdoors)

5. Chase Manhattan Plaza—near Liberty and William Sts., Financial District (outdoors)

6. IBM Garden—Madison Ave., between 56th and 57th Sts. (indoors)

7. World Trade Plaza—Chambers St. (outdoors)

8. South Street Seaport—East River, near Fulton St. (indoors)

9. Bryant Park—42nd St., between Fifth and Sixth Aves. (outdoors)

10. World Wide Plaza—49th and 50th Sts., between Eighth and Ninth Aves. (outdoors)

*New York Stock Exchange*   212-656-5165
20 Broad Street (ticket booth), FD

Here you can watch all the trading-floor action from a glassed-in observation deck. There are also interactive exhibits explaining how the market works (in a very general sense) and a short film about the NYSE past and present. Very early arrival may earn you a ticket that allows you inside in time to see the opening bell (at 9:30 A.M.) when the whole place goes berserk.

**Exchange hours:** Monday through Friday 9:15 A.M.– 4:00 P.M.; closed national holidays.

**Admission:** Tickets are free, but rationed (3,000 per day) and usable only for specified time slots, so arrive early (the ticket booth opens at 8:45 A.M.).

---

### *Rockefeller Center*                    212-632-3975
### 47th–50th Streets (between Fifth and Sixth Aves.), MT

Most of Rockefeller Center was built in the 1930s, at the height of the Art Deco era. It is the world's largest such complex, with 18 buildings on 21 acres of extremely valuable New York City land. If you stand on Fifth Avenue between 49th and 50th Streets, you're looking at the Promenade, which leads to the Lower Plaza, encircled by the flags of every United Nations member country, where you'll find the famous Rockefeller Center ice-skating rink (in winter) and Paul Manship's bronze statue of Prometheus. Also along the Promenade and Lower Plaza are numerous shops and restaurants. This is also where, in Christmas season, you'll find the famous New York City Christmas tree.

Inside Rockefeller Center:

@ The **ice-skating rink** is open October through March. Call 212-332-7654 for details.

@ The focal point of the complex is the seventy-story **General Electric Building,** at 30 Rockefeller Plaza, where you can grab a walking-tour brochure at the main information desk.

@ **Radio City Music Hall,** at 1260 Sixth Avenue (at 50th St.), is the crown jewel of Rockefeller Center. See Arts for details.

@ Many NBC television shows are broadcast from the network's Rockefeller Center studios: *Saturday Night Live,* the *Rosie O'Donnell Show,* and *Late Night with Conan O'Brien.* **NBC Studio Tours** run every 15 minutes daily from 9:15 A.M. to 4:30 P.M., Easter through Labor Day and Thanksgiving through New Year's, and every 30 minutes Monday through Saturday during the rest of the year. Tickets: $10 all ages (no children under 6 admitted). Call 212-664-7174 for details.

@ *The Today Show* broadcasts live from a glassed-in studio on the southwest corner of 49th Street and Rockefeller Plaza on weekdays from 7 A.M. to 9 A.M.

@ And don't miss the **International Building,** on Fifth Avenue between 50th and 51st Streets, with its world-famous statue of Atlas holding up the globe.

| | |
|---|---|
| *Saint Patrick's Cathedral* | **212-753-2261** |
| **Fifth Avenue (at 50th St.), MTE** | |

Saint Patrick's is the largest Catholic cathedral in the United States and the headquarters of the Archdiocese of New York. Designed by James Renwick, it took from 1858 until 1906 to complete. It's named for the patron saint of the Irish, one of New York's principal ethnic groups. A major landmark, its front steps are a great place to meet and people-watch in Midtown. There is, incidentally, a wonderful view of Saint Patrick's from the SFA Café on the top floor of the Saks Fifth Avenue department store across the street.

   **Hours:** Open daily 8:00 A.M.–8:45 P.M.

*Shearith Israel Spanish and*          **212-873-0300**
*Portuguese Synagogue*
**2 West 70th Street (at Columbus Ave. and Central Park West), UWS**

The oldest Jewish congregation in the United States, Shearith Israel was founded in 1654 by refugees from the Spanish Inquisition. The current building dates back to 1897 and is noteworthy for, among other things, its Tiffany windows.

*South Street Seaport*          **212-SEAPORT**
**At Water and South Streets, FD**
**www.southstseaport.org**

The South Street Seaport overlooks the East River and the Brooklyn Bridge and consists of eleven square blocks of historic buildings and piers, plus shops, restaurants, and a museum. It's a great refuge for families, because unlike most of Manhattan, the Seaport is relatively manageable.

Within the Seaport:

- The Seaport hosts **free events** all summer, including concerts, fireworks, and dancing. Call 212-SEAPORT or 212-809-6080 for schedules.

- The **Pier 17 shopping complex** contains numerous shops and a food court, with a panoramic view that includes the Statue of Liberty and Brooklyn Bridge.

- The **Fulton Fish Market,** on Fulton Street at the East River, is the nation's largest wholesale fish market. It operates only in the middle of the night, roughly from 12 A.M. to 6 A.M. You can barely tell it's there during the day (except for the smell)!

@ The *Titanic* **Memorial Lighthouse,** at Fulton and Water Streets, commemorates the passengers who lost their lives on 15 April 1912. The *Titanic* was bound for New York on that fateful voyage.

@ The circa-1885 cargo schooner, ***Pioneer***, offers two-hour cruises daily from May through September. Tickets: $20 for adults, $15 seniors, $12 for children. Call 212-748-8786 to confirm times and make reservations.

@ The Seaport is also home to a small but interesting museum, which focuses on maritime history. Museum hours: from April to September, Friday through Wednesday 10 A.M.–6 P.M., Thursday 10 A.M.–8 P.M.; from October to March, Wednesday through Sunday 10 A.M.–5 P.M. Tickets: $6 adults, $5 seniors, $3 children. Call 212-748-8600.

| ★*Statue of Liberty* | 212-363-3200 general info |
|---|---|
| On Liberty Island in | 212-269-5755 ticket/ferry info |
| New York Harbor | |
| www.nps.gov/stli | |

A gift from France to the United States, the Statue of Liberty was designed by sculptor Frédéric-Auguste Bartholdi, and the engineering was the brainchild of Alexandre-Gustave Eiffel (of Eiffel Tower fame). It is the definitive icon of New York and America. The statue weighs 225 tons and is 152 feet from foot to torch. The nose is 4½ feet long; the index finger, 8 feet. It's a 354-step (22 story) climb to the observation deck in the crown, though you can take the elevator the first 10 stories. There are several other observation decks, including one in the pedestal that requires minimal stair climbing. The ferry ride takes about 20 minutes and offers great views of the

Manhattan skyline. The ferry also stops at Ellis Island (included in the fare), though the last ferry of the day will only take you to one destination.

**Hours:** Ferries leave daily every half-hour to 45 minutes from 9:30 A.M. to 3:15 P.M., with more frequent ferries in the morning and extended hours in summer.

**Admission:** The ferry ticket plus admission to the Statue of Liberty and Ellis Island is $7 adults, $6 seniors, $3 children under 17.

**Transportation:** *Subway:* 4, 5 subway to Bowling Green, or the 1, 9 to South Ferry. Walk downtown (south) through Battery Park to Castle Clinton, where you line up for ferry tickets; you'll then have to wait on a separate line for the ferry (there is a nearby playground where kids can kill some of the time).

## Helpful Hint

The Statue of Liberty is one of New York's most popular attractions, so you need to be clever to beat the crowds. Go first thing in the morning or risk having to wait an hour or more to climb the stairs. In summer, the National Park Service sometimes limits crown access to only those visitors on the 8:30 A.M. boat. There is a ferry to the Statue of Liberty from New Jersey, which leaves from the front of the Liberty Science Center (see Museums). This ferry is much less crowded than the Manhattan one. Combine your Statue of Liberty visit with a Liberty Science Center expedition for a great day—and save a lot of time. The least busy time of year to visit the statue is in January and February.

## Temple Emanu-El                          212-744-1400
### 1 East 65th Street (at Fifth Ave.), UES
www.emanuelnyc.org

This is the largest Reform synagogue in the world, and the most important. The architecture is a mix of Moorish and Romanesque, which is meant to evoke the commingling of Eastern and Western cultures. Within is a small museum, the Bernard Museum, which has a world-class Judaica collection, including Hanukkah lamps from the fourteenth to twentieth centuries.

**Hours:** Open daily 10 A.M.–5 P.M.

## ★ Theodore Roosevelt Birthplace         212-260-1616
### 28 East 20th Street (between Broadway and Park Ave.), GP
www.nps.gov/thrb

I consider this to be one of New York's most delightful attractions. It's small, intimate, and manageable, and the kids can really learn something without feeling oppressed or overwhelmed. President Theodore Roosevelt was born on this site in 1858. The house contains period furniture, beautiful rooms, and a collection of Roosevelt memorabilia.

**Hours:** Wednesday through Sunday 9 A.M.–5 P.M.; closed national holidays. Tours on the hour; last tour at 4 P.M.

**Admission:** $2 adults, children under 17 free

**Transportation:** *Subway:* Lexington Avenue 6 train to 23rd Street (which, here, stops on Park Avenue)

## Times Square
### 42nd Street (at Broadway)

It's actually a triangle formed by 42nd Street, Seventh Avenue, and Broadway (which runs at a diagonal), but it's nonetheless

one of New York's central landmarks. There isn't exactly anything to do here, but you have to see it—preferably at night.

### United Nations                          212-963-8687
**First Avenue (at 46th St.), MTE**
**www.un.org**

When you're in the United Nations, you're not technically in the
United States. You're in an international zone over which only
the United Nations is sovereign. The complex covers 18 acres
along the East River. John D. Rockefeller Jr. donated the land in
1946. There is a beautiful riverside promenade, a rose garden
with 1,400 rosebushes, and sculptures donated by member nations (whose 180 flags fly in alphabetical order in the plaza). You
can have lunch weekdays at the Delegates' Dining Room, where
you'll have a beautiful view of the river, though you may or may
not see actual delegates. Call 212-963-7625 for reservations. The
gift shop sells flags and other international memorabilia. The
UN post office is a must-visit for budding numismatists.

   **Hours:** Guided tours (one-hour long) cover the General As-
sembly Hall, the Security Council Chamber, the Chagall stained-
glass windows, and more. Daily tours every 30 minutes, 9:15
A.M.–4:45 P.M. (closed weekends in January and February).

   **Admission:** $7.50 adults, $5.50 seniors, $4.50 students,
$3.50 children (children under 5 not permitted)

### World Financial Center
**Hudson River (between Vesey and Liberty Sts.), FD**
**www.worldfinancialcenter.com**

One of the great monuments to New York's urban renewal, the
World Financial Center—which sits right behind the World
Trade Center (to which it is connected by an overpass)—is a

gorgeous, 14-acre, 6-million-square-foot complex of glass atriums, office buildings, shops, restaurants, and a marina. The buildings sit on landfill produced in part by the excavation for the World Trade Center Towers. In the Winter Garden there are sixteen palm trees from the Sonoma Desert in Arizona. Though the World Financial Center isn't a tourist attraction as such, it's a great place to get some climate-controlled, indoor peace and quiet, plus a snack and a beverage, when you're exploring downtown. There are free concerts and performances throughout the year; check the Web site for schedules.

★ *World Trade Center* 212-323-2340 observation deck
Between Church, Vesey,    212-435-4170 general info
Liberty, and West Streets, FD
www.wtc-top.com

The ticket lines at Two World Trade Center can be long, but once you're on an elevator it's only 58 seconds to the top. The outdoor observation platform, 107 stories high, is New York's highest, and affords as much as a 55-mile view on a clear day. The platform is often closed, however (it's only open when weather and wind conditions are just right), so don't be disappointed if you have to do your looking from inside. Also on the observation deck you'll find a six-minute simulated Manhattan helicopter tour, a food court, and some interesting exhibits. If you're downtown and you're having trouble finding the World Trade Center, don't forget to look up! It's visible from almost any intersection in the neighborhood.

**Hours:** September through May, daily 9:30 A.M.–9:30 P.M.; June through August, daily 9:30 A.M.–11:30 P.M.

**Admission:** $12 adults, $9 seniors, $6 children under 12
**Transportation:** *Subway:* 1, 9 to WTC

## Helpful Hint

There are three restaurants: Windows on the World, Wild Blue, and the Greatest Bar on Earth, all of which sit atop One World Trade Center (the tower opposite the one with the observation deck). Though these places are expensive, and the food isn't all that great, it's sometimes possible to finagle your way in for a snack or a drink or just a look around—and the same views you'd get from the observation levels across the way.

## Museums

Many people come from around the world for the sole purpose of visiting New York's museums. And, whether you're visiting with toddlers or teens, there's something for *everyone*. Because you're confronted with a dizzying number of museums, I've tried to help by narrowing down the selection and indicating my top picks by arranging the museums into three categories of appropriateness:

- ℮ The two must-visit museums, Best for Children and Families, are my top picks and are listed first. These are the Metropolitan Museum of Art and the American Museum of Natural History (which contains the Rose Center for Earth and Space). I have found that these museums are the odds-on favorites of the greatest number of children and families. I've devoted the longest and most detailed descriptions to these museums, because I want you to be able to use this book as a mini-guide and educational tool. Unless you have a very specific agenda, the truth is that—on a typical New York City vacation—

it's possible you won't have the time or inclination to visit any museums other than these.

ꙅ The Best of the Rest includes museums that are excellent and highly worthwhile, but, as much as I love every one of these museums, I can't honestly tell you to drag the kids to all of them. You'll have to make choices based on interest, attention span, and availability of time. I provide the highlights of each museum, but the descriptions aren't as in-depth as for my top picks.

ꙅ Specialty Museums are also extremely worthy attractions. I don't mean to judge the value of these museums by placing them in this category, and were I writing a guide for adults, my choices might be different. But I wouldn't necessarily recommend these places for a first-time visitor on a short vacation unless you or your child has a special interest in the particular subject area. These museums tend to be very specialized, off the beaten path, or grownup-oriented. Therefore, these listings are shortest.

Of course, if you're looking for information about a specific museum, you needn't hunt through the categories—all listings are cross-referenced and indexed as well.

## Best for Children and Families

★*American Museum of Natural History* 212-769-5100 *and Rose Center for Earth and Space*
**Central Park West (between 77th and 81st Sts.), UWS**
**www.amnh.org**

Any way you slice it, this museum is a winner for everyone. My favorite museum since I was a young child, the American

Museum of Natural History (AMNH) offers something for children of all ages and all interests. With 42 exhibition halls, the world's largest dinosaur collection, the 563-carat Star of India sapphire, the Hall of Biodiversity, and the replica of the 94-foot blue whale (everyone's favorite), whether you spend thirty minutes or all day, this museum is a must. Still, although you could easily spend a couple of years exploring this museum, if you have young children, plan to spend, at most, one hour. No matter how enticing the dioramas and the giant elephants are, small legs (the museum is gigantic) get tired, and attention spans wane (you'll be exhausted just *reading* about everything that's in this place!). If it's a real hit, you can always return later.

For children under 10, the favorites are the whale in the Ocean Life room (first floor), the dioramas (everywhere), the dinosaurs (fourth floor), the African Mammals (third and fourth floors), and the Asian Mammals (second floor). Even toddlers can appreciate the dioramas and will get a kick out of the animals in their "natural" environments.

Here's a quick look at what AMNH has to offer:

@ Starting with the first floor main entrance, you'll see the ancient dioramas of the **Pilgrims and Native Americans** in old New York.

@ Next, the **Hall of Biodiversity** is dark and soothing. On the right is a giant clamshell. The giant squid and octopus have been the sources of many great novels and bad movies. Children who are in school, and especially those learning about biology, will get a kick (and good grasp) from the classification system on the wall. Younger children will enjoy the specimens (turtles, mammals, birds) that are mounted on the wall. *Note the sea creatures hanging from the ceiling.*

- The **Dzanga-Sangha African Rainforest** project is an example of what is being done to help preserve the vanishing rainforest. Walk through and even sit down in the rainforest. Even the very young can appreciate the foliage and dim lighting—it simply feels different. Older children can read about and look at pictures of grasslands and savannas and islands. High school students can ponder questions like, *What is an integrated conservation development project?*

- Moving along into the **Hall of North American Forests.** This is primarily a pass-through, except for the diorama with the giant earthworm and millipede and the incredible cross-section of the sequoia. This tree, which was cut in 1891, has 1,342 annual rings. It is enormous. After digesting the size and age of the specimen, look at the pointers. Each of those pointers specifies what was happening in history at the time that the tree was that many years old. When put in that perspective, it is mind-boggling.

- Refuel at **Café 77** if you need a break, drinks, or light fare.

- By the entrance to the **Northwest Coast Indians** is the Haida Indian Canoe. It was made from a single red cedar log. It is 63 feet long and just over 8 feet wide at its widest point. In the canoe are models of Haida Indians, active in their frozen state, paddling the canoe. Young children will delight in this specimen.

- Also good for a walk-through (and more if your child has special interests in this area) is the dark, cool **Northwest Coast Indian Hall.** Huge totems line the galleries, each of which has been set up in a separate alcove differentiating specimens and tribes. The collection is vast and varied.

◉ The **Hall of Human Biology and Evolution** starts with simple dioramas of prehistoric people and goes on to the more advanced model of the double helix and 3-D holograms of the human body. This hall can be a great area for learning. If attention spans are waning, it's still worth a walk-through, if only for the dioramas and holograms and what it leads you to . . .

◉ The **Halls of Meteorites, Minerals, and Gems** are fascinating to children of all ages. The specimens are shiny, and you can touch some of them. Kids in grade school through high school who have spent any time at all studying rocks and minerals will be amazed by the vast collection. The hundreds of labeled specimens are astonishing even to the most avid collector. In this section, my favorite specimens are the petrified trees. Laid out on the floor, without protective glass, are what used to be tree trunks and are now ostensibly rocks.

◉ On the fourth floor, the first stop should be the **Saurischian Dinosaurs,** but en route, walk through the **Vertebrate Origins Hall.** You don't even have to stop, but kids might want to check out the skeletons and shells of the giant sea turtles and crocodiles. As you walk from one hall to the next, as your children likely race ahead, the walls of the passageway are lined with black-and-white photographs of various dinosaur excavations. Projects all over the world are featured, including some in Mongolia, Wyoming, and Egypt.

◉ As you walk into the dinosaur hall (the room gets lots of natural light, so it's an extremely pleasant place to spend some time), you'll likely hear exclamations of "cool!" or "excellent!" As well as squeals of delight. These guys are gigantic. To put things in perspective a little, take a few moments to have a discussion. Ask younger kids: *If you stood next to the Apatosaurus skeleton, how high could you reach? Compare your leg with his. How many times bigger are his bones than yours? Who do you think is smarter, you or the dinosaur?*

@ Around the corner is the **Dinostore,** which seems as good a place as any to buy a museum souvenir if you're planning to do so. The selection includes books, tee shirts, stuffed animals, jewelry, mugs, postcards, pens, and so forth.

@ The third floor has two highlights: The first is the **Reptiles and Amphibians** exhibit. You can view this room in five minutes. The big attractions are the 23-foot skeleton of the reticulated python; the Komodo dragon; the 14-foot, 7-inch American crocodile; the Galapagos tortoise; and the 12-inch American alligator. Ask your children: *How many vertebrae do you think this python has? How about in its tail? How many does a human have?* (The python has 321 vertebrae in the body and 91 in the tail; humans have 24 total.)

@ Second, and perhaps most beloved in the museum by the young, is the **Hall of African Mammals.** From the third floor you get a good view of the eight East African elephants standing in the middle of the enormous room, a hint of what's coming downstairs. Take a quick spin around to view the dioramas upstairs—warthogs, ostriches, and cheetahs—but spend most of your time below on the second floor with the close-up view of the elephants and the other animals. At the far end of the room is a pair of tusks, found in Kenya in 1939 and weighing in at 169 pounds. *For younger children, an excellent school report or presentation topic is the difference between African and Asian elephants.*

If you're overwhelmed or don't have a lot of time, you can take one of the museum's free highlights tours. They're offered daily at quarter after the hour from 10:15 A.M. to 3:15 P.M. Of the host of other tours and programs, many are free, so be sure to stop by an information desk when you arrive at the museum. Even if you aren't interested in a tour (and with toddlers and younger children, I'd advise that you're best off on your own), at least you'll know in case you want to join one. For those interested in a self-guided highlights tour, pick up a copy of the World Culture Hour Tour. You can always skip ahead or skip some exhibits altogether if the troops are getting restless.

At all times the museum has special exhibits, such as the recent fighting dinosaurs and the comeback of the Butterfly Conservatory: Tropical Butterflies Alive in Winter (tropical butterflies free-flying in a walk-in vivarium), as well as two feature IMAX films. There is an additional charge for special exhibits and IMAX films.

If that isn't enough, the AMNH also offers educational programs, workshops, and field trips on such topics as bird watching, wildlife in art, and dinosaur shadow theater. These programs are usually on weekends and have fees starting at $15 for one adult with one child. Check the Web site or call ahead to have a schedule mailed.

**The Rose Center for Earth and Space** has received a tremendous amount of attention since the opening of its new multimillion-dollar facility. Truly a sight to behold at any hour, it is especially striking when illuminated at night. Entry into the Rose Center is included with admission to the AMNH. But the biggest attraction—the Space Show in the Space Theater—costs extra. Narrated by Tom Hanks, this twenty-minute show brings audiences "the clearest possible images of the night sky, along with a three-dimensional visual exploration." But be warned: This show is very advanced—most kids won't be able to keep up, no matter how soothing Tom Hanks' voice is—and it's very expensive ($19.00 for adults, $14.00 for seniors and students, and $11.50 for children, including admission to the museum). So, unless your children are extremely interested in astronomy or are at least 10 years old, I'd say save it for the next trip, when they can appreciate it more. Better just to have a walk around the Rose Center (which offers many free exhibits) and see the Big Bang show (which is also free) and pick up a copy of *Our Place in Space, A Kid's Guide to the Universe.* But there's already so much to see and do in the AMNH that unless your kids are in the double digits agewise, I'd be inclined to spend most of my time elsewhere.

**Hours:** Sunday through Thursday 10 A.M.–5:45 P.M., Friday through Saturday 10 A.M.–8:45 P.M.

**Suggested admission:** $8 adults, $6 seniors/students, $4.50 children 2–12

**Transportation:** *Subway:* B, C to 81st Street; 1, 9 to 79th Street. *Bus:* M79 to CPW

★*Metropolitan Museum of Art*                    212-535-7710
**Fifth Avenue (at 82nd St.), UES**
**www.metmuseum.org**

Some would argue that the Met, with three million works of art, is the most magnificent art museum in the world. Though it is not quite as large as the Louvre or the British Art Museum, certainly it has the most encyclopedic collection on the planet. So, what do you do? How do you tackle this monster? How do you get the most out of your visit to the Met with your children?

The best strategy is to select a couple of galleries or a handful of works on which you'd like to concentrate, view those, and call it a day. The thing about the Met is that you can't see the whole thing—not in a day, a week, or a month. It's just that big, which is why children and adults alike should relax and concentrate on what they enjoy most or what they'd like to learn about. Once you've figured out what interests you most, you can set about focusing on those few things.

Still, with *three million* works of art (and rotating special exhibits), how do you narrow down the selection? It's actually not as difficult as you might think. There are four ways to handle it:

1. If you don't want to do any advanced planning (though to get the most out of your visit, you might want to reconsider), pick up a floor plan and select one of the tried-and-true exhibits, like the Arms and Armor gallery on the first floor. This will be a guaranteed hit with most children ages 4 and up. Other favorites include the Temple of Dendur and the costume collection.

2. Go to the Met's Web site (www.metmuseum.org), select a few pieces of art, and learn about them. You don't need to learn enough to write a dissertation, just enough to help your children appreciate and enjoy the art and encourage them to think about the pieces they're seeing. Ask them some questions: *How does this piece make you*

*feel? What do you think it's made of? How old do you think this work of art is? Have you seen anything else that reminds you of this mask/costume/painting?* Beyond toddlers, children of any age can answer most of these questions, and, as they do, they'll be thinking about the art and looking at it more carefully than if they just stood before it with no guidance at all. This way, you are helping your child absorb and enjoy the art, not just dragging him or her around the museum by the hand.

3. Join one of the programs for kids. These programs, usually run on weekends, are free with admission to the museum. "Look Again!" is a family program that takes place on Saturday and Sunday. There is usually a tour and discussion of three or four works of art (while standing or sitting in front of each piece), followed by a storyteller or a drawing project, followed by a related movie for those who are still interested. Children are first engaged by the two team leaders with a description on the piece, then further lured in with pointed questions to get them involved, thinking, and interested. The program is for children ages 5 through 12, though a few younger ones sometimes participate, as well as older siblings (it was plenty interesting for the adults who were in tow, too). Weekend family films are 30 minutes, and special events include multihour celebrations and festivals ("Greek Family Festival" and "Mexico: A Spanish Family Program" are two of many examples) where your children can stay for as long as they're interested. Other programs include "Hello, Met!" "Discoveries," and *"Programas en Español para las Familias"* (programs in Spanish for families). And new programs are being added all the time. Call in

advance (212-570-3932) for a listing of family programs, check the Web site, or ask to be added to the mailing list. The programs are real winners for children, and adults will find that they learn plenty, too.

4. Enter the museum at the Uris Center for Education (at 80th Street—this is also where all of the children's and family programs begin) and read through or pick up some of the special educational guides. There's *Kids Pick, 10 Works of Art,* a particularly useful brochure that highlights children's top ten picks in the museum, including a photo and description of each piece. *Museum Kids* is available, as is *Rooms with a View, A Museum Search* (in both English and Spanish), which is sort of like a treasure hunt through the museum (without the running, touching, and racing). *Family Guides* are also extremely worthwhile. One recent family guide, set up in the form of a hunt, focused on tea sets. There are four objects. The "clue" for the fourth says: "Walk down the corridor, past the canopied bed, until you are in a gallery with two lion sculptures. In the corner just at your right, look for a teapot with a dragon spout. This one is made of real gold and a sparkling material called rock crystal." The guide also specifies all the pertinent details, such as where the pot originated, when it was made, and how the museum acquired it. Also near the Uris Center entrance is a library with plenty of resources and a good collection of children's books, perfect for a break after the museum or before. Another great trick about entering through the Uris Center is that it's far less crowded; there is a coat and stroller check (again, fewer people); bathrooms right by the entrance (not so by the main door); and the li-

brary, ideal for a story or a break. This alone is worth the slight detour.

I've found that younger kids respond better to three-dimensional objects than they do to paintings. Thus, with small children, it may make sense to focus your visit on sculptures and artifacts, rather than on paintings, drawings, and other two-dimensional renditions.

The museum is enormous, and it's easy to get lost, so don't be afraid to ask for directions *before* your kids start to lose it. Don't push the envelope. Budget a realistic amount of time to spend in the museum (about an hour is reasonable) and stick to it—if you have to leave early, do it. If you've got young kids in tow (even teens), and you've been in the museum for an hour and they're still doing well, it's still time to get out and onto the next thing. It's difficult for children (and adults) to spend much more than an hour looking at works of art and better they should leave wanting more than leave never wanting to return.

Remind children that:

@ The museum and the art are there for them to enjoy, but a museum is a *quiet place,* like a library. Other people, many of whom are serious students and lovers of art, don't appreciate loud, shrieking children running around the galleries.

@ The art, no matter how big, small, or nice it is, is for viewing with the eyes and is not to be touched. There are alarms on many pieces, not for theft, but as warning to guards and viewers that they've had "a touch." Explain that the reason is not for the guards at the museum to be mean, but rather because the oils from our hands, no matter how clean we are and how much we wash, damage art. Over time, the more people touch the art, the more damage is done, and the art deteriorates and disintegrates. Obviously, we don't want that to happen, so please: no touching.

@ Running in the museum is not appropriate behavior. If your children are too young to understand this, you might want to let them enjoy the comforts of their strollers (which are allowed every day except for Sunday) for the hour while you enjoy the art. If they are in the running phase, you may want to skip the visit altogether because obviously, if they can't stand still, they can't focus on the art. Don't forget, a museum can be a difficult place for a young child, and only you know whether it's appropriate for yours.

I encourage your children to read *From the Mixed-Up Files of Mrs. Basil E. Franweiler,* by E. L. Konigsburg, if they haven't already (or they can watch the film version, *The Hideaways).* It's perfect for children ages 9 to 12, but younger readers will get it too, and older children will read it in a breeze. I guarantee they'll all appreciate the museum more after reading the book. And, for those who are too young to read, or aren't motivated to do so, start the book a few weeks before departure and read a chapter to the kids each night. It's well worth the effort, and you'll enjoy the exercise (and the story), too.

**Hours:** Tuesday through Thursday and Sunday 9:30 A.M.–5:15 P.M., Friday and Saturday 9:30 A.M.–8:45 P.M. No strollers allowed Sunday (back carriers available at 81st St. entrance coat-check area)

**Admission** (includes same-day entrance to the Cloisters): $10 adults, $5 seniors and students, free for children under 12 when accompanied by an adult

**Transportation:** *Subway:* 4, 5, 6 to 86th Street.

## The Best of the Rest

*American Museum of the Moving Image*  718-784-0077
35 Avenue (at 36th St.)  718-784-4777
Astoria, Q
www.ammi.org

Recently home to *Sesame Street, The Cosby Show,* and earlier to the Marx Brothers, the Museum of the Moving Image makes its home in what is part of the Kaufman Astoria Studios. "Behind the Screen" is the central exhibit in the museum, which details, from start to finish, how a movie is made, marketed, and showcased. For those who are more inclined to *do* rather than to *look,* there are interactive elements. Learning about and trying out sound-effects editing is always a hit with older kids—especially when put in the context of film production. The collection has more than 1,000 items on display, from costumes to high-tech gadgets and nostalgia kitsch. Screenings are free with the cost of admission. Free exhibition tours are offered Tuesday through Saturday at 3 P.M.

**Hours:** Tuesday through Friday 12 P.M.–5 P.M., Saturday and Sunday 11 A.M.–6 P.M.

**Admission:** $8.50 adults, $5.50 seniors and college students, $4.50 children 5–18

**Transportation:** *Subway:* R to Steinway Street

*Brooklyn Children's Museum (BCM)*  718-735-4400
145 Brooklyn Avenue  museum hotline
(between Saint Marks and
Prospect Pl.), BR
www.bchildmus.org

The first children's museum in the world, the Brooklyn Children's Museum has been the benchmark of children's interactive and innovative exhibits for more than one hundred years. If you can get beyond the one major drawback—it's between two subway lines (and close to neither) and difficult to get to without a car—it's a great destination for kids.

From the moment your children climb the steps, they'll be drawn to the museum like bees to honey. The entrance is a turn-of-the-century (nineteenth century, that is) subway kiosk, and directly inside the door kids are enticed into the heart of the museum by the "people tube," a huge drainage pipe, that runs to the depths of the 35,000 square foot, four-floor underground facility, complete with neon accents and a stream.

Brooklyn Children's
Museum

The wonderful thing about the BCM (and the now-more-than 200 others around the country and the world that have used the BCM as a model for their own children's museums) is that it's about hands-on, interactive exploration and learning. This is not the "hush, don't talk, don't touch, don't run" kind of a place nor is it the "clobber your kid over the head with educational programming" kind of a place. What the BCM is, is a place where children, from toddlers to teens, can learn about life and the world around them, their neighbors, the environment, culture, arts, and science through exhibits, touching, special educational and/or family programs, and exploration.

Though a best-kept secret (perhaps because of it's less-than-ideal location), BCM continues to strive to keep pace—changing and evolving with the world and the needs of children as we embark upon the twenty-first century. Some favorite activities and exhibits include Can You Tell Me How to Get to Sesame Street?, Make a Pizza, Sing a Rap Song, Around the Block, Jump Rope, All Bark, MusicMix, Plants and People, the Mystery of Things, Produce a Movie, and Together in the City.

During the summer, the museum holds many special events. The Early Learner Performance Series with Puppet Theatre Inside Out and Fun on Sesame Street are big hits. But these exhibits and programs change, so if one of the above programs is gone by the time you arrive, don't despair; something equally exciting and entertaining will have replaced it.

**Hours:** BCM is always closed on Tuesday. Summer hours: Saturday and Sunday 10:00 A.M.–5:00 P.M., Monday, Wednesday, Thursday 12:00 P.M.–5:00 P.M., Friday 12:00 P.M.–6:30 P.M.; September through June, closed Monday and Tuesday.

**Admission:** $4.00

**Transportation:** *Trolley:* Free shuttle service from Grand Army Plaza to BCM at fifteen minutes past the hour from 10:15 A.M. to 4:15 P.M., Saturday and Sunday. *Subway:* Take the 3, C, or A train. *Bus:* Take the B43 or B44 to Saint Mark's Avenue, or take the B45, B65, or B25 to Brooklyn Avenue.

*Brooklyn Museum of Art*                    718-638-5000
200 Eastern Parkway (at Washington Ave.), BR
www.brooklynart.org

If you're only going to visit one art museum on your visit to
New York City (and you're staying in Manhattan), I'd have to
suggest the Met, because, well, it's *the Met.* The Brooklyn Museum of Art (BMoA), however, is a tremendous museum in its
own right, with a magnificent edifice housing its equally grand
art collection. What you'll find in the collection is far more extensive than what you'd see in most other cities in the country.
It's only because it sits in the shadow of the Met that the Brooklyn Museum of Art does not get the recognition that it deserves
(of course, on the plus side, that makes for smaller crowds, too).

The permanent collection includes about two dozen
American period rooms (1675–1928), which is still popular
with kids, although always frustrating because you can't actually go in, walk around, touch, and sit on the pieces. It helps to
put history and time in perspective. The Egyptian collection,
especially the mummies, is always a big hit, and the Impressionists—Monet, Degas, Cézanne—are not to be overlooked.

Most recently, the BMoA received a tremendous splash
of attention for a controversial exhibit involving dung and images of religious figures. For less controversial exhibits, the
BMoA has also received a great deal of press and recognition
for its temporary exhibits: Monet and the Mediterranean,
Maxfield Parrish 1870–1966, Impressionists in Winter, Mas-
terpieces of Fashion (a great costume exhibit), The Jewels of
the Romanovs, and modern works like From Hip to Hip
Hop: Black Fashion and the Culture of Influence.

"First Saturday," a program that runs (you guessed it) on
the first Saturday of each month, is something your older

teens might get a kick out of. It's from 5 P.M. to 11 P.M. Admission is free, and the program includes some form of entertainment. It could be film, poetry, jazz, dance, and so forth. I'd certainly call first to see what's on the calendar, because it can be pretty weird stuff—experimental, sort of out there, you know, the stuff that New York City is known for. There are also special programs for kids, so call ahead or check the Web site for information.

**Hours:** Wednesday through Friday 10 A.M.–5 P.M., first Saturday of the month 11 A.M.–11 P.M., each Saturday thereafter 11 A.M.–6 P.M., Sunday 11 A.M.–6 P.M.

**Suggested admission:** $4 adults, $1.50 seniors and students, children under 12 free

**Transportation:** *Subway:* 2, 3 to Eastern Pkwy/Brooklyn Museum

★ *Children's Museum of Manhattan*    212-721-1234
**212 West 83rd Street (between Broadway and
Amsterdam Ave.), UWS**
**www.cmom.org**

The Children's Museum of Manhattan is a great destination for kids to touch, learn, and play. Designed specifically *for* kids (they say ages 2 to 12, but it's more like 2 to 8 or 10), this museum encourages hands-on participation. Exhibits like Body Odyssey are presented in language and formats that kids can understand—it's scientific discovery rather than textbook discourse. There's plenty of stuff for toddlers (and even babies) in the 4-and-under play area, and the carpeted reading room is a nice place for a break if energy levels are getting too high, or too low. The Early Childhood Center has a range of activities too. Time Warner Media Center is a hit with older kids—especially when they get to produce their own television show or videos. The animation program is also popular. Every day there is a calendar of events with special programs: Storytellers, face painting, and holiday projects entertain and delight just as much as the regular collection. Here, as at all museums, exhibits change: Dr. Seuss, John Lennon's Real Love: Drawings for Sean, Maira Kalman's Max (A Dog), and WordPlay are a few of the recent winners. If they're gone when you arrive, something equally wonderful will be in their place. *Note:* The museum is very popular with locals, so to avoid the crowds, don't visit it on weekends and holidays if at all possible.

**Hours:** Wednesday through Sunday 10 A.M.–5 P.M.

**Admission:** $5 children and adults, $2.50 seniors

**Transportation:** *Subway:* 1, 9 to 86th Street

---

★*Intrepid Sea-Air-Space Museum*          212-245-0072
**West 46th Street (at Twelfth Ave.), Pier 86, MTW**
**www.intrepidmuseum.org**

---

It takes a while for the facts to sink in: This, the USS *Intrepid,* what is now a museum (and National Historic Landmark) sitting in the Hudson River, was once an active aircraft carrier from which fighter planes actually took off and—harder still—upon which they landed. It's not until you go up on the flight deck that the vastness of the vessel begins to register (especially when the kids have to walk from one end to the other—or run, as the case may be) and yet ironically, at the same time, it seems oddly small: How exactly is it that pilots landed fighter jets on this so-called runway? (Very carefully!)

I had never visited the *Intrepid* before I started working on this book. It didn't strike me as interesting. But having been there I can't believe it took me so long—this is simply an amazing spot for kids.

*Intrepid Sea-Air-Space Museum*

There's plenty of great stuff to see before you venture up to the flight deck, and a lot of it is participatory. This museum, in particular, is a good one at which to arrive early, otherwise your kids will either have to wait on long lines (to do things like sit in the cockpit of the A-6) or worse, skip some of the attractions altogether.

- After you pay admission and climb the stairs to the **Hangar Deck,** directly inside is the **A-6 cockpit challenge.** It's a simulated flight program used to train A-6 pilots to land planes on aircraft carriers. Anyone can sit in the cockpit, and adults and children alike are eager to give it a go.

- Nearby are mannequins adorned in uniforms; there's the landing signal officer, marine detachment, steward's mate, and hell-diver pilot. You'll see more uniforms throughout the exhibit, and they're worth a quick look in passing (and longer with kids who are really into this sort of thing).

- The **cockpit orientation trainer** allows you to climb into a 4D-2N and check out the cockpit. It's amazing how small the space is considering how tall our pilots are. Then there's the Sparrow, which you can also climb into (which is billed as the "free world's most versatile medium range radar guided missile").

℮ Take time to pause at the **Iwo Jima Monument,** which was sculpted after the famous photo (Raising the flag atop Mount Suribachi, 23 February 1945). *If your child is old enough to understand the implications of bombs and war, this might be a good time to have a short discussion.*

℮ The **Famous Flying Machines** exhibit is pure fun. The basket for the hot air balloon (climb on in) and the Human Powered Flight Challenge encourage you to pedal your way to flight. Read the panel about Bryan Allen, who pedaled the Gossamer Albatross (similar to what your child has or is about to climb into) 22.5 miles across the English Channel. It makes the experience that much more interesting and educational.

℮ For older children, there are computer information stations where with the press of a button (entertaining for youngsters too, just for the button pushing), you can access files of photographs, videos, and print information on all of the armed services. For military junkies, there is also a station with narrated videos on aircraft carriers, tanks, helicopters, fighter planes (Blue Angels and Joint Strike fighters are but a few), and attack submarines.

℮ The two things that are available at an extra charge are the **dog tags** from $0.95 to $4.95 (for military stainless steel and upward) and the **Intrepid flight simulator.** The flight simulator gets the longest lines by far, so if the museum is crowded and your kids are determined to get on board, go there first. The cost of the ride is $5.00, and as much as some kids love it, others (and parents) don't. A sign explains: "The simulator is used to test and train commercial airline pilots. Simulator training helps produce more skilled up-to-date pilots, which result in safer operations."

There is also a telling notice posted out front: "Dynamic, high speed motion simulation. You must be able bodied to ride this simulator. You must hold tightly to the rails and do not stand or smoke during the flight. You should not enter the simulator if any of the following apply: (1) Prone to motion sickness; (2) neck, back, or heart problems; (3) you're pregnant; (4) claustrophobia; (5) under 3 years old. Simulates acceleration, deceleration, slow and sharp turns, and dives. Motion is synchronized to a computer-generated film. It runs 5 minutes and holds 15 people." Sounds horrible, but many kids love it.

@ Before you go upstairs to the flight deck, walk straight back to the outside deck. If it's a nice day, you'll get a great view of the river and downtown to the World Trade Towers. If you're having lunch, you can grab something from the **Stars & Stripes Café** or eat what you've packed along and have a seat. There are tables and coke machines for a nice outside lunch.

@ Upstairs are the main attractions, especially for the little ones. Outside voices are acceptable here, and there's plenty of room for burning off some extra energy. Look for the **A-12 Blackbird**, "the world's fastest airplane." If everyone isn't completely exhausted, there's also the submarine USS *Growler* and the destroyer USS *Edson*.

**Hours:** May through September, Monday through Saturday 10 A.M.–5 p.m., Sunday 10 A.M.–6 P.M.; October through April, Wednesday through Sunday 10 A.M.–5 P.M.

**Admission:** $10 adults; $7.50 veterans, seniors, and students; $5 children 6–11; first child under 6 free, each extra child $1

**Transportation:** *Subway:* A, C, F to 42nd Street. *Bus:* M42 crosstown

### ★ *Liberty Science Center (LSC)*          201-200-1000
**251 Phillip Street**
**Liberty State Park, Jersey City, NJ**
**www.lsc.org**

It's well worth the trip to the LSC (and it's a fun ride on the ferry, too), and it can easily be combined with a trip to the Statue of Liberty and Ellis Island to boot (see Statue of Liberty, in City Sights, for details). LSC is a great opportunity for hands-on learning and play, all within the framework of science and technology. The building itself looks really "cool" and futuristic, and your kids will get the futuristic feel simply by walking inside. IMAX films are a big draw, as are the exhibits, temporary and permanent. There's no shortage of things to see and do. Specials like Animal Eyes: What Do Animals Really See?, Scream Machines: The Science of Roller Coasters, and Electric Space really get kids (and parents) excited about learning (probably because they think they're just having fun). Call in advance for special programs and activities or check the Web site.

**Hours:** Daily 9:30 A.M.–5:30 P.M.

**Admission:** $9.50 adults, $7.50 seniors and children

**Transportation:** *Ferry* from World Financial Center to Colgate Center. Connect to Lafayette-Greenville bus to LSC.

### ★ *Lower East Side Tenement Museum*  212-431-0233
**90 Orchard Street (at Broome St.), LES**
**www.tenement.org**

This museum is an excellent depiction of what life was like for the multitudes of poor immigrants arriving in America, many of them not speaking as much as a word of English. They expected to find streets paved with gold, but instead encountered hard work and squalor. Here, in this five-story tenement house, there lived, from 1863 to 1935, 10,000 people from 25 countries. A visit here will help your children imagine the hardships of the immigrant's life and also illustrate the City's earlier history. If you've had a visit to Ellis Island, don't forget to point out that this, the Lower East Side, is where many of the immigrants made their first homes before moving on to a better life.

You can see the museum only with a guided tour, and because group size and tours are limited, it helps to reserve ahead of time. Each of the tours (there are three) lasts an hour and highlights different aspects of life. The Visitors' Center also has a few small exhibits, including photos, videos, and a model tenement, so it's worthwhile to arrive a bit early and check those out.

**Hours:** Tenement tours depart Tuesday through Friday at 1 P.M. and every half-hour to 4 P.M., Thursday hourly 6 P.M.–9 P.M.; Saturday and Sunday every half-hour 11 A.M.–4:30 P.M.

**Admission for one tenement tour:** $9 adults, $7 seniors and students

**Transportation:** *Subway:* F to Delancey Street; B, D, Q to Grand Street

*Museum of the City of New York*       212-534-1672
**1220 Fifth Avenue (at 103rd St.), UES**
**www.mcny.org**

This is the place to be if you're interested in exploring New York's long history, starting with its modest beginnings as a Dutch trading post in the seventeenth century to its current incarnation as the most visited city in the world. Through photographs, maps, costumes, memorabilia, toys, furniture, and other artifacts, the museum cleverly links the past to the present (and the future). Kids will be especially drawn to New York Toy Stories, a collection of toys and dolls that were owned (and well loved) by generations of New York children.

**Hours:** Wednesday through Saturday 10 A.M.–5 P.M., Sunday 12 P.M.–5 P.M.

**Suggested admission:** $5 adults, $4 seniors, students, and children, $10 families

**Transportation:** *Subway:* 6 to 103rd Street

---

### *Museum of Jewish Heritage—*     212-968-1800
### *A Living Memorial to the Holocaust*
**18 First Place, Battery Park City, FD**
**www.mjhnyc.org**

---

More than fifty years after the MoJH was proposed, it was finally born. Everything about it is striking: its location (on the water at the south end of Battery Park), its six-sided building, and its contents. Jewish Life a Century Ago, The War Against the Jews, and Jewish Renewal are all within the permanent exhibits. Moving in their simplicity, stories are told through life's simple objects, photographs, and documents. The videotaped testimonies of Holocaust victims, survivors, and their families (all of which were chronicled by Steven Spielberg's Survivors of the Shoah Visual History Foundation) are especially powerful. Special exhibits are also scheduled, recently including Roman Vishniac's gripping Children of a Vanished World.

**Hours:** Sunday through Wednesday 9 A.M.–5 P.M., Thursday 9 A.M.–8 P.M., Friday and evenings of Jewish holidays 9 A.M.–3 P.M.

**Admission:** $7 adults, $5 seniors and students, children under 5 free.

**Transportation:** *Subway:* 1, 9 to South Ferry; 4, 5 to Bowling Green

★*Museum of Modern Art*      212-708-9400
11 West 53rd Street (between Fifth and Sixth Aves.), MTW
www.moma.org

MoMA is widely recognized as the world's premiere showcase for art of the twentieth century. If your children have any interest in art at all, chances are good they've heard of and seen (at least in books) some of the artists that are represented here. From Van Gogh (try *Starry Night*) to Picasso, Monet (*Water Lilies* will move even the toughest critics) to Matisse and Warhol, Hopper, Klimt, Raunschenberg—the list goes on. Equally interesting are the extensive collections of photography (and special exhibits), drawings, sculpture, furniture, and anything else that is representative of art in the twentieth century (including film and video).

Selecting a few special works to view is a good strategy, maybe a Calder mobile, a Van Gogh, and a Rodin sculpture, broken up by a trip outside to the peaceful patio and sculpture garden. Another option is the self-guided highlights tour, for which each stop was chosen by the different departments' curators. A third option would be coordinating your visit with one of the special programs that MoMA offers, many of which are family-oriented and all of which last one hour. Gallery talks, like Music to My Eyes: Matisse and More, make modern art accessible to the entire family. For an updated listing of family programs, call ahead to the museum or check the Web site.

**Hours:** Saturday through Tuesday, Thursday 10:30 A.M.–5:45 P.M., Friday 10:30 A.M.–8:15 P.M.

**Admission:** $10 adults, $6.50 seniors and students, under 16 free when accompanied by adult; Friday 4:30 P.M.–8:15 P.M., pay what you wish.

**Transportation:** *Subway:* E, F to Fifth Avenue; B, D, F, Q to Rockefeller Center. *Bus:* M1, M2, M3, M4, M5 to 53rd Street

| *Museum of Television & Radio* | 212-621-6800 |
|---|---|
| **25 West 52nd Street (between Fifth** | 212-621-6600 |
| **and Sixth Aves.), MTW** | **operator assistance** |

Ideal for malcontent teens, kids who need a TV break (while satisfying parents who want culture), and those who especially enjoy television and radio as art, the Museum of Television & Radio will be a sure hit. Here there are no pictures on the walls, plaques to read, or people telling you not to touch and to hush. Here at the Museum of TV&R you can take one of the daily tours if you so desire or, better yet, pick up a copy of the day's schedule and either pop into one of the screening rooms or select programs (from among the more than 100,000) that you've always wanted to see again or wished you had seen in the first place. Those who are overwhelmed with the selection and unsure of what to choose can try the highlights option (only 500 selections of TV and radio programs), from which you can break your selection down further by category, title, search, and so forth. Ideal for children who can sit still quietly (you sit in a room with a bunch of TV monitors, each person or group of people watching their own programs with headsets), selections range from *Sesame Street* to *Star Trek* to *Gilligan's Island.* If all of this seems like a little too much fluff (it really is culture though, like it or not), during your two-hour time slot at the monitor, you can also select great moments in history. Search for the Beatles' first appearance on the *Ed Sullivan Show,* old television commercials like Dinah Shore singing about Chevrolet (a total hoot), Roosevelt's address to Congress in 1941 (after the bombing at Pearl Harbor) about entering WWII, footage of the first astronauts walking on the moon, and TV classics that capture an era: *MASH, Leave it to Beaver, I Love Lucy* (chocolate factory), and *Mr. Rogers.* Everyone except perhaps toddlers will find something that appeals, and it's a nice chance to bring the family together—or to allow children to sit at their own consoles with their own selections—doing something the kids most likely won't associate with museums and culture. But I warn you, when you return home and ask the kids to turn off the TV, be prepared to hear, "But television is culture; I'm educating myself here!"

**Hours:** Tuesday, Wednesday, and Friday through Sunday 12 P.M.–6 P.M., Thursday 12 P.M.–8 P.M.

**Admission:** $6 adults, $4 seniors and students, $3 children under 13

**Transportation:** *Subway:* B, D, F, Q to 47th–50th Streets/Rockefeller Center; N, R to 49th Street

★*New York City Fire Museum*        212-691-1303
**278 Spring Street (between Varick and Hudson Sts.), SH**
**www.nyfd.com/museum.html**

Always a huge hit with the little kids (and the big ones too, when no one's looking), the Fire Museum features vintage trucks and equipment (fire houses, fire boats, fire gear), as well as fire-related folk art, paintings, photographs, and memorabilia. Poles and bells from firehouses—it's the stuff that children's fantasies are made of! Don't miss the fire-safety education tours (call ahead). Nothing makes quite the impact as a lesson on fire safety in this place.

**Hours:** Tuesday through Sunday 10 A.M.–4 P.M.

**Suggested admission (donation):** $4 adults, $2 seniors/students, $1 children under 12

**Transportation:** *Subway:* C, E to Spring; 1, 9 to Houston Street

★ *Solomon R. Guggenheim Museum*    212-423-3500
**1071 Fifth Avenue (between 88th and 89th Sts.), UES**
**www.guggenheim.org**

At this museum, perhaps the most photographed edifice in the neighborhood (Carnegie Hill), it's irresistible *not* to consider the possibility of roller skating, sledding, skateboarding, or banister-riding down the six-story spiral interior that is the Guggenheim Museum.

Designed by Frank Lloyd Wright, the permanent Guggenheim collection and special exhibits feature modern art. Even if you're all arted out, step inside the lobby for a look *up*. The building really is magnificent, and it only enhances the manageable collection of art.

Special exhibits tend to occupy the walls of the central spiral, whereas permanent collection pieces (Chagall, Kandinsky, Picasso, Degas, Van Gogh) are in rooms off the swirl. Special offerings include a free highlights tour daily and free family films (check the Web site or call ahead for the current offerings). Jazz in the rotunda is always a big hit. The exhibits do vary though, so check the calendar before you shell out the big bucks to go in.

You can also visit the Guggenheim Museum SoHo (575 Broadway at Prince St., 212-423-3500), which is trendier but not nearly as impressive.

**Hours:** Sunday through Wednesday 9 A.M.–6 P.M., Friday and Saturday 9 A.M.–8 P.M.

**Admission:** $12 adults, $7 seniors/students, under 12 free; Friday 6 P.M.–8 P.M. pay what you wish

**Transportation:** *Subway:* 4, 5, 6 to 86th Street

| | |
|---|---|
| *Whitney Museum of American Art* | 212-570-3676 |
| 945 Madison Avenue (at 75th St.), UES | 877-WHITNEY |
| www.whitney.org | |

The brainchild of artist Gertrude Vanderbilt Whitney, the Whitney Museum of American Art actually came into being in a somewhat haphazard manner. A collector herself, Whitney offered her collection to the Met, and the Met turned it down (I guess the curators weren't interested in twentieth century American art at the time—wonder how they feel about it now?), so she started her own museum. Unveiled in 1966 in its current incarnation, the Whitney is a striking edifice (if only because it looks to me somewhat like a futuristic prison), especially for Madison Avenue. Dedicated to preserving, collecting, interpreting, and exhibiting twentieth and twenty-first century art, the Whitney is one of the greatest advocates of the art of our times. The museum focuses special attention specifically on the work of living artists (after all, why should the dead ones get all the attention?). If you really want to expose your children to what's au currant, the Whitney is a good bet—and it's very manageable too. The permanent collection includes Georgia O'Keeffe, Edward Hopper, Jasper Johns, George Bellows, Roy Lichtenstein, and many other notable twentieth-century artists. Free gallery tours are offered daily, and the restaurant at the Whitney, Sarabeth's, is a winner, as is the counter service, also catered by Sarabeth's. You can enjoy a great cappuccino outside in the moat, while your children burn off some steam.

**Hours:** Tuesday, Wednesday, Saturday, Sunday 11 A.M.–6 P.M., Thursday 1 P.M.–8 P.M., Friday 11 A.M.–9 P.M.

**Admission:** $10 adults, $8 seniors/students, under 12 free

**Transportation:** *Subway:* 6 to 77th Street. *Bus:* M1, M2, M3, M4 to 75th Street; M79 crosstown

> ### *Whitney Museum of American Art*          212-875-2550
> ### *at Philip Morris (Midtown branch)*
> **120 Park Avenue (at 42nd St.), MT**

Features a small gallery (with changing exhibits), a sculpture court, and free gallery tours.

**Hours:** Monday through Friday 11 A.M.–6 P.M., Thursday 11 A.M.–7:30 P.M.

**Admission:** Free

**Transportation:** *Subway:* 4, 5, 6 to 42nd Street

## Specialty Museums

> ### *American Craft Museum*          212-956-3535 weekdays
> **40 West 53rd Street (between**          212-956-3690 weekends
> **Fifth and Sixth Aves.), MTW**

Depending upon the exhibit, this small museum is a good one to pop into, if only for 15 minutes (children under 12 are free). Founded in 1956, it's the country's oldest establishment to be singularly dedicated to contemporary crafts. The gift shop is great; I've been known to stop in for a browse and leave with a bundle. Gallery talks are regularly scheduled and families are welcome.

**Hours:** Tuesday through Wednesday, Friday through Sunday 10 A.M.–6 P.M., Thursday 10 A.M.–8 P.M.

**Admission:** $5 adults, $2.50 students and seniors, children under 12 free; Thursday 6 P.M.–8 P.M. pay as you wish

**Transportation:** *Subway:* E, F to Fifth Avenue

*Asia Society*                                      212-517-ASIA
725 Park Avenue (at 70th St.), UES
www.asiasociety.org

Specializing in contemporary Asian and Asian American art, the Asia Society was established in 1956 to unite us through art and promote better understanding of and communication among Americans and Asians. Through performances, films, lectures, conferences, and, of course, art exhibits, the Asia Society (including people of Asia and the Pacific) aims to present Asia to Americans.

**Hours:** Tuesday through Saturday 11 A.M.–6 P.M. (to 8 P.M. on Thursday), Sunday 12 P.M.–5 P.M.

**Admission:** $4 adults, $2 seniors, children under 13 free; Thursday 6 P.M.–8 P.M. free

**Transportation:** *Subway:* 6 to 68th Street/Hunter College

*Children's Museum of the Arts*          212-941-9198
182 Lafayette Street (between              212-274-0986
Broome and Grand Sts.), LI

This is definitely a place you'll want to call ahead of time if you want to get involved in one of the special programs. Here workshops designed especially to encourage and bring out kids' (18 months to 10 years) creativity are the biggest draw, but there are also plenty of hands-on activities like dress-up for the younger kids and computer graphics for the older ones. Programs include storytelling, sing-alongs, plays, skits, and art projects like puppet-making.

**Hours:** Wednesday 12 P.M.–7 P.M., Thursday through Sunday 12 P.M.–5 P.M.

**Admission:** $4 weekdays, $5 weekends

**Transportation:** *Subway:* B, D, G, Q to Broadway–Lafayette Street; 6 to Spring Street

---

*The Cloisters*                                    212-923-3700
**Fort Tryon Park (north end), Upper Manhattan**
**www.metmuseum.org**

---

Part of the Met, the Cloisters is a bit of a schlep (it's in northern Manhattan), but you can get there via public transportation, it's included with your entry to the Met (same day), and if your kids (or more likely, you) have always dreamed of seeing the famous unicorn tapestries, this is the only place to do it. The kids will get a kick out of the architecture (there are cloisters from medieval monasteries and a Spanish apse brought *intact* from Europe). Free guided tours are offered Tuesday through Friday at 3 P.M. and Sunday at noon.

**Hours:** November through February, Tuesday through Sunday 9:30 A.M.–4:45 P.M.; March through October, Tuesday through Sunday 9:30 A.M.–5:15 P.M.

**Suggested admission:** $8 adults, $4 seniors and students, free for children under 12 (includes same-day entrance to the Metropolitan Museum of Art and vice versa)

**Transportation:** *Subway:* A to 190th Street, then a 10-minute walk north along Margaret Corgan Drive, or pick up the M4 bus at the station. *Bus:* M4 to Madison Avenue

## Cooper-Hewitt National          212-849-8300
## Design Museum
**2 East 91st Street (at Fifth Ave.), UES**
**www.si.edu/ndm**

Housed in the Carnegie Mansion, this museum is magnificent to look at. I've been known to walk inside just to feel the grandness of the place (a girl can dream, can't she?) and of course pop into the gift shop for a quick browse. The yard alone gives me palpitations. Part of the Smithsonian Institution, the Cooper-Hewitt's exhibits are often funky and offbeat. The exhibit that included brightly colored tents in the yard was unlike any other I had ever seen, as were the toasters. If nothing else (depending upon the exhibit), the art can be engaging and fun and open your eyes and those of your children to a different way of looking at art. And after all, isn't that what it's really all about?

**Hours:** Tuesday 10 A.M.–9 P.M., Wednesday through Saturday 10 A.M.–5 P.M., Sunday 12 P.M.–5 P.M.

**Admission:** $5 adults, $3 seniors and students, free for children under 12; Tuesday 5 P.M.–9 P.M., free to all

**Transportation:** *Subway:* 4, 5, 6 to 86th Street

## Forbes Magazine Galleries          212-206-5548
**62 Fifth Avenue (at 12th St.), GV**

Toy soldiers, model boats, old Monopoly sets, toy cars, and, of course, the bejeweled Fabergé eggs, were all part of Forbes's collection. Even though they can't touch, the kids are sure to be delighted by this collection, and it's free, too (what a guy he was, Mr. Forbes), so everyone can be elated.

**Hours:** Tuesday, Wednesday, Friday, Saturday 10 A.M.–4 P.M.

**Admission:** Free

**Transportation:** *Subway:* L, N, R, 4, 5, 6 to 14th Street/Union Square

---

**The Frick Collection**                    212-288-0700
**1 East 70th Street (at Fifth Ave.), UES**
**www.frick.org**

---

They don't love kids here. Children under 10 aren't even allowed to set foot inside this place (I wonder if they'll card you). So if you're traveling with a young family, this isn't the place for you. That being said, this collection really is magnificent (with works by Picasso, Titian, Rembrandt, Michelangelo, Turner, and Vermeer) and manageable, and the facility itself is breathtaking (it was indeed Frick's residence). Could you just imagine?

**Hours:** Tuesday through Saturday 10 A.M.–6 P.M., Sunday and minor holidays 1 P.M.–6 P.M.

**Admission:** $7 adults, $5 seniors and students. *Children under 10 not admitted;* children under 16 must be accompanied by an adult.

**Transportation:** *Subway:* 6 to 68th Street/Hunter College

---

**International Center of**                 212-860-1777
**Photography (ICP)**
**1130 Fifth Avenue (at 94th St.), UES**
**ICP Midtown**                             212-768-4682
**1133 Sixth Avenue (at 43rd St.), MTW**
**www.icp.org**

---

ICP is New York City's preeminent collector of photography. Dedicated to all aspects of photography, from exhibits to seminars and classes, either of these museums (the one in Midtown is bigger, but the original at 94th Street is more charming) is a must for photo buffs and aspiring photographers.

**Hours:** Tuesday through Thursday 10 A.M.–5 P.M., Friday 10 A.M.–8 P.M., Saturday and Sunday 10 A.M.–6 P.M.

**Admission** (includes both Uptown and Midtown locations): $6 adults, $4 seniors, $1 children under 13; Tuesday 5 P.M.–8 P.M. pay what you wish

**Transportation to ICP:** *Subway:* 6 to 96th Street

**Transportation to ICP Midtown:** *Subway:* B, D, F, Q trains to 42nd Street

---

*Japan Society*               **212-832-1155**
**333 East 47th Street (between First and Second Aves.), MTE**
**www.japansociety.org**

Featuring highly regarded exhibitions of Japanese art, the society also offers programs that include lectures, films, concerts, and classes.

**Hours:** Tuesday through Sunday 9 A.M.–5:30 P.M.

**Suggested admission:** $5

**Transportation:** *Subway:* 6 to 51st Street; E, F to Lexington Avenue

---

*The Jewish Museum*            **212-423-3230**
**1109 Fifth Avenue (at 92nd St.), UES**
**www.jewishmuseum.org**

The collection at the Jewish Museum chronicles 4,000 years of Jewish life. From ancient artifacts to modern art, the two-floor permanent exhibit, Culture and Continuity: The Jewish Journey, is the museum's heart and focal point. Touring exhibits are constantly on display, so there's a continuous flow of regulars as well as guests from out of town. The scope of the exhibits is tremendous—enlightening, overpowering, touching. The gift shop is a worthwhile stop for Judaica, books, and posters.

**Hours:** Sunday, Monday, Wednesday, Thursday 11 A.M.–5:45 P.M., Tuesday 11 A.M.–8 P.M.

**Admission:** $8 adults, $5.50 seniors and students, free for children under 12; Tuesday 5 P.M.–8 P.M. pay as you wish

**Transportation:** *Subway:* 4, 5 to 86th Street; 6 to 96th Street

### *El Museo del Barrio*      212-831-7272
### 1230 Fifth Avenue (at 104th St.), UES
### www.elmuseo.org

The only museum in America whose central focus is Puerto Rican, Latin American, and Caribbean art, El Museo's aim is to preserve the cultural heritage of Puerto Ricans and Latin Americans living in the United States. The permanent collection includes paintings, historical photographs, hand-carved religious figurines *(santos de palo),* sculpture, and other creative displays. New exhibitions highlight contemporary Latin art and artists.

**Hours:** Wednesday through Sunday 11 A.M.–5 P.M.

**Suggested admission:** $4 adults, $2 seniors and students, children under 12 free

**Transportation:** *Subway:* 6 to 103rd Street

### *Museum for African Art*      212-966-1313
### 593 Broadway (between Houston and Prince Sts.), SH
### www.africanart.org

You can't help but be drawn to this museum from the outset. The interior was designed by Maya Lin, the same architect who designed the Vietnam Memorial, and, with exhibits like Hair in African Art and Culture and Liberated Voices: Contemporary Art from South Africa, it's not difficult to see why MfAA is so engaging. A leader in organizing exhibits dedicated to historic and contemporary African art and culture, the MfAA brings to New York its own identity of art and culture.

**Hours:** Tuesday through Friday 10:30 A.M.–5:30 P.M., Saturday 12 P.M.–8 P.M., Sunday 12 P.M.–6 P.M.

**Admission:** $5 adults, $2.50 seniors, children, and students

**Transportation:** *Subway:* N, R to Prince Street

---

### *Museum of American Folk Art*     212-595-9533
**2 Lincoln Square (on Columbus Ave.,
between 65th and 66th Sts.), UWS
www.folkartmuseum.org**

---

If you're passing by, pop into this one for a visit because its collection includes a great representation of the American folk-art tradition—and it's free. The quilts, part of the museum's most popular exhibit (textiles), will make any sentimentalist's fingers start to twitch. These quilts put the sewing class you took in HomeEc into perspective. The gift shop here is full of great originals, and there are usually some nice "dollies," far more authentic and cuddly than those at Toys "R" Us.

*Be sure to call first because the MoAFA is scheduled to open in a new, larger space in 2001.*

**Hours:** Tuesday through Sunday 11:30 A.M.–7:30 P.M.

**Admission:** Free

**Transportation:** *Subway:* 1, 9 to 66th Street.

### National Museum of the American Indian          212-668-6624  212-514-3888
George Gustav Heye Center
1 Bowling Green (at Broadway), FD
www.si.edu/nmai

Housed in the magnificent U.S. Customs House, the collection at the Museum of the American Indian is the oldest and one of the best in the country. Sadly, it's only a temporary fixture in its current home. As part of the Smithsonian Institution, the collection will find its new and permanent home on Independence Mall in Washington, D.C. (in 2002). Until then, there is plenty to see, most of which was collected independently (and eventually donated) by George Gustav Heye. In addition to the comprehensive original collection, there are also special exhibits and programs including storytelling, music, and dance presentations. Not to be missed are the Especially for Kids events. Call ahead for a calendar of current programs.

**Hours:** Sunday through Wednesday and Friday through Saturday 10 A.M.–5 P.M., Thursday 10 A.M.–8 P.M.

**Admission:** Free

**Transportation:** *Subway:* 1, 9 to South Ferry; 4, 5 to Bowling Green

### New York Hall of Science          718-699-0005
47-01 111th Street
Flushing Meadows/Corona Park, Q
www.nyhallsci.org

The NYHoS touts itself as New York's only Science Playground and backs the claim with the largest collection of hands-on science and technology exhibits in the City. It's a big hit with kids because it's all hands-on. There are 200 interactive exhibits to examine, touch, and explore, and every child will definitely find something of interest. A few all-time favorites include being "swallowed" by a giant bubble, the anti-gravity mirror (can you guess what will happen?), and composing music by dancing in front of light beams. During the summer, the Outdoor Science Playground is open. Geared toward children 6 and up, the playground outside has plenty of room and opportunity to slide, seesaw, spin, jump, and climb—all lessons in physics but, more important, tons of fun. And for the under-5 set, don't overlook the Discover Place play area, designed especially with them in mind. *Note:* If you're traveling with older kids, those who have seen the movie *Men In Black,* keep a look out for the Unisphere, it really does exist, and no, it wasn't actually destroyed in the movie.

**Hours:** Monday through Wednesday 9:30 A.M.–2:00 P.M., Thursday through Sunday 9:30 A.M.–5:00 P.M.

**Admission:** $7.50 adults, $5.00 children and seniors; Thursday through Friday 2 P.M.–5 P.M. free

**Transportation:** *Subway:* 7 to 111th Street, Queens

*The New-York Historical Society*          212-873-3400
**2 West 77th Street (at Central Park West), UWS**
**www.nyhistory.org**

Since 1804, the New-York Historical Society has been the definitive repository of New York. The collection includes manuscripts, sculpture, paintings, books, decorative arts, photographs, prints, architectural documents, and other objects that catalog the city's history. The focus, though primarily on New York, also includes general American history, culture, and art. Ongoing exhibits include Kid City and Glimmers of the

Past. If you get a chance to see Times Square in Pictures, you'll view the fascinating evolution of Times Square from what it was a century ago to its current incarnation.

**Hours:** Tuesday through Sunday 11 A.M.–5 P.M.

**Admission:** $5 adults, $3 seniors/students, under 12 free

**Transportation:** *Subway:* B, C to 81st Street; 1, 9 to 79th Street

---

### *Pierpont Morgan Library*          212-685-0008
### 29 East 36th Street (at Madison Ave.), MTE
### www.morganlibrary.org

---

This is one of my personal favorite museum spaces in the City. Interestingly enough, the Morgan Library remains something of an undiscovered New York treasure. It not only houses one of the world's most important collections of rare books and bindings, master drawings, original manuscripts, and personal writings (including a working draft of the U.S. Constitution with handwritten notes; handwritten scores by Beethoven, Mozart, and Puccini; and Voltaire's personal household account books), but it also features special exhibitions. Recent exhibits include From Bruegel to Rubens, Treasures from the Royal Tombs of Ur, and Collecting for the Centuries. The building alone is worth a look inside (a grand old mansion), and it's also a great place for a light lunch or afternoon tea.

**Hours:** Tuesday through Thursday 10:30 A.M.–5:00 P.M., Friday 10:30 A.M.–8:00 P.M., Saturday 10:30 A.M.–6:00 P.M., Sunday 12 P.M.–6 P.M.

**Suggested admission:** $7 adults, $5 seniors/students, children under 12 free.

**Transportation:** *Subway:* 6 to 33rd Street. *Bus:* M2, M3, M4, Q32 to 36th Street

### P.S. 1 Contemporary Art Center          718-784-2084
22-25 Jackson Avenue (at 46th Ave.)
Long Island City, Q
www.queensmuse.org

Originally a public school (hence the name), P.S. 1 is the world's largest contemporary art museum. What's featured here is art from the United States and abroad that's so contemporary, it's not yet collected in most other museums. If you have a budding artist in the family, this museum could be an interesting stop—and most definitely unlike any other your child has probably ever seen. A high-profile merger with the Museum of Modern Art was announced recently, so P.S. 1 should start getting more attention soon.

**Hours:** Wednesday through Sunday 12 P.M.–6 P.M. (Hours vary in summer, so call ahead.)

**Suggested admission:** $5 adults, $2 seniors/students/artists

**Transportation:** *Subway:* E, F to 23rd Street/Ely Avenue; 7 to Court House Square/45th Road

## Helpful Hint

Insider's Hour, a program coordinated by the New York Convention and Visitors' Bureau, runs 1 July–30 September. Many of the City's top cultural institutions participate: The American Museum of Natural History, Guggenheim, Intrepid, New York Botanical Garden, and more. The one-hour tours give a quick exposure to the best that each institution has to offer. Pick up a Summer Insider's Hour brochure at the NYC Visitor Information Center (Seventh Ave. at 53rd St.) or contact www.nycvisit.com to get a brochure by mail.

## Tips for Getting the Most Out of New York's Art Galleries

@ Before coming to town, consult the Friday *New York Times* "Weekend" section for a listing of shows that will be on during your visit. If you want to do more in-depth research, take a look at the *Art Now Gallery Guide,* published monthly or online at www.gallery guideonline.com. Plan your gallery itinerary around what you learn from your research.

@ Plan to wander around a single gallery neighborhood, stopping in for a few minutes at each of several nearby galleries. The major clusters of galleries are in SoHo, along 57th Street, and along upper Madison Avenue (there are also many galleries in Chelsea and the East Village). In certain gallery-rich buildings, like 41 East 57th Street, you can get into the elevator and just go from floor to floor, sampling what's of interest and passing over what isn't.

@ Don't be discouraged from visiting galleries by their reputation for being snooty or unfriendly. The truth is that if you visit at a time when they aren't busy (mid-week; first thing in the morning), any given gallery's staff will give you a nice greeting—and maybe even show you around a little.

@ Children under 12 should be extra-carefully super-vised, because galleries have no barriers between observers and the art.

# Galleries: The Museum Alternative

As opposed to art museums, which are in the business of *preserving* art, galleries are in the business of *selling* art—by showcasing the most important artists, especially new ones. Thus, for those children—teens in particular—who have an exceptionally high level of interest in art, New York's dizzying array of art galleries (we have more galleries even than museums—in other words, a whole lot) are a resource you shouldn't pass up. Most galleries have no problem with children, as long as they're well behaved. An added bonus: Galleries charge no admission!

## A Few Key Galleries in the Major Gallery Districts

*A ★ indicates a gallery that has been particularly excellent over the years, though individual shows may vary in quality.*

### 57th Street Galleries

ACA Galleries
41 East 57th Street (at Madison Ave.)
212-644-8300

Andre Emmerich
41 East 57th Street (between Madison and Fifth Aves.)
212-752-0124

Blum-Helman
20 West 57th Street (between Fifth and Sixth Aves.)
212-245-2888

Marchian Goodman Gallery
24 West 57th Street (between Fifth and Sixth Aves.)
212-977-7160

Marchlborough
40 West 57th Street (between Fifth and Sixth Aves.)
212-541-4900

★PaceWildenstein
32 East 57th Street (between Park and Madison Aves.)
212-421-3292

Robert Miller
41 East 57th Street (at Madison Ave.)
212-980-5454

★Sidney Janis Gallery
110 West 57th Street (between Sixth and Seventh Aves.)
212-586-0110

Tatistcheff and Company
50 West 57th Street (between Fifth and Sixth Aves.),
8th floor
212-664-0907

### *Madison Avenue Galleries*

Gagosian
980 Madison Avenue (at 76th St.)
212-744-2313

Hirschl & Adler Galleries
21 East 70th Street (at Madison Ave.)
212-535-8810

★M Knoedler & Company
19 East 70th Street (between Madison and Fifth Aves.)
212-794-0550

## Learning Tip

A visit to a gallery makes a great topic for a school report. Ask the gallery for a brochure, which will contain detailed information about the works on display, and focus the report on the work of one artist.

Terry Dintenfass
20 East 79th Street (at Fifth Ave.)
212-581-2268

### *SoHo Galleries*

Barbara Gladstone
99 Greene Street (between Prince and Spring Sts.)
212-431-3334

Charles Cowles
420 West Broadway (between Prince and Spring Sts.)
212-925-3500

Curt Marcus Gallery
578 Broadway (between Houston and Prince Sts.)
212-226-3200

Gagosian
136 Wooster Street (between Houston and Prince Sts.)
212-228-2828

John Weber
142 Greene Street (between Houston and Prince Sts.),
3rd floor
212-966-6115

★Leo Castelli
420 West Broadway (between Spring and Prince Sts.)
212-431-5160

Mary Boone Gallery
417 West Broadway (between Spring and Prince Sts.)
212-431-1818

★Max Protetch Gallery
560 Broadway (at Prince St.)
212-966-5454

Metro Pictures
150 Greene Street (between Houston and Prince Sts.)
212-925-8335

★Paula Cooper
155 Wooster Street (between Houston and Prince Sts.)
212-674-0766

Postmasters
80 Greene Street (at Spring St.), 2nd floor
212-941-5711

PPOW
532 Broadway (at Spring St.), 3rd floor
212-941-8642

★Sonnabend Gallery
420 West Broadway (between Spring and Prince Sts.)
212-966-6160

Sperone Westwater
142 Greene Street (between Houston and Prince Sts.)
212-431-3685

## Insider's Tip

"Younger people are typically interested in art that's closer to their own age, style, or aesthetic. Galleries that show the younger, or emerging, artists are particularly suitable. The larger galleries tend to show more contemporary or modern art and are easier for the uninitiated to visit. Smaller galleries, or galleries specializing in, say, Old Master drawings, will be more intimidating and less fun for younger people."
—*Robert Schonfeld, art dealer*

In addition to galleries, don't forget the auction houses, which are among the best free entertainment in town and often have objects on view that are of interest to kids (carousel animals, toys, baseball cards, rock-and-roll memorabilia, etc.).

Christie's
20 Rockefeller Plaza
212-636-2408
www.christies.com

Sotheby's
1334 York Avenue (at 72nd St.)
212-606-7000
www.sothebys.com

William Doyle Galleries
175 East 87th Street (between Lexington and
Third Aves.)
212-427-2730
www.doylenewyork.com

## Zoos and Gardens

You wouldn't think such a densely populated urban area
would have so much open space, but New York has some
amazing—and huge—zoos and gardens. The jewel in the
crown is the Bronx Zoo, of which New Yorkers are under-
standably proud. To this I give the lengthiest coverage. Remember, you can
combine your Bronx Zoo visit
with a New York Botanical
Garden visit and a trip to
Arthur Avenue (see chapter 3)
for a full, wonderful day in the
too-often-overlooked Bronx.
Likewise, you can combine the
Aquarium with Coney Island and
Little Odessa/Brighton Beach (see
chapter 3) for a great Brooklyn
adventure.

*Coney Island*

## *Bronx Botanical Garden—*
## See New York Botanical Garden

## ★*Bronx Zoo Wildlife Conservation Park* 718-367-1010
## Fordham Road (at Bronx River Pkwy.), BX
## www.wcs.org

Set on 265 acres of woods, ponds, streams, and parkland, with more than 6,000 animals from 665 species, the Bronx Zoo is every child's fantasyland (and the nation's largest urban zoo). Because of the zoo's enormous size, you really need a strategy for your visit, lest you find that the troops have run out of gas before they've seen the things they'll enjoy most.

Highlights of the zoo include the Congo Gorilla Forest (for which there is an additional charge of $3), the Children's Zoo (additional charge of $2), the World of Reptiles, Africa, Jungle World, and Wild Asia. This is not even the tip of the iceberg. Everyone has a personal greatest-hits list, but these are some of the favorites of the more than two million visitors coming through the zoo each year.

*Note:* If you're on a tight budget and don't wish to/can't spring for the exhibits with extra fees, don't feel compelled to do so. Your children will still have a great zoo experience—there is *plenty* to see and do without paying the extra fees. If you are going to pay for one extra, for youngsters I'd suggest the Children's Zoo; for older kids I'd go for Congo. On the bright side, during the winter months the fee for Congo drops to $1 to compensate for the reduced number of animals you can view.

If you're coming via public transportation on the bus or subway, you'll enter through gate B, which is a perfect place to begin. You can start with the Monkey House, the Zoo Center (elephants, rhinos, and tapirs), and the Children's Zoo. Here's a good basic itinerary, beginning at the Children's Zoo.

- The **Children's Zoo** has some animals for petting, like goats and chickens, in a farmlike setting (pens and barns), and you can buy feed to really endear yourself to the animals. There are also some great climbing apparatus, like the rope spider web and the tree house with swirling slide. One of the most amusing things (to me, at least) is the prairie dog burrow. Prairie dogs are running around on this hill, and if the children go underneath the hill, they can poke their heads through Lucite domes and at once be like a prairie dog poking its head out of its burrow, and at the same time, watch the real prairie dogs scurrying around their habitat. Another nice feature of the Children's Zoo is the opportunity for learning. Children can compare their jumping distance with that of a bullfrog or sit down in a heron's nest. Want to see what it feels like to be a turtle? Slide into one of the brassy shells. Along the pathways are questions on plaques; as you proceed, the questions are answered. The signs are easy to read and understand.

- The star of the **Elephant House** has to be Samuel R. II, a young female elephant who made her first appearance in 1993. She is watched over by Tus, the matriarch of the herd. Nearby neighbors include the tapirs, Carrie and Snuffles, who are a part of the zoo's participation in the Species Survival Plan.

- If you need a ride, the **Zoo Shuttle** is right outside the Zoo Center (which houses the elephants). Transportation options within the zoo include the Zoo Shuttle train, the Skyfari aerial tram, and the Bengali Express Monorail (all of which cost $2 each way). The different shuttle options each go to different destinations.

℮ When you need a break: The zoo has plenty of picnic areas, and you're free to bring in any food, snacks, and drinks you like—but be warned, carrying too much heavy stuff will become a burden quickly because the zoo is both huge and hilly.

℮ If you're still on foot, **World of Reptiles** isn't too far away, and it's a nice dark, cool building with lots of slithering, hopping residents. Probably the most famous of the reptiles is Samantha, the 25-foot reticulated python, who weighs in at a handsome 223 pounds. When the zoo acquired Samantha, she was only 23 feet long. I am also a big fan of the fluorescent tree frogs—blue, green, or red with black spots—it's sort of like being in Alice's Wonderland.

℮ Have a look around the **Himalayan Highlands.** This exhibit's star is the endangered and elusive snow leopard. The Bronx Zoo has had snow leopards since 1903, with seven generations of cubs born at the zoo—78 in all so far! As you look at the snow leopards with your kids, share this: Bronx Zoo snow leopard cubs have been sent to zoos in Australia, Canada, England, Russia, and Japan, as well as many zoos within the country! If your child is missing school and needs to write a report, suggest pertinent snow leopard topics (the history of the species, the conservation efforts, the countries in which it now lives). The zoo is a great place to start doing that research firsthand.

℮ The **Big Bears** are back to back with the snow leopards, and kids always love the grizzlies and polar bears. If it's summertime, don't expect the bears to be too active during the day. Look in the dark shady places to spot them or try to visit the exhibit early or later in the day when temperatures are a bit more agreeable to the creatures with fur coats.

◉ This might be a good time to make your way to the **Wild Asia** exhibit and hop on the Bengali Express Monorail (May through October) for a narrated ride. The trick here is that you've got to keep your eyes peeled for the animals, or you'll miss them as you travel slowly by (the monorail snakes along on a track above the animals). In this exhibit are the hard-to-miss Asian elephants, Indian rhinoceros, red pandas, Gaurs, a selection of deer (don't expect too much excitement here even if there is a great variety—most children have the attitude that "if you've seen one deer, you've seen 'em all").

◉ **Jungle World,** which re-creates an Indonesian scrub forest, isn't far and with as many as 780 animals from 99 species, everyone should be able to find something to love. Jungle World has 280 reptiles, amphibians, and fish, including Indian gharials and mudskippers—you'll have to find them to find out what they are. The 55 mammals include white-cheeked gibbons and black leopards. Ah, and the birds. The 100 birds are complete with laughing thrushes, hornbills, and Bali mynahs. If the Reptile House didn't satisfy all desire for scales and slithers, there is also a collection of arthropods—350 animals to be exact, with millipedes topping the list. Anyone feel like counting the millipede's feet?

◉ Over in **Africa** you'll find the timeless favorites. Who doesn't love the lions, cheetahs, and giraffes? Zebras, blesboks, nyalas, okapis, and ostriches are on hand, too. The names alone are the stuff that entertainment is made of.

*Stretching some limbs at the Bronx Zoo's Children's Zoo*

So, what's left? Plenty, but the final must-see exhibit is the **Congo Gorilla Forest.** For starters, the money you pay as you enter the door is actually donated to projects funded by the WCS (Wildlife Conservation Society, founded in 1895 as the New York Zoological Society and the consortium of the Bronx Zoo, New York Aquarium, Central Park Wildlife Center, Queens Wildlife Center, and Prospect Park Wildlife Center) and better still, as you exit the exhibit, you get to choose how your dollars are spent. This is a good platform from which to discuss the notion of conservation with your children if you haven't already done so.

As you walk along the path you'll see a sign telling you to look for hidden signs of life: dung, anthills, skeletons, and so forth. Who can spot the skull just behind the sign? How about the millipede farther along the trail, embedded into the dirt wall? Look for the colobus monkey forest—can you spot the monkeys in the trees? What colors are they? What feature helped *you* to spot *them?* The Red River hogs are wonderfully ugly to the point of being adorable. Do you see that dirt area right in front of the glass (in which they're probably sleeping)? Every night, when the hogs are most active, they root around and dig up that entire area. Each morning the zookeepers have to put the dirt back in place!

An eight-minute film describes a little bit about what the WCS does, and then the curtain goes up, and you get the dramatic exposure of the gorillas. They're in their habitat, hidden from view first by the movie screen and then by the black curtains. When the curtains part, there's an audible gasp from the audience, and everyone rushes along the path to see the (we're glassed in, not them) gorillas. Another hit of the Congo exhibit is the pygmy marmosets. They are the smallest primates in the world. You could easily cup one in the palm of your hand. It's dark and they're small, so they're a bit difficult to spot, but they're extremely active, so a minute or two of dedicated watching should prove fruitful. Nearby, games like Compare Your Weight to a Primate, Create a Gorilla Reserve, and Measuring Up (comparing your handprint with those of the inhabitants) bring the animals closer to home and make the experience more personal.

A day at the zoo is magnificent and exhausting. Some tips to help you avoid the crowds: Avoid free Wednesday, if at all possible. If you want to capitalize on the free entry (who doesn't), winter, spring, and fall are certainly going to be better than summer. If you are visiting in peak season (summer), arrive as early as possible so that you can enjoy at least some of your time at the zoo with fewer human inhabitants. And, try to schedule your visit during the week, when there's less human traffic. During winter months, not only are crowds sparser and rates lower, but grizzlies, snow leopards, and Mexican gray wolves are also more active. Some animals are not on exhibit because of the temperatures, but you'll find that there's still plenty to see and do. And you can always schedule an Insider's Hour tour (January to March and July to September) by calling 718-220-5141.

**Hours:** November through March, daily 10:00 A.M.–4:30 P.M.; April through October, Monday through Friday 10 A.M.–5 P.M., weekends and federal holidays 10 A.M.–5:30 P.M.

**Admission:** January 3rd through March $5 adults, $3 seniors and children under 12; April through October $9 adults, $5 seniors and children under 12; November through January 3rd $7 adults, $4 seniors and children under 12; Wednesdays free all year

**Transportation:** *Bus:* If you're not driving, the Liberty Line's BxM11 express bus is by far the easiest, most comfortable, and safest way to get from Manhattan right to the zoo's entrance gate. Pick-up points are along Madison Avenue, the cost is $3.00 each way, and you can use your MetroCard to pay (if it isn't an unlimited card). Call 718-652-8400 for a schedule and updated prices.

---

### *Brooklyn Botanic Garden*                    718-623-7200
**1000 Washington Avenue (Eastern Pkwy.), BR**
**www.bbg.org**

---

With names to lure you like Daffodil Hill, Shakespeare Garden, Lily Pool Terrace, Bluebell Wood, and Children's Garden, how can you stay away? Just down the road a piece from the Brooklyn Museum of Art, you'll find this beautiful garden oasis in the middle of Brooklyn. Regardless of what time of year you arrive—though many claim that the garden is at its most spectacular in May when the cherry trees are in blossom—you'll find plenty to see and smell (take the kids to the Fragrance Garden, designed especially for the blind—perhaps they'd like to try sniffing their way through the garden with their eyes closed, rather than seeing their way through). Have an interest in bonsai trees (perhaps on account of watching the *Karate Kid* too many times)? The Steinhardt Conservatory is home to the renowned Bonsai Museum. Whether you're indoors or out, the 12,000 plant specimens should keep everyone happily engaged, at least for a while. Free tours are conducted at 1:00 P.M. on Saturday and Sunday. Call in advance for tours in languages other than English.

**Hours:** April through September, Tuesday through Friday 8 A.M.–6 P.M., Saturday and Sunday 10 A.M.–6 P.M.; October through March, Tuesday through Friday 8:00 A.M.–4:30 P.M., Saturday and Sunday 10:00 A.M.–4:30 P.M.

**Admission:** $3 adults, under 16 free; Tuesday and Saturday 10 A.M.–12 P.M. free

**Transportation:** *Subway:* 2, 3 to Eastern Parkway/Brooklyn Museum; D to Prospect Park

---

★ *Central Park Wildlife Center/*          212-861-6030
*Tisch Children's Zoo (Central Park Zoo)*
**Fifth Avenue (at 64th St., in the Park)**
**www.wcs.org/zoos**

---

The Central Park Zoo (that's what we locals call it; this "Wildlife Center" business is new, and we're not too quick to change) is the perfect zoo destination for young children. Smack dab in the middle of the City and lower Central Park, this zoo is a perennial favorite because it's small, manageable, easily accessible (so it doesn't really matter if kids get cranky after an hour, or even 15 minutes), and specifically geared toward kids. The setup is extremely engaging: Just inside the gate, kids are met with a view of sea lions gliding around their spacious (and glass—ideal for peering and for short people) tank, and just beyond there are monkeys who are far less interested in us than we are in them. Nearby are the famed polar bears (one of whom made headline news—no small feat in New York—due to his obsessive "pacing" and resulting psychiatric analysis; and no, Woody Allen didn't write the story) and perky penguins. The Tropic Zone is a junglelike environment in which the humans are the trespassers. Birds of every imaginable color fly and chirp overhead. If you're lucky, one might land near enough for one of the kids to snap a picture. Don't miss the daily sea lion and penguin feedings, either.

Among preschoolers, the Tisch Children's Zoo is a great hit. Complete with a playground, animal exhibits, and a petting zoo, no child (big or small) can resist the call of the . . . llamas, potbellied pigs, goats, bunnies, and other gentle creatures.

**Hours:** April through October, Monday through Friday 10 A.M.–5 P.M., Saturday and Sunday 10:30 A.M.–5:30 P.M.; November through March, daily 10:00 A.M.–4:30 P.M.

**Admission:** $3.50 adults, $1.25 seniors, $0.50 children 3–12, under 3 free

**Transportation:** *Bus:* M1, M2, M3, M4 to 65th; M66 to Fifth Avenue

**★*New York Aquarium***                    718-265-3400
**West 8th Street (at Surf Ave.), Coney Island, BR**
**www.wcs.org**

Because of the travel time from Manhattan (60 to 90 minutes depending upon where in Manhattan you're coming from), it's best to coordinate a visit to the aquarium with a trip to the amusement park (this is no Six Flags—expect more of a roving carnival atmosphere than a Disney World) and beach at Coney Island, the nearby playgrounds, and a wander around Little Odessa (see chapter 3). The whole package is ideal for a full summer's day outing, but the fall and spring are also very nice

*Crabbing at New York Aquarium*

times to visit. The tradeoff for fewer people in fall and spring, however, is that most of the rides and games aren't open. A nice, mild winter day is not to be overlooked either. Chances are you'll have the clean beach all to yourself, perfect for building sand castles and playing on the jungle gyms. Most of the aquarium's exhibits are indoors.

The New York Aquarium, though not the best in the country, is actually perfect for young children who have short attention spans and delight in the big sea creatures—as well as in the simple pleasures of seeing colorful tropical fish.

- Upon entering the aquarium, the **shark tank** will impress even the jaded teens who are tagging along. Circling the large tank are large sharks—big enough so that you wouldn't want to encounter them anywhere else— and rays as big as any I've ever seen. When the kids have sated their viewing needs, wander through the darkened den of tanks. The squeals of delight let loose by toddlers echo through the hall and entertain older children and adults equally.

- Outside, the **California sea otters** steal the show. Oh, how I wish I could swim like that! You can also view the penguins, seals, and walruses from the outside viewing area and then go inside to the underwater viewing to get a good look at all of the same creatures in action. Seeing them swim around like that really puts your child's swim team in perspective. The same underwater viewing area also holds some magnificent visual treats like the sea-horses—especially the dragon seahorses from Australia. Just try to spot one of those. Also not to be missed is the octopus tank with two enormous octopuses. It might take everyone's eyes a few minutes to adjust to the dark-ness of the tank, but it's worth the effort to try to spot them. The inhabitants are surprisingly large and certainly the stuff that stories of the deep are made of.

@ From April through October, the **touch tanks** are active with horseshoe crabs and other nonstinging creatures. Children can "pet" and pick up the creatures, as long as they treat them very gently.

@ One of the best exhibits for its educational value is **Dis-covery Cove.** Here there are sea creatures coupled with questions and information to enhance the aquarium ex-perience and to help children think about the creatures and their environment. Exhibits include Different Ways to Breathe, Different Mouths for Different Diets, Protec-tion, Vision, Bottom Walkers, and Hearing (listen to aquatic sounds like the "singing" of dolphins and whales).

@ Outside are more big hits: The **beluga whale tank,** with plenty of belugas for everyone to see (did you know that *beluga* means "white" in Russian?), and the **dolphins** are highlights. During the winter, the dolphins reside in the Oceanic Exhibit.

@ From an educational point of view, the exhibit on the **Hudson River** is a great tool, especially for older children. The big map on the wall details the route of the Hudson River and how it flows from way upstate (it starts up in Canada, actually) down into New York City and the Atlantic Ocean. This would make a great report topic for an older child. It also places the aquarium in the context of the New York region and brings the exhibits a little closer to home.

*Note:* The zoo has plenty of outdoor picnic areas for breaks and lunch (packed or purchased) and also *lots* of clean bathrooms. Be sure that everyone uses one before you head to the boardwalk because, there, bathrooms are few and far between at best.

**Hours:** Daily 10 A.M.–5 P.M.

**Admission:** $8.75 adults, $4.50 seniors and children 2–12, free for children under 2

**Transportation:** *Subway:* D, F to West 8th Street in Brooklyn

---

★*New York Botanical Garden*        718-817-8700
**200th Street (at Southern Blvd.), BX**
**www.nybg.org**

---

If I had to choose only one botanical garden to visit on my trip to New York City, it would have to be this one. A National Historic Landmark, the 250-acre New York Botanical Garden is one of America's most beautiful and engaging (public) gardens. The beautifully manicured grounds are ideal for an autumn stroll or a spring fling, and the ponds, waterfalls, streams, wetlands, and grassy knolls are only the beginning. What lies beyond are the 28 specialty gardens and plant collections, the Enid A. Haupt *A World of Plants* Conservatory, and, perhaps best of all, the Everett Children's Adventure Garden with forty hands-on plant discovery activities (spread throughout 12 acres of gardens and wetlands) and the Family Garden, where kids can plant, water, weed, and compost firsthand.

Because the garden is so big and the travelers range in size from small to tall, you should consider the transportation options within the garden before you set out. To be sure, if you don't want to hoof it entirely, it's best to call ahead to be certain the tram is running.

**Hours:** April through October, Tuesday through Sunday and Monday holidays 10 A.M.–6 P.M.; November through March, Tuesday through Sunday and Monday holidays 10 A.M.–4 P.M.

**Admission:** $3 adults, $2 seniors and students, $1 children 2–12; Wednesday and Saturday 10 A.M.–12 P.M. free; extra charges for Everett Children's Adventure Garden, Enid A. Haupt Conservatory, and T. H. Everett Rock Garden and Native Plant Garden

**Transportation:** The easiest way is by Garden Shuttle (running weekends, April through October) between the Museum of Natural History, the Met, and the Botanical Garden—call 718-817-8700 for reservations and information. *Train:* Take Metro North 212-532-4900 from Grand Central Station to the New York Botanical Garden station. *Subway:* take the D or 4 train to Bedford Park Boulevard and walk east eight long blocks.

# Parks

## A Guide to Central Park

The south and north borders of Central Park are 59th Street to 110th Street. Fifth Avenue and Central Park West mark the park's east and west boundaries.

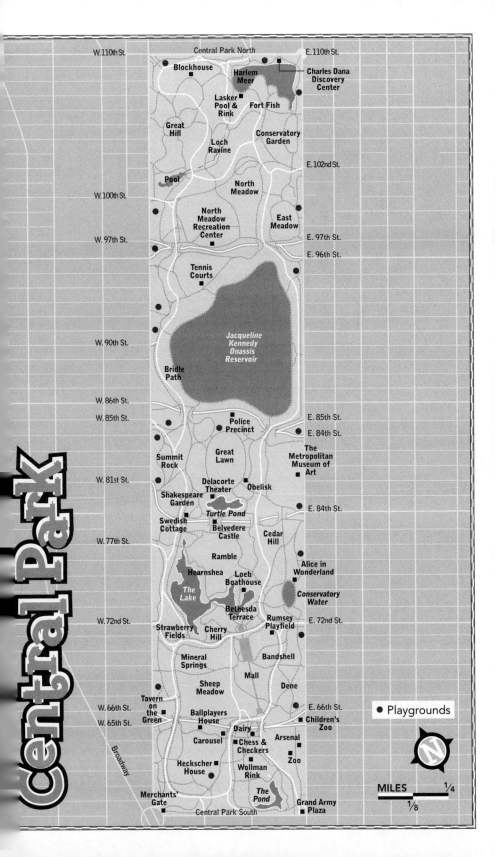

## Top Ten Favorite Things to Do in Central Park

1. Ride the carousel
2. Visit the Central Park Zoo
3. Go ice-skating at Wollman Rink
4. Take a horse-drawn carriage ride
5. Lookout from the Belvedere Castle
6. Take in a puppet show at the cottage
7. Play at the Hippopotamus Playground
8. Visit Strawberry Fields
9. Rent inline skates or bikes and ride along the park drive
10. Visit (and climb on) the statues of Alice in Wonderland

Whenever people ask me, "How can you stand living in Manhattan, surrounded by all those tall buildings?" I answer: "Central Park!"

Occupying 843 acres, Central Park is more than a park to most city dwellers—it's a lifeline to a quiet refuge, culture, sports, wildlife, and nature. It's also where New Yorkers do most of their plain old hanging out.

Designed by Frederick Law Olmsted and Calvert Vaux as the first such park in the City, Central Park was intended to be a refuge from the hustle and bustle of city life right from the beginning. The prophetic Olmsted, as if he were gazing into a crystal ball, predicted in the late 1850s that the City would become built up and that, with no natural environments left, Central Park would be the oasis that it has become for City dwellers.

Personally, I use the park almost every day for a run or a walk or just some peace and quiet. As soon as the plan was approved, people began using the park. The lower end was developed first with the children's district, and the work progressed north from there. The park was actually completed in 1872. By that time there were already a recorded several million visitors per year utilizing the grand open space. Now reports estimate that 20 million visitors pass through Central Park annually.

In the south the park gets more concentrated traffic (both pedestrian and vehicular), and as you progress north, the numbers tend to dwindle (except when there are concerts and special events in and around the north meadow). Circling the entire park is a paved road called the Park Drive. The Park Drive is a six-mile loop, and it is open to vehicular traffic during morning and afternoon rush-hour periods. The roadway transverse cutting across the park at 72nd Street makes up what is known as the "lower loop." The lower loop has extended hours for vehicular traffic and is also the primary route of horse-drawn carriages (otherwise known as Hansom cabs).

Central Park is a place in which you could easily get lost—in a good way. At the same time, there are always plenty of people about (especially on spring, summer, and fall weekends) within shouting distance, even if not in view, if you should find yourself ready to exit the park and in need of directions. But Central Park works pretty much the same as the rest of the City, with main east-west arteries to get from one side of the park to the other (in this case, paved paths) and north-south pathways, too. The paths may meander a bit, but generally, when you come to a clearing, especially in winter, you should be able to spy the city skyline and orient yourself in the direction you wish to be going. If all else fails, just ask. I get stopped for directions almost every time I enter the park and not only do I not mind helping, but also I actually enjoy pointing people in the right direction and answering their questions (if I can).

Working from the south, favorite attractions (and, really, these are only my favorites!) include:

- **Wollman Rink,** which is open for ice-skating in the winter, is located parallel to 63rd Street.

- The **Dairy,** a great source of information, postcards, and calendars of park events, is also housed in a lovely little cottage (formerly a dairy) and is on the 65th Street crosstown path.

- Just in from Fifth Avenue (coming off of Fifth is the best way to enter, unless you're meandering your way down through the park along the path that parallels Fifth Avenue) at 64th Street is the **Central Park Zoo,** a guaranteed winner (see Zoos).

- Right off the Park Drive (at about 64th St.) from the East Side is the famed **Carousel.** The Carousel is by far one of the greatest rides around. It costs $1 per ride, and don't be surprised if your kids ask to ride again and again. I never pass up an opportunity to ride the Carousel in Central Park—and it goes really fast, too.

- On the West Side at 66th Street is **Tavern on the Green.** It's pretty when it's all lit up (the restaurant keeps lights on its trees all year round), especially in winter when the trees are barren without their leaves.

- Directly across from Tavern is the **Sheep Meadow,** a huge green field where people come to relax with books, for picnics, and to take naps.

@ Just in from the Central Park West (CPW) entrance at 72nd Street is the famous **Strawberry Fields.** The commemorative plaque is surrounded by benches where people often come to ruminate about the Beatles and John Lennon's awful demise. No matter what time of year, you'll always find bouquets of flowers (just outside the park is the Dakota, where John and Yoko lived and in front of which John was murdered in 1980).

@ The 72nd Street transverse, which has along side of it a paved sidewalk shaded by giant old trees, is a good route to take to get to the Bethesda Terrace, which overlooks the **Bethesda Fountain.** This is a great place to take a break, to watch the people wander by, to eat an ice cream, to play with the dogs that so love the fountain, and to watch the rower's go by.

@ Just north of the fountain along the pathway is the **Loeb Boathouse,** where you can rent rowboats and bicycles for use in the park.

@ At 74th Street (across the Park Drive toward Fifth) on the East Side is the **Model Boat Pond.** Here children play with remote-controlled boats (many of which are rented at the building on the pond) that are set up on the water during the week. On weekends, the heavy hitters come out, and it's mostly adults (who, in my opinion, take themselves a bit too seriously) who navigate their remote-controlled sailboats around the pond. All of those boats (many of which really are magnificent—remember, they take themselves and their boats *very* seriously) gliding about are quite a sight.

@ Directly north of the Boat Pond is perhaps the most beloved statue in all of Central Park: **Alice in Wonder-**

**land,** with the mushroom and some of her compatriots. Well loved and well rubbed, these brass statues are climbed upon, photographed, and polished by adults and children alike, who insist upon a lengthy visit with the Wonderland characters.

ℯ Just below the Great Lawn (between 81st and 85th Sts.), where people relax and play ball games (also where many of the free concerts in Central Park are held), is **Belvedere Castle.** To the right or left of the southern end of the lawn, follow the pathway that leads up to the castle. After the short climb, you'll be rewarded with not only great views of the park and the City skyline, but also the opportunity to bird-watch and peek into the small museum/information center that is housed inside. Pick up one of the brochures, such as *Birds from Belvedere,* which not only shows some of the many birds that you can see in the park, but also identifies the buildings that dot the skyline and other points of interest in the park.

ℯ Below the castle is **Turtle Pond** and to the left (looking down from the castle) is the Delacorte Theater, which is home to free Shakespeare in the Park performances during summer.

ℯ Off the West Side's Park Drive (at 79th St.) is the **Swedish Cottage Marionette Theater.** A touring company since 1939, the puppeteers settled into the Swedish Cottage in 1947 but continued to tour until 1971, when the cottage was turned into a theater, and the company kicked off it's first season at home with *Cinderella.* The cottage was renovated in 1997 to be more historically accurate, and, at the same time, state-of-the-art stage and lighting equipment was installed. The company does one production per year, which changes annually in October. Reservations are required (tickets are $4.00 per child and $5.00 per adult). Recent productions include *Jack and the Beanstalk* and *Sleeping Beauty.*

e If you were to exit the park on the 81st Street Path to the West Side (the one that runs south of the Great Lawn, across the Park Drive and west), you would come out at Central Park West and 81st Street, or the northern reaches of the **Museum of Natural History.**

e On the East Side, at about 81st Street, is **Cleopatra's Needle,** commonly referred to simply as "The Obelisk." The Obelisk was a gift from Egypt and is the oldest single non-natural thing in Central Park. It dates back to 1600 B.C.

e On the other side of Park Drive is the unmistakable and unmissable **Metropolitan Museum of Art.** At 85th Street on the transverse (the roadway that runs from one side of the park to the other) is the Police Precinct.

e Just above the precinct, at about 87th Street, is the southern end of the **Central Park Reservoir,** where each day thousands of people come to run (including presidents when they're in town). The dirt track around the reservoir is 1.6 miles long, with two water fountains at the southern end. A nice view (and a favorite of tourists) is at the 90th Street entrance to the park. Cross the Park Drive and walk up the stairs to see the reservoir and the skyline that peeks out from the West Side.

e North of the reservoir are the **East Meadow, North Meadow Recreation Center (NMRC),** and **North Meadow** (all at approximately 97th Street, from east to west). The NMRC offers all sorts of wonderful free family programs (such as woods and water hikes, family sports and fitness), so be sure to call ahead or pick up a copy of the calendar at the Dairy. The North Meadow is a playing field, and both the North and East Meadows have been the site of many free concerts and speakers (Garth Brooks, Sting, and the Dalai Lama have been here).

@ At East 105th Street on Fifth Avenue is the **Conservatory Garden.** This magnificent gated garden is a favorite destination of brides and grooms and wedding photographers—and it's easy to see why. You'll be hard-pressed to get out of the garden without seeing at least one, if not two or three, wedding parties in pose. Obviously, depending upon the season, the number of blooming plants will vary, but the roses are lovely, as are the blossoming trees and even the little lily pond.

@ Even farther north, though very few tourists ever venture up here, is the **Lasker Pool and Rink** (in the summer it's an outdoor public pool and in the winter it's a skating rink) and the Charles A. Dana Discovery Center. The Dana Center offers free family programs, the favorite and most well known of which is probably the Catch-and-Release Fish Identification & Fly Tying Demonstrations, but Songs of Central Park and Beats of the Trees are also hits.

@ Throughout the park are sprinkled twenty **playgrounds.** Most are on the periphery so that you can reach them easily from the streets and avenues without having to traipse into the center of the park for playtime. There are two north of Tavern on the Green, one just south of 72nd Street off Fifth Avenue, another at about 76th Street, one at the bottom of the Met, and one just above it. Four additional playgrounds are situated along Fifth

Avenue just inside Central Park. On the West Side bordering Central Park West, going north from Tavern on the Green, is a playground (located at 81st St.) and two more around 85th Street. There is one at 90th Street near the reservoir (look for the Hippopotamus Playground), another at 91st Street, and a third at about 97th Street. Two more playgrounds north of 97th Street border the Park. For more details, stop by the Dairy, which has maps of Central Park, complete with playground locations. Also stop by the Dairy to pick up a schedule of free walking tours of Central Park, which go year-round, rain or shine (call 212-360-2726 two hours in advance for a status report if the weather is really extreme).

If you can believe it, these are really only the highlights of Central Park. There's always so much going on in all the different corners that it's easy to stumble upon something any day of the week.

*An important word of caution:* Central Park, though extremely safe during the daylight hours, should not be entered at night. It's not even that there have been many unfortunate incidents in Central Park in recent years, but it's nevertheless a vast open space that is deserted at night, and there's no reason to tempt fate. So unless you're attending one of the concerts or special events at night (to which hundreds and thousands of people flock and where you'll have plenty of company), it's best to stay out of the park from sunset to sunup.

### Contact Information

Central Park Conservancy General Information: 212-360-3444; 800-281-5722 for the hearing impaired

Alice in Wonderland Statue: just north of Boat Pond

Belvedere Castle, The Henry Luce Nature Observatory (midpark at 79th St.): 212-772-0210

The Charles A. Dana Discovery Center (110th St. and 5th Ave.): 212-860-1370

The Dairy (midpark at 65th St.): 212-794-6564

Bicycle Rental (at the Boathouse): 212-517-3623

Boathouse (boat rentals and gondolas): 212-517-3623

Carousel: 212-879-0244

Conservatory Garden: 212-360-2766

Conservatory Water (Model Boat Pond at 74th St.): 212-673-1102

Fishing at Harlem Meer—Catch & Release: 212-860-1370

Harlem Meer Performance Festival: 212-860-1370

Horseback Riding (Claremont Stables): 212-724-5100

Metropolitan Opera in Central Park: 212-362-6000

New York Philharmonic in Central Park: 212-875-5709

North Meadow Recreation Center (midpark at 97th St.): 212-348-4867

Shakespeare in the Park (Delacorte at the Public Theater): 212-539-8655

Skating—Lasker Rink: 212-534-7639

Skating (ice skating & inline skating at Wollman Rink): 212-396-9203

SummerStage Music Festival: 212-360-2777

Swedish Cottage Marionette Theater: 212-988-9093

Tennis Courts: 212-280-0205

Weddings Hotline: 212-360-2766

Wildlife Center & Tisch Children's Zoo: 212-439-6500

The Central Park Conservancy is a not-for-profit organization founded in 1980 that manages Central Park under a contract with the City of New York/Parks & Recreation.

## Other Parks

### *Battery Park*
**State Street and New York Harbor, FD**

As you weave your way through the skyscrapers that make up downtown, it's hard to imagine that there is a park nearby. But there, on the West Side, hidden from view and tucked along the Hudson River, is Battery Park. You might find yourself here almost by accident if you're headed for the ferry to the Statue of Liberty (Castle Clinton National Monument—an early fort—is where you buy tickets). A fine place for a break, picnic, or stroll, Battery Park is well used by people from all walks of life (which is why it's such a great place for people-watching)—Wall Street's most promising and prominent, tourists, and residents of Battery Park City. If your kids are old enough to have seen *Desperately Seeking Susan* (Madonna's first, and most awful, movie), many scenes from the movie were filmed right here.

**Transportation:** *Subway:* N, R to Whitehall Street; 1, 9 to South Ferry; 4, 5 to Bowling Green

*Prospect Park*                          718-965-8951
Grand Army Plaza (borders: Prospect Park West/
Parkside Ave./Flatbush Ave.), BR
www.prospectpark.org

Many Manhattanites never venture to parks beyond the borders of the small island. And it's a shame, because Prospect Park, approximately two-thirds the size (562 acres) of Central Park, is less crowded and equally as enticing as Central Park. Also designed by the famed team of Olmsted and Vaux *after* the completion of Central Park, Prospect Park is viewed by many people as being as nice as (if not nicer than) Central Park. Its fans consider it the jewel of Brooklyn.

From Grand Army Plaza, you'll enter through (under, around, in-sight-of) the Soldiers' and Sailors' Memorial Arch (1892) honoring Union veterans. Park highlights include the Litchfield Villa on Prospect Park West, the Lefferts Homestead (718-965-6505), and a Dutch farmhouse dating back to 1777 (it's now a museum specializing in children's education programs). The Friends' Cemetery, a Quaker burial ground, is worth a look if anyone in your group is into that sort of thing (ancient headstones can be pretty fascinating). And not to be missed are the carousel and the Prospect Park Wildlife Conservation Center (450 Flatbush Ave., 718-399-7339, www .wcs.org) where kids can be kids and enjoy the animals (wallabies, baboons, prairie dogs, red pandas, sea lions, and domestic animals) and special programs at the zoo ($3.50 adults, $1.25 seniors, $0.50 children 3–12, under 3 free).

**Transportation:** *Subway:* 2, 3 to Grand Army Plaza (walk 3 blocks down Plaza Street West to Prospect Park West)

## *Riverside Park*
### 72nd to 158th Streets

Riverside Park is an oasis along the Hudson River. And guess who designed it? Once again, it's Olmsted and Vaux. Olmsted brilliantly planned this refuge for city dwellers in what is now one of the world's most populated urban environments. Especially nice for a walk along the waterfront (my favorite walk is along the public marina—where people actually live on houseboats!), there are also lots of places to play: basketball, tennis, and volleyball courts; softball fields; and playgrounds.

## *Snug Harbor Cultural Center*          718-448-2500
### 1000 Richmond Terrace (between Tysen and Snug Harbor Rd.), SI

Only about 2 miles from the ferry landing, Snug Harbor Cultural Center houses the Art Lab, a historical museum, Staten Island Botanical Garden, Staten Island Children's Museum, Performing Arts, Education Center, and the Newhouse Center for Contemporary Art. Entry to the grounds is free, and it's worth a wander around to have a look at the 28 historic buildings, a collection of nineteenth-century Greek Revival, Beaux Arts, Second Empire, and Italianate architecture.

What used to be the Sailors' Snug Harbor maritime home and hospital for retired sailors is now a thriving 83-acre parkland and cultural center. It's best to call ahead before you make the trip to find out about special programs, concerts, activities, and exhibits, of which there are plenty, especially for kids.

**Transportation:** Staten Island Ferry to SI. Pick up the S-40 bus (ask to be let off at Snug Harbor) or a taxi.

## Union Square Park
### 14th–17th Streets (north and south) and Park Avenue South–Broadway (east and west), US

In reality, there isn't all that much park to Union Square Park, but to see it alive and bustling on greenmarket days (Monday, Wednesday, Friday, and Saturday), you can understand just how important this small park is to us city folk. Aside from the greenmarket, probably my favorite things about this park are the dog runs; there's one for big dogs and one for small. I enjoy staking out a nearby bench, perhaps with a drink, a friend, or both, and watching the dogs at play (after all, they live in a crowded city, too). If that's a little too mundane for your kids (or they're petrified of dogs, as I was as a tot), the park is often full of performers of various sorts, and it's a welcome place to take a break in the midst of all the hustle and bustle.

**Transportation:** *Subway:* 4, 5, 6, L, N, R to 14th Street/Union Square

*Union Square Green-market*

## Washington Square Park
**At the bottom of Fifth Avenue, bordered by Washington Square North, Washington Square South, MacDougal Street, Wooster Street, GV**

This is another park without all that much green, but it is an open area (with dog runs) and lots of activity. Many famous movies have been filmed here, including *Searching for Bobby Fisher* (this is where all of the chess game scenes in the park take place—look around, it's for real) and the opener in *When Harry Met Sally* (when Meg Ryan, after driving from University of Chicago with Billy Crystal, drops him off in front of the Washington Arch). Older kids might be impressed by the Greenwich Village scene that thrives here: Lots of kids dressed in black with pierced everything, New York University students, skateboarders, musicians, and the occasional unsavory character. Although perfectly safe during the day, this park is best avoided after dark.

**Transportation:** *Subway:* A, C, E, B, D, F, Q to West 4th Street/Washington Square

## Wave Hill                    718-549-3200
**West 249th or 252nd Street (at Independence Ave.), BX**
**www.wavehill.org**

This 28-acre public garden and cultural center (situated north of Manhattan in the Bronx) overlooks the Hudson River. If you should be so lucky as to visit on a sunny afternoon, a crisp autumn day, or a balmy spring morning, you'll perhaps see why the likes of Mark Twain and Theodore Roosevelt decided to make their homes here. Perhaps because of its location, this remains one of the city's best-kept secrets. A dream for botanical garden lovers, Wave Hill offers all sorts of special programs for children and families (like Family Art Project, where kids explore the gardens with an artist/naturalist and then create paintings and collages with their own inspiration). Other programs touch upon forestry, horticulture, environmental education, performing arts, and landscape history.

**Hours:** Tuesday through Sunday 9:00 A.M.–4:30 P.M.; extended in summer (check ahead)

**Admission:** $4 adults, $2 seniors and students; free in winter and Saturday and Tuesday mornings during summer

**Transportation:** *Subway:* 1, 9 subway to 231st Street; transfer to the bus, Bx7 or Bx10; ask to be let off by Wave Hill. Liberty Lines' Manhattan-Riverdale *Express Bus:* (718-652-8400) BxM1 or BxM2 to 252nd Street and walk west across the parkway bridge, following the signs.

# Theater and Shows

Many people feel that a trip to New York City isn't complete without a visit to a Broadway show. But with tickets nowadays starting at $60 for the cheapest seats, and with the most desirable shows requiring booking months in advance (or payment of exorbitant markups to ticket agents), you need to have a plan.

The two most effective strategies for getting tickets are:

1. Plan far, far ahead—this will allow you to get good seats at exactly the show you want, though you'll pay full price.

2. Make a last-minute decision—in which case your reward for flexibility will be great savings.

The best ways to get discounted tickets:

@ The Theater Development Fund (TDF) operates two TKTS half-price booths, one in Duffy Square (five blocks straight up Broadway from Times Square) and the other at Two World Trade Center. You can't decide what you're going to see in advance—you just have to go to one of the two TKTS booths, read what's on the board for the day, and wing it. It helps to familiarize yourself with all the major shows in advance (pick up a copy of *New York Magazine* or *Time Out New York*) because you'll have to make an on-the-spot, split-second decision. Tickets for Broadway and off-Broadway performances are half price (plus a service charge of $2.50 per ticket). Cash only. Call 212-221-0885 or visit www.tdf .org for the most up-to-date information.

℮ For the Duffy Square TKTS branch, located at 47th Street and Broadway, hours are Monday through Saturday (for evening tickets) 3 P.M.–8 P.M., Wednesday and Saturday (for matinee tickets) 10 A.M.–2 P.M., Sunday (matinee and evening tickets) 11 A.M. to closing.

## Helpful Hint
If you don't mind splitting up the family, one adult can wait on line for TKTS tickets, while another takes the kids to the World Trade Center Observation Deck (see City Sights). Whoever finishes first can browse the nearby Borders bookstore or hang out by the World Trade Center plaza water fountain until the rest of the family catches up.

℮ The Lower Manhattan TKTS branch is on the mezzanine of Two World Trade Center. In addition to day-of-performance tickets, a limited number of matinee tickets are sold one day prior to performance date at the Lower

Manhattan TKTS only. Hours are Monday through Friday 11:00 A.M.–5:30 P.M.; Saturday 11:00 A.M.–3:30 P.M. Closed Sunday. Unlike the Duffy Square branch, the Lower Manhattan TKTS doesn't have special hours for sale of matinee versus evening tickets—all tickets are sold at all times. Lines also tend to be quite a bit shorter (though you should still plan to spend a half-hour or more waiting) at the Lower Manhattan branch.

### Insider's Tip

"Afternoon matinee performances are usually much better for most kids than evening performances. At night, a show may not end until 10:30 P.M. or later, and kids can get tired, cranky, and fidgety. Most shows have their matinees on Wednesday and on weekends." —*Jane Matthews, Educator*

Remember, though, Broadway isn't the be-all and end-all of New York theater. The City is also rich in off-Broadway and off-off-Broadway theaters, where the spectacles tend to be less elaborate and less expensive, but no less fun. And there are also some theaters that cater specifically to kids and families. Sometimes you'll find the best experiences at these alternate venues. For current listings see *New York Magazine, Time Out New York,* the *Village Voice,* or the Friday *New York Times* "Weekend" section.

## Theaters for Kids and Families

| *Grove Street Playhouse* | 212-741-6436 |
|---|---|
| **39 Grove Street (between Bedford and Bleecker Sts.), WV** | |

Specializes in comedies, with heavy audience participation.

★*New Victory Theater*       212-382-4020
**209 West 42nd Street (between Seventh and Eighth Aves.), TD**
**www.newvictory.org**

Theater targeted exclusively toward kids and families. A range of performances, including plays, music, dance, puppetry, mime, and circus arts. Performers come from around the world to perform at New Victory.

*New York Youth Theater*       212-242-2822
**547 Greenwich Street, GV**

Mostly family-oriented musicals with both child and adult performers.

*Paper Bag Players, at Hunter College*  212-772-4448
**68th Street (between Park and Lexington Aves.), UES**

Eccentric performances using paper bags and cardboard boxes as props. January through March only.

★*Tada! Youth Ensemble Theater*    212-627-1732
**120 West 28th Street (between Sixth and Seventh Aves.), GP**
**www.tadatheater.com**

Performances by kids for kids, as opposed to most children's theater, which uses adult actors. The performances are very professional.

> **_Theatreworks USA_**                    **212-627-7373**
> **2162 Broadway (at West 76th St.), UWS**
> **www.theatreworksusa.org**

Classic children's plays *(Oliver Twist, Treasure Island)* every weekend from September through March.

## Finding the Broadway Theaters

Ambassador Theater
215 West 49th Street (between Broadway and Eighth Ave.)
212-239-6200

American Place Theater
11 West 46th Street (between Sixth and Seventh Aves.)
212-840-2960

Belasco Theater
111 West 44th Street (between Sixth and Seventh Aves.)
212-239-6200

Biltmore Theater
261 West 47th Street (between Broadway and Eighth Ave.)
212-239-6200

Booth Theater
222 West 45th Street (between Broadway and Eighth Ave.)
212-239-6200

Broadhurst Theater
235 West 44th Street (between Broadway and Eighth Ave.)
212-239-6200

Broadway Theater
1681 Broadway (between 52nd and 53rd Sts.)
212-239-6200

Brooks Atkinson Theater
256 West 47th Street (between Broadway and Eighth Ave.)
212-719-4099

Circle in the Square Theater
1633 Broadway (between 50th and 51st Sts.)
212-307-2700

Cort Theater
138 West 48th Street (between Sixth and Seventh Aves.)
212-239-6200

Criterion Center Theater
1530 Broadway (between Broadway and Eighth Ave.)
212-239-6200

Edison Theater
240 West 47th Street (between Broadway and Eighth Ave.)
212-302-2302

Ethel Barrymore Theater
243 West 47th Street (between Broadway and Eighth Ave.)
212-239-6200

Eugene O'Neill
230 West 49th Street (between Broadway and Eighth Ave.)
212-246-0220

45th Street Theater
234 West 45th Street (between Eighth and Ninth Aves.)
212-333-7421

Gershwin Theater
222 West 51st Street (between Broadway and Eighth Ave.)
212-586-6510

Golden Theater
252 West 45th Street (between Broadway and Eighth Ave.)
212-239-6200

Helen Hayes Theater
240 West 44th Street (between Broadway and Eighth Ave.)
212-944-9450

Imperial Theater
249 West 45th Street (between Broadway and Eighth Ave.)
212-239-6200

Lamb's Theater
130 West 44th Street (between Sixth and Seventh Aves.)
212-997-1780

Longacre Theater
220 West 48th Street (between Broadway and Eighth Ave.)
212-307-2700

Lunt Fontanne Theater
205 West 46th Street (between Broadway and Eighth Ave.)
212-575-9200

Lyceum Theater
149 West 45th Street (between Sixth and Seventh Aves.)
212-239-6200

Majestic Theater
247 West 44th Street (between Broadway and Eighth Ave.)
212-239-6200

Manhattan Theater Club
131 West 55th Street (between Sixth and Seventh Aves.)
212-246-8989

Mark Hellinger Theater
237 West 51st Street (between Broadway and Eighth Ave.)
212-757-7064

Marquis Theater
1700 Broadway (between 45th and 46th Sts.)
212-382-0100

Martin Beck Theater
302 West 45th Street (between Eighth and Ninth Aves.)
212-974-9736

Minskoff Theater
Broadway (at 45th St.)
212-869-0550

Music Box Theater
239 West 45th Street (between Broadway and Eighth Ave.)
212-239-6200

Nederlander Theater
208 West 41st Street (between Seventh and Eighth Aves.)
212-921-8000

Neil Simon Theater
250 West 52nd Street (between Broadway and Eighth Ave.)
212-757-8646

Palace Theater
Broadway (at 47th St.)
212-730-8200

Plymouth Theater
236 West 45th Street (between Broadway and Eighth Ave.)
212-239-6200

Richard Rogers Theater
226 West 45th Street (between Broadway and Eighth Ave.)
212-239-6200

Royal Theater
242 West 45th Street (between Broadway and Eighth Ave.)
212-239-6200

Saint James Theater
246 West 44th Street (between Broadway and Eighth Ave.)
212-398-0280

Shubert Theater
225 West 44th Street (between Broadway and Eighth Ave.)
212-398-0280

Virginia Theater
245 West 52nd Street (between Broadway and Eighth Ave.)
212-977-9370

Walter Kerr Theater
219 West 48th Street (between Broadway and Eighth Ave.)
212-582-4022

Winter Garden Theater
1634 Broadway (between 50th and 51st Sts.)
212-239-6200

## Finding the Off-Broadway and Off-Off-Broadway Theaters

Actors Playhouse
100 Seventh Avenue (at Sheridan Sq.)
212-691-6226

Astor Place
434 Lafayette Street (at Astor Pl.)
212-254-4370

Cherry Lane
38 Commerce Street (between Bedford and Barrow Sts.)
212-989-2020

Circle in the Square Downtown
159 Bleecker Street (at Sullivan St.)
212-254-6330

Circle Repertory Company
99 Seventh Avenue (at Sheridan Sq.)
212-924-7100

Delacorte Theater
81st Street (in Central Park)
212-598-7100

Douglas Fairbanks Theater
432 West 42nd Street (between Ninth and Tenth Aves.)
212-239-4321

Ensemble Studio Theater
549 West 52nd Street (between Ninth and Tenth Aves.)
212-247-3405

Gramercy Arts Theater
138 East 27th Street (between Madison and Park Aves.)
212-889-2850

Harold Clurman Theater
412 West 42nd Street (between Ninth and Tenth Aves.)
212-695-3401

Hudson Guild
441 West 26th Street (between Ninth and Tenth Aves.)
212-760-9810

John Houseman Theater
450 West 42nd Street (between Ninth and Tenth Aves.)
212-564-8038

Kaufman Theater
534 West 42nd Street (between Tenth and Eleventh Aves.)
212-554-8038

Minetta Lane
18 Minetta Lane (at MacDougal St.)
212-420-8000

Mitzi Newhouse Theater
64th Street and Broadway (at Lincoln Center)
212-362-7600

Nat Horne Theater
Ninth Avenue (at 42nd St.)
212-279-4200

Pearl Theater Company
125 West 22nd Street (between Sixth and Seventh Aves.)
212-645-7708

Players
115 MacDougal Street (at Minetta Ln.)
212-254-5076

Playhouse 91
361 East 91st Street (between First and Second Aves.)
212-831-2000

Public Theater
425 Lafayette Street (at Astor Pl.)
212-598-7150

Roundabout Theater
100 East 17th Street (at Park Ave.)
212-460-1883

Samuel Beckett Theater
410 West 42nd Street (between Ninth and Tenth Aves.)
212-594-2828

SoHo Repertory Theater
27 Barrow Street (between Bedford and Bleecker Sts.)
212-925-2588

Sullivan Street Playhouse
181 Sullivan Street (between Bleecker and Houston Sts.)
212-674-3838

Top of the Gate
160 Bleecker Street (at Sullivan St.)
212-475-5120

Vivian Beaumont Theatre
64th Street and Broadway (at Lincoln Center)
212-787-6868

# The Arts

New York City is the world capital of the performing arts, and you could easily see a different musical performance every night of the year. As with all aspects of planning your vacation, when selecting arts performances, it helps to do your homework and be selective. *Time Out New York* tends to have the best arts listings, along with *New York Magazine* and the Friday *New York Times* "Weekend" section.

## Music

**Brooklyn Academy of Music**       718-636-4111
30 Lafayette Avenue, BR
www.bam.org

BAM, as we call it, is a mecca for dance, film, music, theater, and opera seven days a week. Though you'll have to schlep to Brooklyn to experience the wonders of BAM, it's almost always worth the trip. A real gem for those who are willing to wander off the beaten path, BAM offers several family-appropriate performances each month.

**Carnegie Hall**       212-247-7800
156 West 57th Street (between Broadway and
Seventh Ave.), MTW
www.carnegiehall.org

One of America's most beloved and beautiful concert halls, the William Barnet Tuthill–designed Carnegie Hall is one of the most acoustically wonderful performance venues in the world. Acts range from classical to jazz. Carnegie Hall presents several Saturday afternoon children's concerts each year—call for schedules. There's also an hour-long tour available Monday, Tuesday, Thursday, and Friday at 11:30 A.M., 2:00 P.M., and 3:00 P.M. (performance schedule permitting).

### Learning Tip
Named for Andrew Carnegie, who paid for most of the construction, Carnegie Hall opened in 1891. If you had been alive then, you could have gone to Carnegie Hall to see Tchaikovsky conduct his own works!

## Lincoln Center                                    212-875-5000
**Broadway, from 62nd to 65th Sts., and beyond, UWS**
**www.lincolncenter.org**

Lincoln Center took six years (1962–1968) to build and is currently the largest performing arts center in the world. The various venues within have a total of 18,000 seats. Standing on Broadway (the avenue) and facing the fountain, to your left is the New York State Theater, where the New York City Ballet and New York City Opera perform. The central building is the Metropolitan Opera House, home to the Metropolitan Opera and American Ballet Theatre (the murals you see through the arched windows are by Marc Chagall). To your right is Avery Fisher Hall, where you'll find the New York Philharmonic Orchestra. Also within the complex are several additional performance areas for theater, film, and music. Lincoln Center has several very active youth programs, including the Little Orchestra Society and Young People's Concerts at Avery Fisher Hall; Growing Up With Opera at the Metropolitan Opera House; and Jazz for Young People and Meet the Music at Alice Tully Hall. And of course there are frequent tours. Call for schedules.

## 92nd Street Y                                    212-415-5607
**1395 Lexington Avenue**
**New York, NY 10128**
**www.92ndsty.org**

A major New York cultural institution, this is a great place to expose kids to the riches of New York intellectual life—you won't find many tourists here. The Y is famous for its lectures and interviews, readings by award-wining authors, dance performances, and concerts, including classical, cabaret, jazz, and popular music.

| | |
|---|---|
| ***Radio City Music Hall*** | 212-247-4777 |
| **1260 Sixth Avenue (at 50th St.), MT** | 212-632-4041 |
| **www.radiocity.com** | |

With 6,000 seats, Radio City is America's largest indoor theater. The chandeliers weigh 2 tons! Best known for the Rockettes and its Christmas and Easter extravaganzas, Radio City also plays host to concerts and events year-round. One-hour tours ($16 adults, $10 children under 12) usually leave from the main lobby every half-hour Monday through Saturday 10 A.M.–5 P.M. and Sunday 11 A.M.–5 P.M. Call for schedules.

## Dance

| | |
|---|---|
| ***Alvin Ailey American Dance Theater*** | 212-247-0430 |
| **Performances at City Center** | 212-767-0590 |
| **130 West 56th Street, MTW** | schedules and details |
| **www.alvinailey.org** | |

The amazing Alvin Ailey dancers—unquestionably the foremost African American dance company—perform at City Center as well as at other venues, including Lincoln Center.

| | |
|---|---|
| ***American Ballet Theater*** | 212-362-6000 |
| **Lincoln Center (see Music) at the Metropolitan** | |
| **Opera House** | |
| **www.abt.org** | |

Though the company is artistically considered the lesser (by just a little bit) of the two Lincoln Center ballet troupes, many viewers find these performances more pleasant and accessible (there isn't as much experimental dance going on here as at the New York City Ballet). Performance season is May through June.

### Joyce Theater                          212-242-0800
**175 Eighth Avenue (at 19th St.), CH**
**www.joyce.org**

A world-class modern dance theater, with a particularly strong children's outreach program.

### New York City Ballet                   212-870-5570
**Lincoln Center (see Music) at the New York State Theater**
**www.nycballet.com**

The New York City Ballet needs no introduction. This is where the legendary George Balanchine created his masterworks, and where the *Nutcracker* is performed every December. Just be sure you choose your show carefully—many of the performances are very modern and abstract, and may not appeal to kids other than die-hard dance fanatics. Performance seasons are April through June and November through February.

## Film

You'll find no shortage of movie theaters in New York City (all local papers have complete listings, as does 777-FILM), but frankly it seems a waste of time to see the same movie in New York City that you could see at your local cineplex. There are, however, three gigantic IMAX theaters in the area, which you might not find as easily at home.

**IMAX Dome Theater at the**               201-200-1000
**Liberty Science Center**
**Liberty State Park, Jersey City, NJ**
**www.lsc.org**

See the separate entry on Liberty Science Center under Museums.

**IMAX Theater at the**                    212-769-5100
**American Museum of Natural History**
**79th Street (at Central Park West), UWS**
**www.amnh.org**

See the separate entry on the Museum of Natural History under Museums.

**★ Sony IMAX Theater**                    212-336-5000
**68th Street (at Broadway), UWS**

The biggest (eight stories high) and best, with many 3-D offerings.

In addition, check with Lincoln Center (see Music) for the latest schedules for the weekend Movies for Kids series, which emphasizes the classics. There are also weekend children's film series at the Metropolitan Museum of Art (see Museums) and the New York Public Library (see City Sights).

## Puppetry

In Central Park, don't miss the Crowtations on weekend afternoons at the Bethesda Fountain (at the middle of the 72nd St. transverse) and the shows at the Swedish Cottage (Park Drive West at 81st St.). See Central Park.

### The Children's Aid Society
**219 Sullivan Street (between 3rd and Bleecker Sts.), GV**

Year-round weekend performances, with an emphasis on classic children's stories.

### Lenny Suib Puppet Playhouse     212-369-8890
**Asphalt Green Center**
**555 East 90th Street (between York and East End Aves.)**
**www.asphaltgreen.org**

Weekend puppet shows from the legendary Lenny Suib, who has been delighting audiences for decades.

### The Puppet Company     212-741-1646
**31 Union Square (at 16th St.), Loft 2b, US**

A tiny, 35-seat theater, with performances on weekends from October to April.

### Puppetworks—Park Slope     718-965-3391
**338 Sixth Avenue (at 4th St.), Park Slope, BR**
**www.puppetworks.org**

Classic fairy and folk tales performed daily. Puppetworks uses all hand-carved wooden marionettes. Shows sell out far in advance, especially on weekdays when school groups often take up all the seats. So plan ahead. Audience members can mingle with the puppets and puppeteers after the show.

## Circuses

Three major circus troupes come to New York City annually. Locations and show times vary, so check with each circus for up-to-the-minute schedule information.

### The Big Apple Circus                    212-268-2500
ww.bigapplecircus.org

The most kid-friendly and intimate of the New York circuses, everybody loves this one.

### Cirque du Soleil
www.cirquedusoleil.com

The famous French circus, now a multinational franchise. It's the most adult of the circuses, and younger children may even find parts of it too scary.

### Ringling Bros. Barnum &              800-755-4000
### Bailey Circus
www.ringling.com

The original three-ring circus extravaganza. It can be a bit over-whelming—it's huge—but it's not called the Greatest Show on Earth for nothing. At Madison Square Garden every spring.

## Just for Kids–Or Maybe Not!

### Crafts

### The Craft Studio                        212-831-6626
1657 Third Avenue (between 92nd and 93rd Sts.), UES

Stop in for an arts and crafts project, and the kids take their completed work with them. Each child selects a plain plaster ($11.95 and up), wood, or terra cotta ($14.95 and up) piece. You pay by the piece, and everything is covered in that price, including supplies and time. Kids can paint, glue, sparkle, and adorn their piece until they are satisfied with the outcome. Afterward the art is sprayed with a shellac coating and voila! The project is ready for the road.

> ★ *Little Shop of Plaster*          **212-717-6636**
> **431 East 73rd Street (between First and York Aves.), UES**

If I had to choose one of the three shops for a craft outing, I'd most likely go with this one, especially if the kids are varied in age. It offers a variety of materials to work with—pottery (which starts at $17.95), tee shirts ($14.95 and up), and plaster pieces ($11.95 and up). Your artist can take the piece home when it's complete, except for the pottery, which has to be fired here (and usually takes a week, but shipping arrangements can be made).

> *Our Name Is Mud*
> **1566 Second Avenue (between**          **212-570-6868**
> **81st and 82nd Sts.), UES**
> **506 Amsterdam Avenue (between**          **212-579-5575**
> **84th and 85th Sts.), UWS**
> **59 Greenwich Avenue (Seventh**          **212-647-7899**
> **Ave. at 11th St.), WV**
> **www.ournameismud.com**

Kids love this! Our Name Is Mud is a great activity for any age kids, especially on a rainy day. You buy a piece of ready-made pottery and paint it at the "Paint Bar" any way you want. You pay for the piece and $5.00 per half-hour for the time. The only catch is that usually the pieces aren't ready for a week (because they have to fire them). If your visit is a short one, call in advance and ask about exceptions—sometimes pieces get fired more quickly, depending upon volume.

## Makeup Makeovers

One of the greatest activities of all time for young and teen girls has got to be the opportunity to have a makeover. Girls who wear no makeup at all and those who wear it all the time will appreciate the exercise because it's so much fun. All of the big department stores do makeovers by appointment (and charge a fee), and some do casual makeup application at the counter if you catch a representative in the right mood (no appointment). A few places that are especially good with kids follow. In all instances, be sure to *call well in advance for an appointment* to avoid disappointment.

### *Barney's*     212-826-8900
### Madison Avenue (at 61st St.), UES

If you're planning on buying any makeup, the women who work the makeup counters at Barney's are very generous with their time. When I went to buy makeup for my wedding at the Clinique counter, the woman who helped me was extremely kind and patient (she didn't talk down to me) and helped me not only with lipstick (about which I was totally ignorant), but with some other products as well. Even though I'm an extreme cynic (I know that the more she helps me, the more she sells and the better for her), I appreciated her efforts and attention. She did her job well, and I walked away a satisfied (and made-over) customer—having only bought one lipstick. For the best shot at the most attention (smaller crowds), go during the day and midweek, when only the idle rich (and the other half of New York with odd schedules) are at play.

### Bloomingdale's  212-355-5900
**1000 Third Avenue (between 59th and 60th Sts.), UES**

Numerous makeup artists work their magic in the Bloomingdale's makeup department. You might want to describe your daughter a bit when you make your reservation (age, if she wears makeup, and how much) so that you get the best person for the job.

### Face, Stockholm
**226 Columbus Avenue  212-769-1420**
**(at 70th St.), UWS**
**687 Madison Avenue (at 62nd St.), UES  212-207-8833**
**110 Prince Street (at Green St.), SH  212-966-9110**

The staff could not be nicer at this minimalist makeup gallery. They look a little bit intimidating from the outside, but the moment you enter the store, you're made to feel welcome.

### Henri Bendel  212-247-1100
**712 Fifth Avenue (at 55th St.), MTE**

Ok, so I admit it. This is where I had my makeover when I turned sixteen. My older cousin, who lived in Brooklyn at the time, decided that it would be the perfect gift for my sweet sixteen—me, the short-haired athlete who could barely spare the time to towel dry my hair (let alone apply makeup). She took me to Bendel's, a store I had never so much as set foot in, and we had a total field day. Because of my coloring (fair skin, fair hair), I didn't end up looking that much different than when I started, but that was a good thing—they checked me out, realized I had never worn any makeup at all, and worked from there. Of course, I got suckered into buying all sorts of expensive and fancy makeup (with my hard-earned babysitting money), but you don't have to, and to this day I still use one of the products that I discovered there.

> **_Laura Geller Make-Up Studios_**     **212-570-LIPS**
> **1044 Lexington Avenue (between 74th and 75th Sts.), UES**

At Geller, beauty is the name of the game. Laura is the big gun here, so if you want a lesson with her, you'll have to pay big bucks to get it ($150 for an hour). But there are also plenty of other makeup artists in the studio with whom you can book an appointment, and the price tag, though still a bit steep, is half as much. They also offer makeup parties for children and teens. While you're at it, if anyone needs a facial, they do those too. Call ahead for appointments.

## High-Tech Fun

> **_Lazer Park_**     **212-398-3060**
> **163 West 46th Street (at Broadway), MTW**

Lazer Park's digital entertainment center includes high-tech hits like Lazer Tag, BattleTech, and loads of outrageous video games.

> **_Sony Wonder Technology Lab,_**     **212-833-8100**
> **_Sony Plaza_**
> **550 Madison Avenue (at 56th St.), MTE**
> **www.sonywondertechlab.com**

Sony Wonder is a hit with kids of all ages (except perhaps for pre-kindergarten). It's a cutting-edge, hands-on, interactive technology zone, and it's free! After kids have personalized a "swipe card" at "Log-in," they are free to explore communications technology as a "Media Trainee." Create a musical composition, take a cyber journey, examine the inner workings of innovative technology, experiment with robotics, or experience High Definition in the 72-seat theater. And, upon "Logout," each kid is presented with a graduation certificate for becoming a technology pro. There are also scheduled special events, so call or check the Web calendar for listings.

**Hours:** Tuesday through Saturday 10 A.M.–6 P.M., Thursday 10 A.M.–8 P.M., Sunday 12 P.M.–6 P.M.

**Admission:** Free

**Transportation:** *Bus:* M1, M2, M3, M4, M5, M57. *Subway:* 4, 5, 6 to 59th Street; E, F to Fifth Avenue

## Helpful Hint

For kids who can't live without their video game fix, one of the best selections by far is at ESPN Zone in Times Square. For more information, see the Theme Restaurants section.

| *XS New York* | 212-398-5467 |
|---|---|
| **1457 Broadway (between 41st and 42nd Sts.), MTW** | |

XS is a three-story virtual reality dream come true, complete with Lazer Tag.

## Participatory Sports

| *Chelsea Piers* | 212-336-6666 |
|---|---|
| **23rd Street (on the Hudson River, from 17th to 23rd Sts.), CH** | |
| **www.chelseapiers.com** | |

Chelsea Piers has filled a gap in NYC so big that no one seems to be able to figure out how we managed without this place for so long. I guess it's the old story of you don't know what you're missing until you have it. An enormous 30-acre "sports village," Chelsea Piers has something for everyone in the family. In no other single place in New York City will you find such extensive facilities and equipment dedicated to sports and fitness as here. Choose from among golf, soccer, dance, gymnastics, batting, inline skating, bowling, rock climbing, skate park with ramp, swimming, and lacrosse. Starting to get the idea? Prices vary (and they do run high), so to avoid disappointment and bankruptcy, call in advance for prices and the children's schedule.

> ### *Claremont Riding Academy*     212-724-5100
> ### 175 West 89th Street (between Columbus and
> ### Amsterdam Aves.), UWS

Skilled riders, ages 10 and up, can take a horse out for a ride in Central Park. Claremont is one of the City's unexpected finds. There, right in the middle of the Upper West Side, is a stable and riding academy. These same folks that teach city kids to ride can also set you and your family up with horses for an outing in the park. You've got to follow their rules, which they'll run through with you over the phone *(when you call at least two days in advance to reserve)* and when you get there. Even though the stable's hours are long, park rides are only allowed during daylight hours. Therefore, during the winter, horses have to be in by 4:30 P.M. And safety is a big issue for the staff at Claremont—no riding in the park when the ground is icy and no outings when the mercury is above 90 degrees. Helmets (you can borrow one or bring your own) and hard shoes are required and no shorts or sneakers are allowed (riders will be turned away if they are not appropriately attired). Riders must be experienced in English style; there are no Western saddles available. For avid equestrians, riding in Central Park, with the leaves turning red, yellow, and orange all around, is one of life's great moments.

**Hours:** Monday through Friday 6 A.M.–10 P.M., Saturday and Sunday 6 A.M.–6 P.M.

**Cost:** $40 per hour per horse

**Transportation:** *Subway:* 1, 9, B, C to 86th Street (walk 1½ blocks over, 3 blocks north)

For inline skate rentals, see Blades Board & Skate (under Sports) in chapter 7.

---

*Rockefeller Plaza Rink*                212-332-7654
**Fifth Avenue (between 49th and 50th Sts.), MTE**

---

This is undeniably the most glamorous, famous, and romantic ice skating rink in the city, and maybe even the world. The stuff that Hollywood movies have been made of, lacing up skates and going for a spin is sort of like living in a dream. It's especially wonderful when the Christmas tree is set up and illuminated. The best time to go is early in the morning during the week, before the crowds come. I've often seen people skating before work, and the rink is virtually empty. By far the worst time to skate is during the Christmas/winter vacation, but if you must, call for hours and rise and shine to beat the crowds. Hot Chocolate at Serendipity (if it's open yet) is a perfect finish to the experience.

**Admission:** The prices seem to be changeable (in the upward direction) but last word was: Monday through Thursday $7.50 adults, $6 kids under 12; Friday through Sunday $9 adults, $6.75 kids. Rentals are available. Call for updated details on hours (and prices).

**Transportation:** *Bus:* M1, M2, M3, M4 to 49th Street. *Subway:* B, D, F, Q to 47th–50th/Rockefeller Center.

See also Central Park, in Parks, for ice-skating.

# Family-Friendly Nightlife: Comedy Clubs

Nightlife in major cities isn't typically family-friendly, center-ing as it does around the bar scene. But New York's multitude of comedy clubs can provide the perfect evening of entertain-ment for families, especially those traveling with teens. Be sure to call ahead and learn about the act and the club's specific policies. Some comedians can get pretty raunchy; others keep it clean. It's also important to call ahead because clubs change their admissions policies from time to time, or allow under-18 customers only on certain days or at certain times.

> *Caroline's Comedy Club*                     212-757-4100
> **1626 Broadway (between 49th and 50th Sts.), MT**

Very slick, modern club. Entertainers have included Joy Behar, Sandra Bernhard, and Gilbert Gottfried.

### Helpful Hint

For families traveling with independent teens who have a particular interest in other forms of nightlife, there are some music and dance clubs that allow un-derage patrons to attend at certain times and on cer-tain nights of the week. These fluctuate wildly, so the best way to find out what's going on when you're in town is to check *Time Out New York* and then call the club in question to inquire about its policy.

### Chicago City Limits                    212-888-5233
1105 First Avenue (at East 61st St.), UES

Wonderful improvisational comedy with lots of audience participation.

### Comedy Cellar                          212-254-3480
117 MacDougal Street (between 3rd and Bleecker Sts.), GV

A real old-time comedy club in a basement, in business for twenty years.

### Comic Strip Live                       212-861-9386
1568 Second Avenue (between 81st and 82nd Sts.), UES

Reliable comedy in a neighborhood bar/lounge atmosphere with several acts nightly.

### Dangerfield's                          212-593-1650
1118 First Avenue (between 61st and 62nd Sts.), UES

It is indeed owned by Rodney himself.

### Freestyle Repertory Theater            212-642-8202
Various locations

An utterly zany improv company.

### Gotham Comedy Club                      212-367-9000
34 West 22nd Street (between 5th and 6th Aves.), GP

This Flatiron District club has hosted comedians ranging from Chris Rock to David Brenner.

> ### *Luna Lounge*                          212-260-2323
> **171 Ludlow Street (between Houston and Stanton Sts.),**
> **LES**

Janeane Garofalo has appeared here, though most of the acts are less distinguished. Monday night only.

> ### *Surf Reality*                          212-673-4182
> **172 Allen Street (between Stanton and Rivington Sts.),**
> **LES**

Alternative/avant-garde comedy—not stand-up routines, but rather unusual sketches and performances.

## Professional Sports

There's nothing like attending a sporting event in New York City, where fans are surely the world's most enthusiastic. It's usually pretty easy to get early-season baseball tickets in the upper decks, but basketball and football can be more of a challenge (in some cases impossible without resorting to scalpers). In any event, for the best seats, it's best to plan far ahead.

### *Baseball*

If you're in New York during baseball season, even if you're not a die-hard baseball fan, I strongly recommend attendance at a Mets or Yankees home game as one of the best New York experiences available. I suggest you bring some snacks and sandwiches to avoid paying outrageous sums for stadium junk food, and that you agree with the kids in advance that you won't be purchasing overpriced souvenirs at the ballpark. You can get all that stuff in Manhattan at the clubhouse shops (or you can buy hats and tee shirts for a fraction of the cost, about $5, on the street; see chapter 7).

*The New York Mets*          718-565-4305
Shea Stadium
Flushing, Q
www.mets.com

To get to Shea Stadium, take the #7 train (it stops along 42nd Street in Manhattan) eastbound (toward Queens) to the Willets Point/Shea Stadium stop. Allow for about 45 minutes on the train. There's also a quicker Long Island Railroad commuter train that departs from Penn Station, but you get more of the true fan experience when you take the subway. Shea Stadium also has ample parking for those with cars.

*The New York Yankees*          718-293-4300
Yankee Stadium, BX
www.yankees.com

To get to Yankee Stadium, take the #4 (Lexington Avenue), C (Eighth Avenue), or D (Sixth/Eighth Avenue) trains to 161st Street/Yankee Stadium. Though the neighborhood isn't great, it's safe enough when you're traveling with 60,000 other fans. Driving to Yankee Stadium is not advised, because the parking situation is very inconvenient.

### Basketball

The New York Knickerbockers (Knicks)
Madison Square Garden Center
Seventh Avenue (from 31st to 33rd Sts.)
212-465-6741
212-465-MSG1 for Madison Square Garden info
www.nba.com/knicks
www.thegarden.com

The New York Liberty (WNBA)
Madison Square Garden
212-465-6741
212-465-MSG1 for Madison Square Garden info
www.wnba.com/liberty
www.thegarden.com
*All tickets for events at Madison Square Garden are sold through Ticketmaster (212-307-7171).*

The New Jersey Nets
Continental Airlines Arena
East Rutherford, NJ
800-7NJ-NETS
www.nba.com/nets

### Hockey

New York Islanders
Nassau Coliseum (Long Island)
800-882-ISLES
www.newyorkislanders.com

New York Rangers
Madison Square Garden
212-465-6741
212-465-MSG1 for Madison Square Garden info
www.newyorkrangers.com
www.thegarden.com

New Jersey Devils
Continental Airlines Arena
East Rutherford, NJ
201-935-6050
www.newjerseydevils.com

*Transportation:* For all events at the stadiums and arenas in East Rutherford, NJ (Giants Stadium, Meadowlands, Continental Airlines Arena), buses run from the Port Authority Bus Terminal, located at 42nd Street and Eighth Avenue. New Jersey Transit buses leave two hours before game time, and return up to one hour after the game. $3.25 one-way fare. 20 minute travel time. For more information, call 212-564-8484.

## Football

You'll need good connections or a very large wallet to pry loose even the least desirable football tickets, but for those who simply must attend . . .

> The New York Giants
> Giants Stadium
> East Rutherford, NJ
> 201-935-8111
> www.giants.com

> The New York Jets
> Meadowlands Arena
> East Rutherford, NJ
> 516-560-8200
> www.newyorkjets.com

## Soccer

> Metrostars
> Giants Stadium
> East Rutherford, NJ
> 201-935-8111
> www.metrostars.com

## Tennis

If your kids are into tennis, this is the most incredible spectator tennis experience available in America. Tickets are wickedly expensive, though.

U.S. Open
USTA National Tennis Center
Flushing Meadows-Corona Park
Flushing, NY
212-239-6250 U.S. Open ticket info
888-OPEN-TIX (888-673-6849) tickets through
    Telecharge
*Follow the directions to Shea Stadium.*

# Flea Markets

Visiting New York's flea markets is a great way to combine the best of sightseeing, shopping, and people-watching. The following are some of the best.

### *Annex Antique Fair & Flea Market*    212-243-5343
### *(Chelsea Flea Market)*
### Sixth Avenue (at 26th St.), CH

Antique furniture, jewelry, used clothing, old books, and bric-a-brac (and lots of it) fill the parking lot. Prices are often sharply reduced at dusk.
    **Hours:** Saturday and Sunday, sunrise to sunset.

### *NoHo Flea Market*
### Broadway (between East Fourth and Great Jones Sts.), EV

As a teenager, this was always one of my favorite markets, especially around Christmas time. Jewelry, tee shirts, funky clothes, sky's the limit. Perfect for bringing hip gifts home to give to (and impress) friends.
    **Hours:** Saturday and Sunday

### SoHo Antique Fair            212-682-2000
**Broadway and Grand Street, SH**

A wide range of goods—especially antiques and crafts.
**Hours:** Saturday and Sunday

### Spring Street Flea Market
**Spring and Wooster Streets, SH**

I've browsed this crowded SoHo lot for more than 15 years. The stock is changeable depending upon the season—gloves and hats in winter are standard, as are sunglasses and silver jewelry in summer. Good entertainment and not as pricey as the rest of SoHo.
**Hours:** Saturday and Sunday

### West 76th Street Flea Market (Greenflea)
**Columbus and 76th Street, UWS**

A combination of furniture, vintage clothes and jewels, farm-fresh produce, and crafts, there's nothing especially earth-shattering at this market, but the homemade lemonade is really good.
**Hours:** Saturday

# INDEX TO ATTRACTIONS/ACTIVITIES BY NEIGHBORHOOD

Brooklyn Museum of Art
(p. 206)

*Music*
Brooklyn Academy of
Music (p. 278)

*Parks*
Prospect Park (p. 262)

*Puppetry*
Puppetworks—Park Slope
(p. 283)

*Zoos and Gardens*
Brooklyn Botanic Garden
(p. 244)
★New York Aquarium
(p. 246)

### CENTRAL PARK

*Zoos and Gardens*
★Central Park Wildlife
Center/Tisch Children's
Zoo (Central Park Zoo)
(p. 245)
For more on Central Park, see
pp. 250–261.

### CHELSEA

*Dance*
Joyce Theater (p. 281)

*Flea Markets*
Annex Antique Fair & Flea
Market (p. 298)

*Participatory Sports*
Chelsea Piers (p. 289)

### EAST VILLAGE

*Flea Markets*
NoHo Flea Market (p. 298)

### FINANCIAL DISTRICT

*City Sights*
★Brooklyn Bridge (p. 175)

★Ferry to Ellis Island
(p. 177)
★Ferry to Statue of Liberty
(p. 185)
New York Stock Exchange
(p. 181)
South Street Seaport
(p. 184)
World Financial Center
(p. 188)
★World Trade Center
(p. 189)

*Museums*
Museum of Jewish Her-
itage—A Living Mem-
orial to the Holocaust
(p. 214)
National Museum of the
American Indian (p. 228)

*Parks*
Battery Park (p. 261)

### GRAMERCY PARK/ FLATIRON

*City Sights*
Flatiron Building (p. 179)
★Theodore Roosevelt
Birthplace (p. 187)

*Comedy Clubs*
Gotham Comedy Club
(p. 293)

*Theaters for Families*
★Tada! Youth Ensemble
Theater (p. 269)

### GREENWICH VILLAGE

*Comedy Clubs*
Comedy Cellar (p. 293)

*Museums*
Forbes Magazine Galleries
(p. 223)

*Music*
  Carnegie Hall (p. 278)

**NEW JERSEY**
*Film*
  IMAX Dome Theater at the
    Liberty Science Center
    (p. 282)
*Museum*
  ★Liberty Science Center
    (p. 212)

**QUEENS**
*Museums*
  American Museum of the
    Moving Image (p. 203)
  New York Hall of Science
    (p. 228)
  P.S. 1 Contemporary Art
    Center (p. 231)

**SOHO**
*Flea Markets*
  SoHo Antique Fair (p. 299)
  Spring Street Flea Market
    (p. 299)
*Makeup Makeovers*
  Face, Stockholm (p. 287)
*Museums*
  Museum for African Art
    (p. 226)
  ★New York City Fire Mu-
    seum (p. 217)

**STATEN ISLAND**
*Parks*
  Snug Harbor Cultural Cen-
    ter (p. 263)

**THEATER DISTRICT**
*Theaters for Families*
  ★New Victory Theater
    (p. 269)

**TIMES SQUARE**
*City Sights*
  Times Square (p. 187)

**UNION SQUARE**
*Parks*
  Union Square Park (p. 264)
*Puppetry*
  The Puppet Company
    (p. 283)

**UPPER EAST SIDE**
*City Sights*
  Temple Emanu-El (p. 187)
*Comedy Clubs*
  Chicago City Limits (p. 293)
  Comic Strip Live (p. 293)
  Dangerfield's (p. 293)
*Crafts*
  The Craft Studio (p. 284)
  ★Little Shop of Plaster
    (p. 285)
  Our Name Is Mud (p. 285)
*Makeup Makeovers*
  Barney's (p. 286)
  Bloomingdale's (p. 287)
  Face, Stockholm (p. 287)
  Laura Geller Make-Up
    Studios (p. 288)
*Museums*
  Asia Society (p. 221)
  Cooper-Hewitt National
    Design Museum (p. 223)
  The Frick Collection
    (p. 224)

International Center of Photography (p. 224)
The Jewish Museum (p. 225)
★Metropolitan Museum of Art (p. 197)
El Museo del Barrio (p. 226)
Museum of the City of New York (p. 213)
★Solomon R. Guggenheim Museum (p. 218)
Whitney Museum of American Art (p. 219)

*Theaters for Families*
Paper Bag Players, at Hunter College (p. 269)

## UPPER MANHATTAN

*Museums*
The Cloisters (p. 222)

*Music*
92nd Street Y (p. 279)

*Parks*
Riverside Park (p. 263)

*Puppetry*
Lenny Suib Puppet Playhouse (p. 283)

## UPPER WEST SIDE

*City Sights*
★Cathedral of Saint John the Divine (p. 176)
Shearith Israel Spanish and Portuguese Synagogue (p. 184)

*Crafts*
Our Name Is Mud (p. 285)

*Dance*
American Ballet Theater (p. 280)
New York City Ballet (p. 281)

*Film*
IMAX Theater at the American Museum of Natural History (p. 282)
★Sony IMAX Theater (p. 282)

*Flea Markets*
West 76th Street Flea Market (p. 299)

*Makeup Makeovers*
Face, Stockholm (p. 287)

*Museums*
★American Museum of Natural History and Rose Center for Earth and Space (p. 191)
★Children's Museum of Manhattan (p. 207)
Museum of American Folk Art (p. 227)
The New-York Historical Society (p. 229)

*Music*
Lincoln Center (p. 279)

*Parks*
Riverside Park (p. 263)

*Participatory Sports*
Claremont Riding Academy (p. 290)

*Theaters for Families*
Theatreworks USA (p. 270)

## WEST VILLAGE

*Crafts*
Our Name Is Mud (p. 285)

*Theaters for Families*
Grove Street Playhouse (p. 268)

For Broadway, Off-Broadway, and Off-Off Broadway listings,
    see pp. 270–277.
For Circuses, see the listing on p. 284.
For Galleries, see the listing by neighborhood on
    pp. 233–237.
For information on Professional Sports, see pp. 294–298.

# Dining

# Dining

Map shows highlights only. See chapter text for more listings.

In New York City, every meal is an adventure, which can be a mixed blessing. The pioneering spirit that so many children otherwise display often disappears when it comes to trying unfamiliar foods. Sometimes, kids just want to eat pizza, burgers, or hot dogs. Luckily, New York offers some of the world's finest examples of each of these items.

But if you can push your kids a little farther than usual and get them wrapped up in the culinary adventure of New York City, a world of ethnic food—some of it available nowhere else in America—awaits them. Like Korean barbecue, where you cook your own meat on tabletop grills. Or Brazilian rodizio, where waiters carve unlimited portions of more than twenty meats tableside off gigantic metal skewers. Have you ever been to a real, old-fashioned Romanian Jewish steakhouse, or a Tibetan restaurant, or a Filipino "turo-turo" buffet? You could easily spend a month in New York and eat the cuisine of a different nation every single day.

Of course, the more familiar ethnic cuisines, like Chinese and Italian, are also well represented, but even these come with some unusual twists. One of the greatest activities for kids is Sunday dim sum brunch in Chinatown, where busy waiters wheel steaming carts around the dining room, from which you select your meal, one little dish at a time. And several of New York's Italian restaurants offer family-style dining, where all dishes are meant to be shared.

I recoil at the notion of a "kids' restaurant," and I find most listings of such places to be patronizing and dull. You didn't come all the way to New York City to eat at TGI Friday's or McDonald's (though the flagship McDonald's establishment, in the Financial District, is a must-visit). So I've tried to list restaurants that kids will love, but that are also delicious in their own right. But you should know, if the kids absolutely, positively refuse to eat anything but Burger King, that all the major national fast-food chains are well represented in every neighborhood of Manhattan.

I've organized the restaurant listings in this chapter alphabetically by cuisine (Burgers, Chinese, Indian, Pizza). After the main restaurant listings, look for special sections on ice cream, candy, bakeries, and "grownup" restaurants.

**Helpful Hint**
Eat at off-hours (late lunch; early dinner) to beat the crowds and avoid being rushed through your meal.

I have not, for the most part, included in this chapter the dozens of restaurants in museums and at other popular attractions. Typically, you can't even enter these restaurants unless you've paid admission to the site in question. Thus, where attractions have restaurants attached, they are discussed separately in chapter 5.

But what about the "theme restaurants," like Hard Rock Café and the new WWF restaurant? I've visited all of them—with kids in tow—and I'll tell you my picks and pans in the "Quick Guide to Theme Restaurants."

Finally, remember, you don't have to eat every meal in a restaurant. New York has a wealth of gourmet markets, where you can buy nutritious cheese, fruit, bread, and prepared salads. I've included a list of the City's best markets, so, armed with a sharp knife and a few paper plates and plastic forks, you can feed your family healthy, economical breakfasts and lunches—so you only have to cope with and pay for one restaurant meal per day.

*Note:* Nothing changes more quickly than the New York restaurant scene. The information here was accurate at press time, but definitely call ahead before you make a special journey to any restaurant.

### *What the $ Ratings Mean*

$ = cheap; less than $10 per person
$$ = moderate; $10–$25 per person
$$$ = expensive; $25–$50 per person
$$$$ = luxury; $50 and up per person

The $ ratings represent averages, based on what the typical customer eats at a particular restaurant. You can always spend more, and sometimes less, if you're an atypical consumer.

I've also indicated the neighborhood, using the following abbreviations:

BR: Brooklyn          BX: Bronx
CH: Chelsea           CT: Chinatown
EV: East Village      FD: Financial District

## Top Ten "Grownup" Restaurants that Welcome Kids

1. Union Square Café (p. 318)

2. Gramercy Tavern (p. 317)

3. Mesa Grill (p. 357)

4. Calle Ocho (p. 356)

5. Ruby Foo's (p. 336)

6. Blue Water Grill (p. 313)

7. Café Luxembourg (p. 338)

8. Peter Luger (p. 367)

9. Sparks (p. 367)

10. Oyster Bar (p. 318)

GD: Garment District    GP: Gramercy Park/Flatiron
GV: Greenwich Village    LES: Lower East Side
LI: Little Italy    MT: Midtown
MTE: Midtown East    MTW: Midtown West
Q: Queens    SH: SoHo
SI: Staten Island    TBC: TriBeCa
TD: Theater District    TS: Times Square
UES: Upper East Side    US: Union Square
UWS: Upper West Side    WV: West Village

**Payment:** It's safe to assume that most restaurants where the check is over $10 per person will accept major credit cards, and that most of the less expensive restaurants will not. However, it's always good to call ahead because restaurants occasionally change their policies and some noteworthy moderate-to-expensive restaurants (such as the Carnegie Deli and

Peter Luger Steakhouse) do operate on a cash-only basis. Where this was the case at press time, I have noted it.

**Reservations:** It always helps to call ahead, even where reservations are not available. You can at least assess the wait and find out whether special menu items are available, hours of operation, and the like.

## Insider's Tip

"When it comes to eating at places that don't accept reservations, always have a backup plan so your night doesn't turn into a nightmare. Be aware of at least one other restaurant in the area that you can visit if the wait is too long at your first choice." —*Andrew, father of two*

A ★ indicates a particularly noteworthy restaurant for its price range or type, either because of the excellence of its food or its appeal to kids.

## American

These restaurants serve the food that's most familiar to most American kids, and lots of it. They can be a godsend for parents of picky eaters because the food is simple and the choices numerous. Inspired by the roadside diner menus of old, and very often called "coffee shops" in the local New York City dialect (even though coffee is only a minor part of their business), each of these restaurants has added its own twists to this slice of Americana. *See also the entries on Burgers, Frankfurters, and French Fries.*

### ★*America* $$
9 East 18th Street (between
Broadway and Fifth Ave.), GP

212-505-2110

This mega-eatery offers one of the most extensive menus you've ever seen, including the venerable Fluffernutter (a sandwich made with peanut butter and marshmallow Fluff). The place is loud and rambunctious, and even the loudest kids will blend in here.

**City Fact**

The apple strudel on the menu at Planet Hollywood is made from Arnold Schwarzenegger's mother's recipe.

### *Barking Dog Luncheonette* $$
1678 Third Avenue (at 94th St.), UES      212-831-1800

A more refined version of a diner, with strong seafood selections in addition to the expected items.

### *Bendix Diner* $
219 Eighth Avenue (at 21st St.), CH      212-366-0560
167 First Avenue (between
10th and 11th Sts.), EV      212-260-4220

High-quality diner food, and the price is right.

### *Blue Water Grill* $$$
31 Union Square West, US      212-675-9500

Impeccable seafood. **Although this is a rather grownup restaurant, they do welcome children.**

# Quick Guide to

The restaurants kids ask for most when they come to New York are, overwhelmingly, the nationally publicized and promoted theme restaurants. Just because they're popular, however, doesn't mean they're good—or worth the effort you have to expend to get in. Although some of the theme restaurants can be a

| Restaurant | Address | Phone Number |
|---|---|---|
| **TOP THEME RESTAURANT PICKS** | | |
| ★WWF | 43rd St. and Broadway, TS | 212-398-2563 |
| Jekyll & Hyde | 1409 Sixth Ave. (between 57th and 58th Sts.), MTW | 212-541-9505 |
| ★Mars 2112 | 1633 Broadway (at 51st St.) downstairs, MTW | 212-582-2112 |
| Harley-Davidson Café | 1370 Sixth Ave. (at 56th St.), MTW | 212-245-6000 |
| Mickey Mantle's | 42 Central Park South (between Fifth and Sixth Aves.), MTW | 212-688-7777 |
| **THEME RESTAURANTS YOU CAN SAFELY SKIP** | | |
| ESPN Zone | 1472 Broadway (at 42nd St.), TS | 212-921-3776 |
| Hard Rock Café | 221 West 57th St. (between Broadway and Seventh Ave.), MTW | 212-489-6565 |
| Planet Hollywood | 1540 Broadway (at 45th St.), TS | 212-333-7827 |

# Theme Restaurants

lot of fun, many are just mediocre restaurants with a few thematic pictures on the walls—a total waste of time and a big disappointment for many young visitors. I've tried to separate the wheat from the chaff, so you can make informed decisions about whether or not to visit these restaurants.

| Price Rating | Comments |
|---|---|
| $$ | Great for wrestling fans. TVs run nonstop wrestling bios and matches. On Tuesdays, watch matches that aren't aired publicly until Thursdays. Wrestlers stop in when they're in town. |
| $$ | Not for the faint of heart, this is nevertheless another winner. The horror theme is consistent throughout, and highly interactive. |
| $$ | Get a full-length amusement-park-like ride when you gain entry to this sci-fi restaurant. When you exit, you're in what looks and feels like a cave. |
| $$ | The Harley-Davidson motorcycle theme is as American as apple pie, the decor is original and star studded, and the food is not just edible, but also even good. |
| $$ | A worthwhile, understated restaurant for the avid baseball fan who not only follows the game but has studied baseball history, too. |
| $$ | Offers almost nothing special for kids. A lot of TVs feature sporting events, but most viewing areas are in the bars. |
| $$ | If you've seen one Hard Rock, you've seen them all. |
| $$ | The same rules apply to Planet Hollywood as to Hard Rock, only Planet Hollywood is a copycat with not much in the way of originality or décor. |

316

DINING

**Bubby's**                                        **$$**
120 Hudson Street (at                  212-219-0666
North Moore), TBC

A New York institution, this place is frequented by everybody
who's anybody downtown.

**Chat 'n' Chew**                                  **$$**
10 East 16th Street (between Fifth     212-243-1616
Ave. and Union Square West), GP

You can't help but love the BLT's and pink-frosted chocolate
cake at this contemporary take on the greasy spoon.

**Comfort Diner**                                  **$$**
142 East 86th Street (at               212-426-8600
Lexington Ave.), UES
214 East 45th Street (between          212-867-4555
Second and Third Aves.), MTE

A retro look and modern menu make this one of the best
diner-style restaurants in town.

**Crab House**                                     **$$**
Pier 61 (at Chelsea Pier), CH          212-835-2722

If your kids like seafood, this gigantic restaurant in the newly
restored Chelsea Pier sports complex is a winner.

| ★*EJ's Luncheonette* | $ |
|---|---|
| 1271 Third Avenue (at 73rd St.), UES | 212-472-0600 |
| 447 Amsterdam Avenue (between 81st and 82nd Sts.), UWS | 212-873-3444 |
| 423 Sixth Avenue (between 9th and 10th Sts.), WV | 212-473-5555 |

One of the most popular diners among native New Yorkers; just about everything is good.

| *Googie's* | $$ |
|---|---|
| 1491 Second Avenue (at 78th St.), UES | 212-717-1122 |

This great neighborhood diner also has a slight Italian twist to the menu.

| *Gramercy Tavern* | $$$$ |
|---|---|
| 42 East 20th Street, GP | 212-477-0777 |

The more upscale of Danny Meyer's dynamic duo (see also Union Square Café), Gramercy Tavern will serve you a meal that will be a memory the whole family will cherish. Call far, far in advance for reservations. **Be aware, this is mainly a restaurant for grownups, although it does welcome kids.**

| *Junior's* | $$ |
|---|---|
| 386 Flatbush Avenue (at DeKalb Ave.), BR | 718-852-5257 |

The definitive Brooklyn diner, with orange vinyl banquettes, and some of the world's best cheesecake.

| | |
|---|---|
| *Oyster Bar* | $$$ |
| Grand Central Station, | 212-490-6650 |
| Dining Concourse, MTE | |

A soaring, tiled, arched ceiling and the finest fresh oysters make this one of America's greatest traditional seafood restaurants. Don't miss the made-to-order chowders.

| | |
|---|---|
| ★*Peanut Butter & Co.* | $ |
| 240 Sullivan Street (between | 212-677-3995 |
| Bleecker and West 3rd Sts.), WV | |

Kids love this menu, which contains, among other things, no less than fourteen variations of the peanut-butter sandwich.

| | |
|---|---|
| ★*Screening Room* | $$$ |
| 54 Varick Street (between | 212-334-2100 |
| Canal and Laight Sts.), TBC | |

Yes, you can eat a meal while watching a movie. The schedule varies, and most of the movies are classics. Prices are high, but this place is great, especially for teens who love cinema.

| | |
|---|---|
| *Union Square Café* | $$$$ |
| 21 East 16th Street, US | 212-243-4020 |

Danny Meyer, who also owns Gramercy Tavern, is committed to welcoming kids no matter how popular his restaurants become with adults (they are numbers one and two in the *Zagat Survey*).

# Bagels

Bagels are the signature bread product of New York, and New York bagels will simply blow you away if you've never had the real thing. They're also a great snack—or even a meal—for kids. Of all the foods in the world, I've found that bagels are the ones least likely to be rejected by kids, especially when bagels are fresh out of the oven and particularly when you get them at a real old-fashioned bagel bakery where you can watch the bagels first being boiled (to give them their unique crust) and then baked. The following are my favorite bagel bakeries in New York. Most of these shops will make bagel sandwiches, which make convenient, portable, filling lunches.

Absolute Bagels
2788 Broadway (between 107th and 108th Sts.), UWS
212-932-2052

Bagelry
1380 Madison Avenue (at 96th St.), UES
212-423-9590
1324 Lexington Avenue (between 88th and 89th Sts.),
UES
212-996-0567
1228 Lexington Avenue (at 83rd St.), UES
212-717-2080

B-J's Bagels
130 West 72nd Street (between Columbus Ave. and
Broadway), UWS
212-769-3350

★Columbia Hot Bagels
2836 Broadway (between 110th and 111th Sts.), UWS
212-222-3200

David's Bagels
1651 Second Avenue (between 85th and 86th Sts.), UES
212-439-7887

228 First Avenue (between 13th and 14th Sts.), UES
212-533-8766

★Ess-a-Bagel
359 First Avenue (at 21st St.), GP
212-260-2252
831 Third Avenue (between 50th and 51st Sts.), MTW
212-980-1010

## Learning Tip

*Ess-a-Bagel* means "eat a bagel" in Yiddish, the language (a mix of German, Russian, and Hebrew) that used to be spoken by Eastern European Jews. Term paper idea: Discuss the history of the Yiddish language, where it came from, and how many of its words and expressions *(schlep, oy vay!)* have come into common English usage.

★H&H
2239 Broadway (at 80th St.), UWS
212-595-8003

★Kossar's
367 Grand Street (between Essex and Norfolk Sts.), LES
212-473-4810

Kossar's bialys are the best I have ever tasted. You can watch them being made and eat them straight out of the oven at this Lower East Side bakery.

Pick-a-Bagel
1101 Lexington Avenue (at 77th St.), UES
212-517-6590
200 West 57th Street (at Seventh Ave.), MTW

212-957-5151
1473 Second Avenue
(between 76th and
77th Sts.), UES
212-717-4662
601 Avenue of the
Americas (between
17th and 18th Sts.),
CH
212-924-4999
297 Third Avenue
(between 22nd and
23rd Sts.), GP
212-686-1414

Tal Bagels
333 East 86th Street
(between First and
Second Aves.), UES
212-427-6811
977 First Avenue (be-
tween 53rd and 54th Sts.), MTE
212-753-9080

> **Learning Tip**
> Although you can find
> a bagel—albeit not al-
> ways the best—in vir-
> tually any part of the
> United States, its near
> relative, the bialy, is
> still largely unknown
> outside New York. A
> bialy is a softer, more
> perishable bread with
> an indentation instead
> of a hole in the middle.
> The indentation is filled
> with an onion or garlic
> mixture. Once you've
> tried a hot bialy, you'll
> wonder if it isn't per-
> haps even better
> than a bagel.

# Barbecue and Southern

If you're coming to New York from the South, I can't honestly
recommend that you eat barbecue here. But for everybody
else, you'll find New York's barbecue restaurants to be great al-
lies in feeding your kids. Prices are a little higher than in Lexington, North Carolina, but then again they don't have to pay
New York rents down there.

**Cowgirl Hall of Fame**                              **$$**
519 Hudson Street (at Tenth Ave.), WV    212-633-1133

A slice of the South in Manhattan, this palace of barbecue and corn dogs lures kids with its wild décor.

**★ Dallas BBQ**                                         **$**
1265 Third Avenue (between                212-772-9393
72nd and 73rd Sts.), UES
27 West 72nd Street (between              212-873-2004
Columbus Ave. and Central Park West), UWS
132 West 43rd Street (between             212-221-9000
Broadway and Sixth Ave.), TS
21 University Place (at 8th St.), EV      212-674-4450
132 Second Avenue (at Saint Marks), EV   212-777-5574

Not particularly authentic, but kids love the sweet baby back ribs and tender rotisserie chicken; and parents appreciate the incredibly reasonable prices.

**Tennessee Mountain**                                   **$**
121 West 45th Street (between             212-869-4545
Broadway and Sixth Ave.), TS
143 Spring Street (at Wooster St.), SH    212-431-3993

Good ribs, even better prices.

**★ Virgil's Real BBQ**                              **$$**
152 West 44th Street (between             212-921-9494
Broadway and Sixth Ave.), TS

Perhaps the best and most legitimate barbecue in Manhattan; prices are a little steep, but the atmosphere is perfect for kids—lots of nice Southern touches in a gigantic, roaring Midtown space.

## City Fact
New York City has more than 20,000 restaurants today. If you ate at a different restaurant every day, you couldn't even keep pace with all the new openings, much less make a dent in the 20,000!

# Brazilian

The Brazilian tradition of *rodizio* is ideal for families. Waiters circle the restaurant with meat (more than twenty varieties, ranging from simple steak to more adventurous choices) on gigantic metal skewers, stopping at your table and carving it right on to your plate. One price covers unlimited meat and trips to the salad bar, though drinks are extra.

| *Churrascaria Plantation* | $$ |
| --- | --- |
| 150 Central Park South (between Sixth and Seventh Aves.), MTW | 212-489-7070 |

The most upscale of the rodizios, and not as crowded at Plataforma.

| ★ *Churrascaria Plataforma* | $$ |
| --- | --- |
| 316 West 49th Street (between Eighth and Ninth Aves.), MTW | 212-245-0505 |

The best of the all-you-can eat roasted meat feasts.

| *Riodizio* | $$ |
| --- | --- |
| 417 Lafayette Street (between Astor Pl. and 4th St.), EV | 212-529-1313 |

The original Manhattan rodizio, and the only one in the neighborhood.

# Burgers

If your kids like burgers, they'll have no trouble eating in New York. You'll find fantastic, gigantic burgers of every variety (grilled, fried, and steamed; beef, turkey, and tuna) all over town. These are a few of the best and most reliable, authentic, local burger joints.

| | |
|---|---|
| *Big Nick's* | $ |
| 2175 Broadway (between 76th and 77th Sts.), UWS | 212-362-9238 |
| 70 West 71st Street (at Columbus Ave.), UWS | 212-799-4444 |

Great grilled burgers and an extensive menu of American, Greek, and Italian specialties, including very good pizza.

| | |
|---|---|
| *Burger Heaven* | $ |
| 9 East 53rd Street (between Fifth and Madison Aves.), MTE | 212-752-0340 |
| 20 East 49th Street (between Fifth and Madison Aves.), MTE | 212-755-2166 |
| 291 Madison Avenue (between 40th and 41st Sts.), MTE | 212-685-6250 |
| 536 Madison Avenue (between 54th and 55th Sts.), MTE | 212-753-4214 |

A consistently reliable local chain. Businesspeople with short lunch breaks crowd these places midday, but at all other times they're quite pleasant.

## Fanelli $$
94 Prince Street (at Mercer St.), SH     212-266-9412

Fanelli is one of SoHo's only remaining authentic institutions (not that I have anything against SoHo's many wonderful, new, inauthentic restaurants and shops). It has been around since 1847. Up front, you can grab a flyer that explains the history of the place in exhaustive (and exhausting) detail. In addition to burgers, Fanelli has a full menu of simple, straightforward fare.

## ★Island Burgers and Shakes $
766 Ninth Avenue (between     212-307-7934
51st and 52nd Sts.), MTW

A very casual spot for a quick burger with an incredible selection of toppings. The chicken sandwiches are also excellent, as are the shakes.

## Jackson Hole $

| | |
|---|---|
| 1270 Madison Avenue (at 91st St.), UES | 212-427-2820 |
| 1611 Second Avenue (between 83rd and 84th Sts.), UES | 212-737-8788 |
| 232 East 64th Street (between Second and Third Aves.), UES | 212-371-7187 |
| 517 Columbus Avenue (at 85th St.), UWS | 212-362-5177 |
| 521 Third Avenue (at 35th St.), MTE | 212-679-3264 |
| 69-35 Astoria Boulevard (at 70th St., near LaGuardia Airport), Q | 718-204-7070 |

Jackson Hole serves a big, juicy burger that practically falls apart if you pick it up. Kids love to watch the frenzied griddle activity, where the burgers are steamed/fried under little metal

# Quick Guide to

Weekend brunch is a religion in New York, and at many restaurants it's the busiest time of the week. To beat the crowds, go early—New Yorkers tend to sleep in on weekends, and brunch business doesn't really pick up until late morning. Still, you

| Restaurant | Address | Phone Number |
|---|---|---|
| Friend of a Farmer | 77 Irving Pl. (between 18th and 19th Sts.), GP | 212-477-2188 |
| Good Enough to Eat | 483 Amsterdam Ave. (between 83rd and 84th Sts.), UWS | 212-496-0163 |
| Isabella's | 359 Columbus Ave. (at 77th St.), UWS | 212-724-2100 |
| NoHo Star | 330 Lafayette (at Bleecker St.), EV | 212-925-0070 |
| ★Popover Café | 551 Amsterdam Ave. (between 86th and 87th Sts.), UWS | 212-595-8555 |
| ★Sarabeth's | 1295 Madison Ave. (between 92nd and 93rd Sts.), UES | 212-410-7335 |
| | 945 Madison Ave. (between 75th and the Whitney Museum), UES | 212-570-3670 |
| | 423 Amsterdam Ave. (between 80th and 81st Sts.), UWS | 212-496-6280 |
| Time Café | 2330 Broadway (at 85th St.), UWS | 212-579-5100 |
| | 380 Lafayette St. (at Great Jones), EV | 212-533-7000 |
| ★Treehouse | 436 Hudson St. (at Morton St.), WV | 212-989-1363 |

# Brunch

should always be prepared to wait a few minutes (and sometimes more) for a brunch table in New York City. *Note:* All of
these restaurants are also excellent for other meals. See also
Dim Sum, under Chinese, for another interesting brunch option.

| Price Rating | Comments |
|---|---|
| $$ | A slice of New England in Manhattan, with excellent baked goods. |
| $$ | Comfort food and cozy decor make this a likely family-pleaser. |
| $$ | Huge portions distinguish this neighborhood favorite. |
| $$ | A classic New York downtown crowd makes people-watching the activity of choice at this NoHo favorite. |
| $$ | The popovers are great—and there are teddy bears everywhere for the kids. Very, very popular; go early. |
| $$ | Tourists and New Yorkers alike line up outside Sarabeth's for incredible omelets, porridges, and pastries. |
| $$ | Very reliable, this place is also often not as crowded as some of the others. |
| $$ | A favorite of families, Treehouse has a great menu with something for everyone. |

domes. The menu is full of dozens of interesting topping combinations, with names like the Baldouni Burger.

| | |
|---|---|
| ***Sassy's Sliders*** | **$** |
| **1530 Third Avenue (between** | **212-828-6900** |
| **86th and 87th Sts.), UES** | |

Like White Castle (tiny burgers on tiny buns) but better.

## City Fact
Thought all McDonald's were the same? Wrong! The one at 160 Broadway in the Financial District (212-227-3828, $) is the flagship McDonald's. It has live music on a grand piano, a doorman in topcoat and tails, hostesses, marble tables, a digital stock ticker, a gift shop, flowers, and a dessert menu (including cappuccino and espresso).

# Candy and Nuts

Your kids will not have experienced these stores before, but you'll be transported back to your own childhood when you wander into some of these marvelous New York candy and nut shops.

| | |
|---|---|
| ***Bazzini*** | |
| **339 Greenwich Street (at Jay St.), LES** | **212-227-6241** |

One of the best nut shops in the world. If you've only ever tasted grocery store peanuts, cashews, and pistachios, you're in for a treat. And don't overlook their homemade nut brittles, either.

### ★ *Economy Candy*
**108 Rivington Street (between**     **212-254-1832**
**Essex and Ludlow Sts.), LES**

Arguably my favorite candy store in the world, Economy Candy is every child's (and candy-loving adult's) dream come true. With a selection of everything from candy buttons to hand-dipped chocolates, and prices ranging from a mere 99 cents for large, Easter-sized jelly beans to $3.00 per pound for gummy candies, every child will bounce off the walls with mere anticipation (and that's before they eat the candy).

### *Elk Candy Co.*
**1628 Second Avenue (between**     **212-650-1177**
**84th and 85th Sts.), UES**

Art-quality marzipan and molded chocolates as well as some of the regulars like gummy bears and European candy bars.

### *Li-Lac Chocolates*
**120 Christopher Street (between**     **212-242-7374**
**Hudson and Bleecker Sts.), WV**

The selection is like that of a real old-fashioned penny-candy shop, though nothing costs a penny.

### *Mondel's Chocolates*
**2913 Broadway (at 114th St.), UWS**     **212-864-2111**

Another favorite old-fashioned candy store.

### Nut City
**1585 Second Avenue (between**          **212-772-0659**
**82nd and 83rd Sts.), UES**

These nut, ice cream, and frozen yogurt stores are a dime a dozen around the City. But this one especially has an extremely nice staff, all happy to give samples of yogurt and ice cream to any curious customer—even if they don't ask. Be sure to tell Mafoz (the owner) I sent you.

### Philip's Candy
**1237 Surf Avenue (near Stillwell,**          **718-372-8783**
**next door to the original Nathan's), BR**

The candy apples in Philip's are the crowning touch to every visit to Coney Island. Even the most mature child will revert to being a fun-loving kid. Don't forget the wet naps!

### The Sweet Life
**63 Hester Street (at Ludlow St.), LES**          **212-598-0092**

Specializing in candy, nuts, and dried fruit, a Lower East Side Institution.

### Wolsk's Candy
**181 Ludlow Street (at Delancey St.), LES**          **212-475-0704**

Though this 1940s-era candy store has an impressive inventory of gourmet, old-fashioned, and hard-to-find confections, the real reason to shop here is for the unparalleled selection of nuts and dried fruits. Most nuts are roasted in-house, and many of the dried fruits are available with no additives (which makes them less attractive to look at but doesn't affect the taste).

# Chicken

| *El Pollo* | $ |
|---|---|
| 1746 First Avenue (between | 212-996-7810 |
| 90th and 91st Sts.), UES | |
| 482 Broome Street | 212-431-5666 |
| (at Wooster St.), SH | |

Delicious, slow-cooked Peruvian-style marinated chicken.

| *William's Bar-B-Que* | $ |
|---|---|
| 2350 Broadway (between | 212-877-5384 |
| 85th and 86th Sts.), UWS | |

One of the best rotisserie chickens on the planet, but it has nothing to do with barbecue.

## Money-Saving Tip

Set a limit on the number of drinks your children can order in restaurants and encourage them to take the healthier option of New York City's excellent tap water. Soft drinks in New York are very expensive (sometimes upwards of $2), and refills *are not free,* so the addition of a few extra drinks for each person can easily double your bill.

# Chinese

New York is swimming in Chinese food, and many New Yorkers eat Chinese takeout more often than they eat at home. But a lot of New York Chinese food, especially in Chinatown, can be disappointing, expensive, and (often unpleasantly) surprising. Here are a few of the more predictable, consistent, mid-priced

# Quick Guide to

These gourmet (read: expensive) chocolatiers ostensibly target an adult audience, but I've known many kids, myself as a child included, who absolutely love the display cases packed full of jewel-like European chocolates (for a price, of course).

| Restaurant | Address | Phone Number |
| --- | --- | --- |
| Fifth Avenue Chocolatiere | 510 Madison Ave. (between 52nd and 53rd Sts.), MTE | 212-935-5454 |
| | 120 Park Ave. (at 42nd St.), MTE | 212-370-5355 |
| La Maison du Chocolat | Bergdorf Goodman, 754 Fifth Ave. (between 57th and 58th Sts.), MTE | 212-744-7117 |
| | 1018 Madison Ave. (between 78th and 79th Sts.), UES | |
| Neuchatel | 2 West 59th St. (at Central Park South), MTW | 212-751-7742 |
| | 60 Wall St. (between William and Pearl Sts.), FD | 212-480-3766 |
| Richart | 7 East 55th St. (between Fifth and Madison Ave.), MTE | 212-371-9369 |
| Teuscher Chocolates of Switzerland | Rockefeller Center, 670 Fifth Ave. (between 49th and 50th Sts.), MTW | 212-246-4416 |
| | 25 East 61st St. (at Madison Ave.), UES | 212-751-8482 |

# Grownup Candy Stores

## Comments

The be all and end all of specialized chocolates. With two weeks notice, anything your child can conceive of, from baseball bats to ballerinas, can be sculpted in chocolate. Their caramels are to die for.

By far my favorite. All chocolates are imported from Paris, with shipments arriving several times a week. The macaroons, though very expensive, are among the finest in the world.

Another fine European chocolatier, with beautiful stores. The caramels are particularly noteworthy.

This French chocolate boutique sells incredibly detailed, hand-decorated chocolates. It's almost more of an art gallery than a candy store.

World-renowned for its intense truffles as well as other fine chocolate candies.

options, all of which have extensive menus of the familiar Cantonese, Hunan, and Szechuan specialties, plus some with which you might not be as familiar.

| **China Fun** | **$$** |
| --- | --- |
| **1239 Second Avenue (at 65th St.), UES** | **212-752-0810** |
| **246 Columbus Avenue (between** | **212-580-1516** |
| **71st and 72nd Sts.), UWS** | |
| **1653 Broadway (at 51st St.), MTW** | **212-333-2622** |

### Helpful Hint

Dim sum palaces fascinate kids. Waiters roam the dining room pushing metal carts piled high with dozens of little Chinese dishes. The choices seem infinite, so there's nearly always something for even the pickiest kid to eat. Prices tend to be very reasonable (you pay by the dish, and most are only a couple of dollars).

| **HSF** | **$$** |
| --- | --- |
| **46 Bowery (between Bayard** | **212-374-1319** |
| **and Canal Sts.), CT** | |

Most Chinatown restaurants serve dim sum on only weekends, but HSF does so daily.

| **Jing Fong** | **$$** |
| --- | --- |
| **20 Elizabeth Street (between** | **212-964-5256** |
| **Bayard and Canal Sts.), CT** | |

The largest of the dim sum restaurants, and one of the best.

*Mee*  $
219 First Avenue (at 13th St.), EV    212-995-0333
547 Second Avenue (between    212-779-1596
30th and 31st Sts.), GP
922 Second Avenue (at 49th St.), MTE    212-888-0027
795 Ninth Avenue (at 53rd St.), MTW    212-765-2929

★*New York Noodletown*    $$
28½ Bowery (at Bayard St.), CT    212-349-0923

*Ollie's*    $$
2957 Broadway (at 116th St.), UWS    212-932-3300
2315 Broadway (at 84th St.), UWS    212-362-2712
1991 Broadway (at 67th St.), UWS    212-595-8181
200B West 44th Street (between    212-921-5988
Broadway and Eighth Ave.), TS

★*Pig Heaven*    $$
1540 Second Avenue (between    212-744-4333
80th and 81st Sts.), UES

## Learning Tip

How do dim sum restaurants know what to charge
at the end of a meal? At some restaurants, they use
plates with different designs for each dish; at the
end of the meal, they count the plates. At other
places, you get a little card and each waiter stamps
it to indicate what you ate.

| *Ruby Foo's* | $$$ |
|---|---|
| 2182 Broadway, UWS | 212-724-6700 |
| 1626 Broadway, TS | 212-489-5600 |

A pan-Asian dim sum and sushi fantasy. **A family-friendly restaurant, although mainly for adults.**

| ★ *Triple Eight Palace* | $$ |
|---|---|
| 88 East Broadway (between | 212-941-8886 |
| Division and Market Sts.), CT | |

My favorite dim sum restaurant, with terrific food at low prices.

| *Wu Liang Ye* | $$ |
|---|---|
| 215 East 86th Street (between | 212-534-8899 |
| Second and Third Aves.), UES | |
| 36 West 48th Street (at Fifth | 212-398-2308 |
| and Sixth Aves.), MTW | |
| 338 Lexington Avenue (between | 212-370-9647 |
| 39th and 40th Sts.), MTE | |

## Learning Tip

Did you know that Cuba traditionally had a large Chinese community? Paper topic idea: Trace the history of Chinese immigrants in Cuba, and the unique challenges they faced. And while you're at it, sample the inexpensive, delicious food at La Caridad (2199 Broadway at 78th Street, UWS, 212-874-2780, $).

# Deli and Sandwiches

If you're new to the City's great delis, you'll likely find the sandwiches shocking. Many are impossible to pick up due to their sheer bulk, which in part explains why they can cost in the $10 neighborhood (most adults, much less kids, cannot eat more than a half). But these are also the best sandwiches in the world, and you'll love the uniquely New York atmosphere at our old-time delis.

| | |
|---|---|
| *Artie's New York Delicatessen* | $$ |
| **2290 Broadway (between 82nd and 83rd Sts.), UWS** | **212-579-5959** |

The first good, new New York deli to come along in years, this is a faithful retro reproduction of an old-time Jewish deli. Plus it's brand new and impeccably clean.

| | |
|---|---|
| *Carnegie Deli* | $$ |
| **854 Seventh Avenue (at 55th St.), MTW** | **212-757-2245** |

The second-best pastrami after Katz's Deli, and good renditions of Jewish standbys like matzoh ball soup and potato pancakes. Cash only.

## Learning Tip

Though it is today a Jewish deli mainstay, pastrami was invented by the American Indians. Did you know that pastrami, corned beef, and brisket are all made from the same piece of meat: the beef brisket? The only difference is in the cooking. Pastrami is dry-cured and smoked. Corned beef is cured in brine. Brisket is simply boiled.

### ★ *Italian Food Center*        $
**186 Grand Street (at Mulberry St.), LI    212-925-2954**

The Italian answer to the Jewish deli, with first-rate cold cuts (salami, prosciutto, sopresatta, etc.) served on crusty Italian bread. Friendly countermen complete the experience.

### ★ *Katz's Deli*        $$
**205 Houston Street (at Ludlow St.), LES    212-254-2246**

"Send a Salami to Your Boy in the Army," reads the World War II–era sign up front, but you go to Katz's for the best pastrami available, and also for delicious hot dogs and knishes. Cash only.

### *Second Avenue Deli*        $$
**156 Second Avenue (at 10th St.), EV    212-677-0606**

A real neighborhood deli, with fewer tourists in evidence than at the others. The hot entrees are wonderful. Cash or AmEx only.

### *Stage Deli*        $$
**834 Seventh Avenue (between    212-245-7850
53rd and 54th Sts.), MTW**

The menu is full of sandwiches evocatively named after celebrities, and the portions are gigantic. Not as good as the neighboring Carnegie, in my opinion, but less cramped and crowded.

# Eclectic

### *Café Luxembourg*        $$$
**299 West 70th Street, UWS    212-873-7411**

Gorgeous Art Deco French bistro with some of the best food in the neighborhood. **For adults, but welcomes kids.**

# Quick Guide to Department Store Dining

The restaurants in New York's better department stores—many of which serve excellent food—are some of New York's best-kept secrets. Most New Yorkers won't actually bother to go through the maze of a department store to get lunch, so these restaurants tend to be nice little urban enclaves. And they're all used to handling families with children. So next time you're wandering the stores, consider staying for a meal.

| Restaurant | Address | Phone Number | Price Rating |
|---|---|---|---|
| Cafe American Style at Lord & Taylor | 424 Fifth Ave., MTE | 212-391-3344 | $$ |
| Caffe Linda at Benetton | 597 Fifth Ave., MTE | 212-593-0290 | $$ |
| 59th & Lexington at Bloomingdale's | 1000 Third Ave., UES | 212-705-2000 | $$ |
| Fred's at Barney's | 10 East 61st St., UES | 212-833-2200 | $$ |
| Nicole's at Nicole Farhi | 10 East 60th St., UES | 212-223-2288 | $$ |
| SFA Cafe at Saks Fifth Avenue | 611 Fifth Ave., MTE | 212-940-4080 | $$ |
| The Tea Box at Takashimaya | 693 Fifth Ave., MTE | 212-350-0180 | $$ |

### *Dojo*  $

14 West 4th Street (between  212-505-8934
Broadway and Mercer St.), WV
24-26 St. Marks Place (between  212-674-9821
Second and Third Aves.), EV

Asian-influenced, healthy food at excellent prices.

### *Shopsin's*  $$
63 Bedford Street (at Morton St.), WV  212-924-5160

A really unusual New York institution, with interesting ex-hippie owners and a diverse international menu.

## Money-Saving Tip

Plan ahead for your meals—coordinate them with other activities—so you aren't forced to eat mediocre, overpriced food in your hotel restaurant or at expensive Midtown tourist traps.

### *Yaffa Cafe*  $
97 St. Marks Place (between  212-674-9302
1st St. and A Ave.), EV

Eclectic, Middle Eastern–inspired menu with great salads served twenty-four hours a day, seven days a week.

# Filipino

> **★ Elvie's Turo-Turo**       **$**
> 214 First Avenue (between      212-473-7785
> 12th and 13th Sts.), EV

*Turo-turo* means "point-point," and that's exactly what you do at this Filipino buffet. Just point to what you want, and it's yours.

## Insider's Tip

"Encourage kids to be open minded about eating and try new things; explain to them that it's all about the adventure." —*Penny, grandmother of two*

# Frankfurters

It may sound strange, but the official way to eat a frankfurter in New York City is to wash it down with a glass of papaya juice. It's one of those amazing food combinations you just have to try for yourself, and many kids love the sweetness of the tropical fruit. I urge you to avoid street-vendor frankfurters—they're usually boiled and bland—and seek out one of these places instead. See also Katz's Deli (under Deli and Sandwiches) and F&B (under French Fries).

> **★ Gray's Papaya**       **$**
> 2090 Broadway (at 72nd St.), UWS
> 402 Sixth Avenue (at 8th St.), WV

One of the great dining bargains in the history of humanity: Two delicious grilled hot dogs with all the fixings and a 14-ounce fruit juice (papaya, banana, or coconut—it costs extra for pineapple and fresh-squeezed orange or grapefruit) for $1.95.

### *The Original Nathan's*    $
**Coney Island, BR**

Opened in 1916 by Polish immigrant Nathan Handwerker, Nathan's is the classic New York hot dog stand. Nathan's is now a chain, but the Coney Island branch is the original.

*The Original Nathan's, Coney Island*

### ★*Papaya King*    $
**179 East 86th Street (at Third Ave.), UES**

The hot dogs at Papaya King are similar to those at Gray's (Mr. Gray used to work here). They may even be a little meatier, but they should be—they cost more than twice as much.

## City Fact
The Bryant Park Grill, which seats 1,420 people, is the largest restaurant in NYC, followed by Tavern on the Green, which seats 800. Chinatown's largest restaurant, Jing Fong, is the size of a professional football field.

# French Fries

★*F&B* $
269 West 23rd Street (between     646-486-4441
Seventh and Eighth Aves.), CH

Delicious Belgian-style twice-fried fries and unusual hot dog combinations. Plus, for the parents, there are little soda pop–sized bottles of Champagne.

*Pommes Frites* $
123 Second Avenue (7th St. and     212-674-1234
St. Marks Pl.), EV

Hot, crispy fries served in a paper cone. You have a choice of dozens of toppings (some of which are included in the price of the fries and some of which cost 50 cents). I recommend (as does the staff) a combination of ketchup, mayonnaise-based "frites sauce" and chopped onions—all of which are free.

# German

*Hallo Berlin* $$
402 West 51st Street (between     212-541-6248
Ninth and Tenth Aves.), MTW

A great spot for wurst-loving families.

# Greek

*Aegean* $$
221 Columbus Ave (at 70th St.), UWS     212-873-5057

Moderately priced Greek in a typically overpriced neighborhood.

## Learning Tip

*Haloumi*—A salty, mozzarella-like cheese, usually broiled or fried.

*Kafteri*—Spicy feta cheese spread.

*Melitzanosalata*—Eggplant spread, usually with a liberal application of garlic. Virtually identical to the Middle Eastern babaganouj.

*Saganaki*—Most Greek-American menus translate it as "Flaming Cheese," but it need not be served flaming. The term actually refers to the metal plate on which the cheese is cooked. In many Greek restaurants, the dish will be finished with brandy and served flaming.

*Skordalia*—Mashed potato and garlic spread, served cold.

*Taramosalata*—Fish roe spread. Even though this spread looks as though it must be dairy-based, the main ingredients are simply oil and fish roe (tarama). When whipped, the oil becomes emulsified through the incorporation of air (much as with mayonnaise), accounting for the spread's creaminess.

*Tzatziki*—Yogurt/garlic/cucumber spread, often with a little mint. Although garlic is a standard ingredient, tzatziki provides a cooling effect.

---

### *Delphi*                                                              $$
**109 West Broadway (at Reade St.), TBC    212-227-6322**

Delicious grilled meats.

### *Elias Corner* $$

**2401-2402 31st Street (at 24th Ave.), Q   718-932-1510**

Astoria, Queens, is New York's major Greek neighborhood, and Elias Corner is the best restaurant in the area. Emphasis on fresh seafood.

### ★ *Niko's Mediterranean Grill* $$

**2161 Broadway (at 76th St.), UWS   212-873-7000**

Exceptional food given the low-to-midrange prices. The menu is gigantic, but nothing seems to suffer. Portions are generous, and ingredients are top-notch. Several dishes are identified by their region of origin within Greece, making for an educational and enlightened menu.

### *Uncle Nick's* $$

**747 Ninth Avenue (between   212-245-7992
50th and 51st St.), MTW**

A traditional Greek grilled-fish restaurant, with plenty of other choices for those who don't like seafood.

## Ice Cream

Although old-fashioned ice-cream parlors and soda fountains have gone the way of the buffalo in many parts of America— and New York has lost its fair share as well—a few are still going strong in the City.

### Chinatown Ice Cream Factory    $
65 Bayard Street (between      212-608-4170
Mott and Elizabeth Sts.), CT

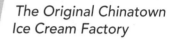

Exotic, fun flavors, like ginger, lychee, mango, almond cookie, and taro.

*The Original Chinatown Ice Cream Factory*

### Ciao Bella    $
27 East 92nd Street (at
Madison Ave.), UES
212-831-5555
262 Mott Street (between
Prince and Houston
Sts.), LI 212-226-7668

Ciao Bella ice cream is only 20 percent air and 10 percent butterfat, making it denser, creamier, and tastier than most.

### Emack & Bolio's    $
56 Seventh Avenue (between      212-727-1198
13th and 14th Sts.), WV
389 Amsterdam Avenue      212-362-2747
(between 78th and 79th Sts.), UWS
151 West 34th Street (in Macy's,      212-494-5853
4th floor), MTW

Made in a small Massachusetts dairy, this is incredibly good ice cream. The chocolate peanut butter cup, vanilla bean speck, and grasshopper pie are all great, and perhaps your family will be large enough to tackle the Emack Attack, a bowl packed with forty scoops (for $40).

| *Peter's Homemade* | $ |
|---|---|
| **185 Atlantic Avenue (at Court St.), BR** | **718-852-3835** |

Delicious, stabilizer-free ice cream in 140 unusual flavors like ginger, pecan pie, Campari-grapefruit sorbet, Vienna fingers, chunky cappuccino brownie, carrot cake, and molasses-ginger snap.

| ★*Serendipity* | $ |
|---|---|
| **225 East 60th Street (between** | **212-838-3531** |
| **Second and Third Aves.), UES** | |

Charming Victorian decor—Tiffany lamps, wire chairs, and an all-white interior—and old-fashioned ice-cream sundaes drowned in gobs of hot fudge.

# Indian

You'll find dozens of Indian restaurants clustered around East 6th Street between First and Second Avenues (Manhattan's "Little India"). You'll also find a smaller group on Lexington Avenue in the 20s and 30s. These places tend to be cheap and the food plentiful, making them ideal for families. These are a few of the better ones.

| *Curry in a Hurry* | $ |
|---|---|
| **119 Lexington Avenue (at 28th St.), GP** | **212-683-0900** |

**Kohinoor Indian Cuisine**　　　　　$
342 East 6th Street (between　　212-533-6622
First and Second Aves.), EV

**Raj Mahal**　　　　　$
322 East 6th Street (between　　212-982-3632
First and Second Aves.), EV

## Helpful Hint

Bring entertainment with you. If you have a game, project, or topic of discussion at the ready in the event of delays, your kids won't mind the wait (for a table or for food) quite so much.

# Indonesian

This cuisine, rarely seen on our shores, features interesting, often spicy food. Kids who already like Chinese food will find plenty of approachable dishes.

**Bali Nusa Indah**　　　　　$
651 Ninth Avenue (between　　212-765-6500
45th and 46th Sts.), MTW

# Italian

Italian food is America's favorite food, and New York has the best Italian food in America. *Buon appetito!*

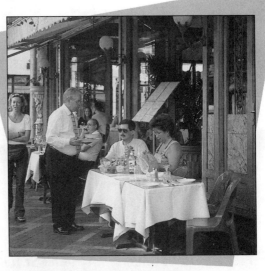

*Lunchtime in
Little Italy*

| ★ *Becco* | $$ |
|---|---|
| 355 West 46th Street (between | 212-397-7597 |
| Eighth and Ninth Aves.), MTW | |

Three varieties of amazing homemade pasta daily, all you can eat. Plus a full Italian menu including excellent fish.

| *Bella Luna* | $$ |
|---|---|
| 584 Columbus Avenue | 212-877-2267 |
| (between 88th and 89th Sts.), UWS | |

Particularly family-friendly neighborhood Italian.

| *Carmine's* | $$ |
|---|---|
| 200 West 44th Street (between | 212-221-3800 |
| Broadway and Eighth Ave.), TS | |
| 2450 Broadway (between | 212-362-2200 |
| 90th and 91st Sts.), UWS | |

The original family-style Italian, Carmine's is always noisy and crowded, but happily so.

## Helpful Hint

The larger your group, the more fun it is to eat at New York's family-style Italian restaurants. Everybody can share the large platters of salads, pastas, and meats, which provides variety for the kids and interest for the folks. Lines tend to be long, but these places will take reservations for parties of six or more.

| ★*Casa Bella Restaurant* | $$ |
| :--- | ---: |
| **127 Mulberry (at Hester St.), LI** | **212-431-4080** |

My favorite Italian in Little Italy, where restaurants are often disappointing tourist traps. But not Casa Bella!

| *Mimi's Macaroni* | $$ |
| :--- | ---: |
| **718 Amsterdam Avenue** | **212-866-6311** |
| **(at 95th St.), UWS** | |

A bin of toys near the front door, a kids' menu, and crayons will keep the young ones occupied, but the food is very grown up. A great place for the family.

| ★**Sambuca** | $$ |
| :--- | ---: |
| **20 West 72nd Street (between Columbus** | **212-787-5656** |
| **Ave. and Central Park West), UWS** | |

With the best food of the family-style Italian restaurants, Sambuca is a little more upscale than the others, but you'll see plenty of kids having a great time.

> ### Tony's $$
> 1606 Second Avenue (between    212-861-8686
> 83rd and 84th Sts.), UES

Not as popular or crowded as the other family-style Italian restaurants—perhaps because of its East Side location—Tony's is a good bet for weekends and other busy times.

> ## Money-Saving Tip
> If you're traveling in a large group, eat at family-style Italian restaurants and at Asian restaurants where it's common to share food. That way, children aren't forced to order entire entrees they won't be able to finish (and you're not forced to pay for them!).

# Japanese

Kids often either like Japanese food, or they don't—or so they think. New York has an embarrassment of riches when it comes to this wonderful cuisine, and we're not just talking sushi. These are a few of the more casual, family-appropriate spots. Also look for the Daikichi Sushi and Teriyaki Boy Japanese fast-food chains; they're not fabulous, but they're cheap and nourishing.

> ### Haru $$
> 433 Amsterdam Avenue    212-579-5654
> (at 81st St.), UWS
> 1329 Third Avenue (at 76th St.), UES    212-452-2230

From the same folks who brought us Carmine's, Artie's Deli, and Polistina's Pizza comes this extremely competent interpretation of a classic American Japanese restaurant, with an emphasis on sushi. Very popular, with friendly service.

### *Menchanko-Tei* $
131 East 45th Street (between 212-986-6805
Third and Lexington Aves.), MTE
43-45 West 55th Street (between 212-247-1585
Fifth and Sixth Aves.), MTW
5 World Trade Center (Concourse 212-432-4210
Level), FD

Hot, steaming, fresh Japanese noodle soups. Perfect for a winter meal on the run.

### ★*Shabu-Tatsu* $$
1414 York Avenue (at 75th St.), UES 212-472-3322
216 East 10th Street (between 212-477-2972
First and Second Aves.), EV

You cook your own food by dunking strips of meat into a pot of boiling broth. A great participatory eating experience for kids.

### *Tsunami* $$
70 West 3rd Street (between 212-475-7770
La Guardia and Thompson Sts.), WV

New York's only floating sushi bar—the chefs put the food in little "boats," which then float around the bar where you pick them up.

# Jewish

*Sammy's Roumanian Jewish Steakhouse*  $$$
157 Chrystie Street                    212-673-0330
(at Delancey St.), LES

Sammy's is a not-to-be-missed, only-in-New-York, rollicking good time. If this is how they eat every day in Romania, I'm moving there!

# Kebabs

The ideal cheap, filling sustenance for families on the move, these skewers of marinated meat really hit the spot.

★*Afghan Kebab House*                   $
764 Ninth Avenue (between              212-307-1612
51st and 52nd Sts.), MTW
155 West 46th Street (between          212-768-3875
Sixth and Seventh Aves.), TS
1345 Second Avenue (between            212-517-2776
70th and 71st Sts.), UES

# Korean

In the "Little Korea" neighborhood, right in the shadow of the Empire State Building, you'll find a whole bunch of restaurants where you can cook your own meat on tabletop grills. Communicating with the largely non-English-speaking waiters can be a little challenging, but as long as you can smile and point, you'll be okay. Of the restaurants, Won Jo and Woo Chon are two of my favorites.

# Quick Guide to Kosher Restaurants

Though New York has many Jewish restaurants and kosher-style delis, not all are strictly kosher according to traditional Jewish dietary laws. Thus, if your beliefs require a higher level of observance, these restaurants all have orthodox supervision.

| Restaurant | Address | Phone Number | Price Rating |
| --- | --- | --- | --- |
| China Shalom | 686 Columbus Ave. (between 93rd and 94th Sts.), UWS | 212-662-9676 | $$ |
| ★Dimple Indian | 11 West 30th St. (between Fifth and Sixth Aves.), MTW | 212-643-9464 | $ |
| Dougie's BBQ & Grill | 222 West 72nd St. (between Broadway and West End Ave.), UWS | 212-724-2222 | $$ |
| Great American Health Bar | 35 West 57th St. (between Fifth and Sixth Aves.), MTW | 212-355-5177 | $ |
| Joseph's | 50 West 72nd St. (between Columbus Ave. and Central Park West), UWS | 212-595-5004 | $$ |
| Kosher Delight | 1365 Broadway (at 36th St.), MTW | 212-563-3366 | $ |
|  | 1156 Sixth Ave. (at 45th St.), MTW | 212-869-6699 |  |

*Dok Suni's*                          $$
119 First Avenue (between             212-477-9506
7th St. and St. Marks Pl.), EV

A more Americanized, hip, downtown version of a Korean
restaurant, with spare ribs to die for.

*Won Jo*                             $$
23 West 32nd Street (between         212-695-5815
Broadway and Fifth Ave.), MTW

★ *Woo Chon*                         $$
8 West 36th Street (between          212-695-0676
Fifth and Sixth Aves.), MTW

# Mexican and Tex-Mex

Mexican food is cheap and familiar, and there's no shortage of
it in New York. These places will fill your family's bellies for
just a few dollars.

★ *Benny's Burritos*                          $
93 Avenue A (at 6th St.), EV          212-254-2054
113 Greenwich Avenue (at Jane St.), WV  212-727-3560

Economical, filling burritos in a great downtown setting.

| *Burritoville* | $ |
|---|---|
| 451 Amsterdam Avenue (between 81st and 82nd Sts.), UWS | 212-787-8181 |
| 141 Second Avenue (between 8th and 9th Sts.), EV | 212-260-3300 |
| 1489 First Avenue (between 77th and 78th Sts.), UES | 212-472-8800 |
| 144 Chambers Street (between West Broadway and Greenwich), TBC | 212-571-1144 |
| 166 West 72nd Street (between Columbus and Amsterdam Aves.), UWS | 212-787-8181 |
| 36 Water Street (at Broad St.), FD | 212-747-1100 |
| 1606 Third Avenue (between 90th and 91st Sts.), UES | 212-410-2255 |

Top-notch burritos filled with brown rice and mostly natural ingredients.

| *Calle Ocho* | $$$ |
|---|---|
| 446 Columbus Avenue, UWS | 212-873-5025 |

Creative Nuevo Latino cuisine in a slick Upper West Side setting. **This chic restaurant is mainly for adults, although it does welcome kids.**

| *Gabriela's* | $$ |
|---|---|
| 685 Amsterdam Avenue (at 93rd St.), UWS | 212-961-0574 |

A little more upscale than the others, Gabriela's serves more complex, nuanced Mexican cuisine. A real treat.

| *Manhattan Chili Company* | $$ |
| 1697 Broadway (between | 212-246-6555 |
| 53rd and 54th Sts.), MTW | |

A real favorite of families, it's one of the best deals in the Theater District.

| *Mary Ann's* | $$ |
| 1503 Second Avenue (between | 212-249-6165 |
| 78th and 79th Sts.), UES | |
| 2452 Broadway (between | 212-877-0132 |
| 90th and 91st Sts.), UWS | |
| 116 Eighth Avenue (at 16th St.), CH | 212-633-0877 |
| 300 East 5th Street (at Second Ave.), EV | 212-475-5939 |

A good Mexican mini-chain with a pro-kids attitude.

| *Mesa Grill* | $$$ |
| 102 Fifth Avenue, CH | 212-807-7400 |

TV Food Network star chef Bobby Flay's Southwestern cuisine never fails to dazzle. **A "grownup" restaurant that welcomes kids.**

| ★*Rocking Horse Cafe Mexicano* | $$ |
| 182 Eighth Avenue (at 19th St.), CH | 212-463-9771 |

Excellent sit-down Mexican. Among the best in town, but not overpriced.

| *Taco Taco* | $ |
| 1726 Second Avenue (between | 212-289-8226 |
| 89th and 90th Sts.), UES | |

My favorite taco spot, with amazing soft-shell tacos.

## Pastries

If you're looking for a snack or dessert, rather than a meal, stop into one of these world-famous pastry shops.

**Bonte Patisserie**
1316 Third Avenue (between          212-535-2360
75th and 76th Sts.), UES

Traditional European patisserie.

**Cupcake Café**
522 Ninth Avenue (at 39th St.), MTW    212-465-1530

Cupcake specialist.

**De Robertis**
176 First Avenue (between          212-674-7137
10th and 11th Sts.), EV

Old-fashioned Italian pastries.

**Ferrara**
195 Grand Street (between          212-226-6150
Mulberry and Mott Sts.), LI

Italian pastries in a grand historic restaurant.

**Sant Ambroeus**
1000 Madison Avenue (between          212-570-2211
77th and 78th Sts.), UES

Fabulous European desserts.

*Soutine*
104 West 70th Street (between          212-496-1450
Columbus Ave. and Broadway), UWS

Handmade, delicious pastries of all kinds.

★ *Veniero's*
342 East 11th Street (between          212-674-4415
First and Second Aves.), EV

My favorite Italian pastry shop. The miniature pastries, aside
from being very inexpensive, are totally addictive.

# Pizza

The New York slice is synonymous with great pizza, and it
seems there's a pizzeria on every block in the City. For pur-
poses of planning a meal, there are really two categories of
pizzeria: ones where you can grab a slice on the go, and ones
where you sit down and order whole pies (you can get a whole
pie at a by-the-slice place, but not vice-versa). The by-the-slice
places tend to offer a thicker, cheesier slice, whereas the sit-
down pizzerias usually bake a thinner-crusted, more gourmet
pie, often in a traditional high-temperature brick oven. No
matter, though—both are great!

★ *Angelo's*                          $
117 West 57th Street (between          212-333-4333
Sixth and Seventh Aves.), MTW

Superb thin-crust pizza (whole pies only) baked in a coal oven.

| *Candido* | $ |
|---|---|
| 1606 First Avenue (between 83rd and 84th Sts.), UES | 212-396-9401 |

Although the service is a bit slow, the coal-fired brick oven turns out beautifully crisp, thin-crust pies. Whole pies only.

| *Freddie & Pepper's* | $ |
|---|---|
| 303 Amsterdam Avenue (between 74th and 75th Sts.), UWS | 212-799-2378 |

This pizza-by-the-slice joint has a superlative, subtly flavored sauce, and the guys in the store are very friendly.

| *John's* | $$ |
|---|---|
| 278 Bleecker Street (between Sixth and Seventh Aves.), WV | 212-243-1680 |
| 498 East 64th Street (between First and York Aves.), UES | 212-935-2895 |
| 48 West 65th Street (between Central Park West and Columbus Ave.), UWS | 212-721-7001 |
| 260 West 44th Street (between Broadway and Eighth Ave.), TS | 212-391-7560 |

John's has expanded lately, building Barnes & Noble–sized pizza superstores in the major uptown neighborhoods, and quality has slipped a little, but it's one of the more useful pizzerias because of its convenient locations and efficient service. The Bleecker Street original is better than the others. Whole pies only.

| *Marco Polo* | $ |
| --- | --- |
| **1289 Madison Avenue** | **212-427-3777** |
| **(between 91st and 92nd Sts.), UES** | |

Marco Polo serves the Classic New York Slice, and the hordes of local private school students lined up at the door for slices every weekday at lunchtime are a testament to consistently good output. Marco Polo may not be the best pizza in New York, but it is the best slice in the neighborhood.

| *Naples 45* | $ |
| --- | --- |
| **200 Park Avenue (at 45th St.), MTE** | **212-972-7001** |

Some of the best thin-crust, whole-pie-only pizza around. *Hint:* Order at the counter and take it to go or eat it at the little tables up front—you'll pay half as much as you would if you sit in the main dining room.

## Insider's Tip
"New Yorkers are used to getting what they want in restaurants, and within reason your kids' needs should be accommodated. Ask for what you want at the time of your order and be specific: If your child wants no sauce on the pizza, make sure to say so up front and most places will happily oblige."
—*Jennifer, mother of two*

362

DINING

| *Patsy's* | $$ |
|---|---|
| 2287-2291 First Avenue | 212-534-9783 |
| (between 117th and 118th Sts.), UES | |
| 1312 Second Avenue (at 69th St.), UES | 212-639-1000 |
| 61 West 74th Street (between | 212-579-3000 |
| Central Park West and Columbus Ave.), UWS | |
| 509 Third Avenue (between | 212-689-7500 |
| 34th and 35th Sts.), MTE | |
| 67 University Place (between | 212-533-3500 |
| 10th and 11th Sts.), EV | |

Another great old pizzeria that didn't reproduce as well as it should have. The 117th Street location is by far the best, but it's in a marginal neighborhood. The others are on par with John's. Whole pies only, and also very good pastas and salads.

| ★ *Polistina's* | $$ |
|---|---|
| 2275 Broadway (between | 212-579-2828 |
| 81st and 82nd Sts.), UWS | |

Polistina's pies are beautiful to behold, the mozzarella cheese is excellent, the toppings are first-rate—especially the mushrooms—and the pizzas all have a little fresh basil sprinkled over them. Whole pies only.

| *Sal & Carmine's* | $ |
|---|---|
| 2671 Broadway (between | 212-663-7651 |
| 101st and 102nd Sts.), UWS | |

Sal & Carmine's serves a very nice classic New York slice with a thin coating of high-quality mozzarella and a well-spiced sauce. Plus, the guys behind the counter are a real hoot. For some unknown reason, the small seating area in the back is decorated with Wallase Ting posters and French fashion advertisements.

| **Stromboli** | **$** |
| --- | --- |
| 112 University Place (between 12th and 13th Sts.), EV | 212-255-0812 |

A good place to grab a slice in the Village.

| **Totonno's** | **$$** |
| --- | --- |
| 1524 Neptune Avenue (between 15th and 16th Sts.), BR | 718-372-8606 |
| 1544 Second Avenue (between 80th and 81st Sts.), UES | 212-327-2800 |

Totonno's mozzarella cheese is truly a cut above the rest. On a good day, Totonno's may very well serve the best pizza in New York. But it can be inconsistent, and the Manhattan branch isn't nearly as good as the Coney Island original. Whole pies only.

| **V&T** | **$** |
| --- | --- |
| 1024 Amsterdam Avenue (between 110th and 111th Sts.), UWS | 212-663-1708 |

An old-fashioned, red-checkered-tablecloth pizzeria. Whole pies only. Very popular with the students at Columbia University.

| **★ Vinnie's** | **$** |
| --- | --- |
| 285 Amsterdam Avenue (between 73rd and 74th Sts.), UWS | 212-874-4382 |

If there is an award for nicest pizza guys, it has to go to the men behind the counter at Vinnie's. And the pizza at Vinnie's is just about the best classic New York slice available today.

## Polish

The Polish American restaurants in the East Village offer large menus that mix American diner staples with Polish and Eastern European classics like pierogies (little meat or cheese dumplings) and blintzes (cheese or fruit rolled in a thin crepe-like dough). Wander up First Avenue and look for other East European restaurants and stores.

| *Christine's* | $ |
|---|---|
| 208 First Avenue (between | 212-254-2474 |
| 12th and 13th Sts.), EV | |

## Soup

Soup has always been a popular New York quick bite, but there has been a veritable explosion of soup sales in the wake of *Seinfeld's* popularization of Soup Kitchen International on West 55th Street. Now, you'll also see stores like Hale & Hearty Soup, Daily Soup, Mr. Soup, and Soup Nutsy, but none are as good (or as rude) as the original. A must-visit for kids who are old enough not to mind getting screamed at.

| ★*Soup Kitchen International* | $ |
|---|---|
| 259-A West 55th Street (between | 212-757-7730 |
| Eighth Ave. and Broadway), MTW | |

## Southeast Asian and Pan-Asian

The cuisines of Southeast Asia are complex and varied, but for the most part kids who already like Chinese food can adapt to the new flavors. For the less adventurous eaters, look for the

## Top Ten Unique and Unusual New York Restaurants

1. Sammy's Roumanian Jewish Steakhouse (p. 353)

2. Screening Room (p. 318)

3. Churrascaria Plataforma (p. 323)

4. Woo Chon (p. 355)

5. Katz's Deli (p. 338)

6. Tsunami (p. 352)

7. Shabu-Tatsu (p. 352)

8. Tibet Shambhala (p. 368)

9. Elvie's Turo-Turo (p. 341)

10. Gray's Papaya (p. 341)

dishes that are pretty similar to familiar Chinese staples, particularly the noodle and fried rice preparations.

| *Holy Basil* | $$ |
|---|---|
| 149 Second Avenue (between | 212-460-5557 |
| 9th and 10th Sts.), EV | |

One of the best Thai restaurants in town, with exceedingly friendly service.

| *Kelley & Ping* | $$ |
|---|---|
| 127 Greene Street (between | 212-228-1212 |
| Houston and Prince Sts.), SH | |

Interesting pan-Asian food and an offbeat, downtown setting make this place popular with teens.

| *Penang* | $$ |
|---|---|
| **109 Spring Street (between Greene and Mercer Sts.), SH** | **212-274-8883** |
| **240 Columbus Avenue (at 71st St.), UWS** | **212-769-3988** |
| **1596 Second Avenue (at 83rd St.), UES** | **212-585-3838** |
| **64 Third Avenue (at 11th St.), EV** | **212-228-7888** |

A reliable Malaysian chain, good for families.

| *Thailand Restaurant* | $$ |
|---|---|
| **106 Bayard Street (between Baxter and Mulberry Sts.), CT** | **212-349-3132** |

Very popular with employees of the New York court system by day and with families by night.

## Steak

Steak at the top New York steakhouses can be expensive—$30 and up for the basic steak, without any appetizers or sides—and the portions are too large for most kids other than football-playing teens. Listed here are a few steakhouses that combine quality and value, and also happen to be especially kid-friendly—plus a couple of the more expensive classics.

| *Chimichurri Grill* | $$ |
|---|---|
| **606 Ninth Avenue (between 43rd and 44th Sts.), MTW** | **212-586-8655** |

An Argentinean steakhouse, which means a festive atmosphere and quality steaks at reasonable prices. The chimichurri steak sauce (garlic, parsley, olive oil, and spices) is out of this world.

| *Christos Hasapo-Taverna* | $$$ |
|---|---|
| 41-08 23rd Avenue (at 41st St.), Q | 718-726-5195 |

A Greek steakhouse and butcher shop in Astoria, Queens. Great dry-aged steaks at much lower prices than you'd pay in Manhattan.

| *Dan Maxwell's* | $$$ |
|---|---|
| 1708 Second Avenue (between | 212-426-7688 |
| 88th and 89th Sts.), UES | |

The best of the moderately priced New York steakhouses.

| *Peter Luger* | $$$$ |
|---|---|
| 178 Broadway, Williamsburg, BR | 718-387-7400 |

Considered by many to be the finest steakhouse in America. **Although it does welcome kids, this is definitely a "grown-up" restaurant.**

| *Sparks* | $$$$ |
|---|---|
| 210 East 46th Street, MTE | 212-687-4855 |

If you can't make it to Peter Luger in Brooklyn, Sparks, in Manhattan, is almost as good. **It welcomes kids, although it is definitely a "grownup" restaurant.** World-class wine list.

# Tibetan

Tibet is pretty much sandwiched between India and China, so, as you might imagine, Tibetan cuisine is a bit like a cross between Indian and Chinese. You'll recognize dishes from both cultures (Indian curry, Chinese dumplings), but the food has its own charms as well. Many kids find it less "scary" than either Chinese or Indian, because the preparations tend to be simpler. These three restaurants (yes, New York has multiple Tibetan restaurants) are my top picks:

| | |
|---|---|
| **_Lhasa_** | **$$** |
| **96 Second Avenue (between 5th and 6th Sts.), EV** | **212-674-5870** |

| | |
|---|---|
| **_Tibet on Houston_** | **$$** |
| **136 West Houston Street (between MacDougal and Sullivan Sts.), WV** | **212-995-5884** |

| | |
|---|---|
| **★ _Tibet Shambhala_** | **$$** |
| **488 Amsterdam Avenue (between 83rd and 84th Sts.), UWS** | **212-721-1270** |

### Learning Tip

The Benetton boutique used to be a completely different establishment: A famous bookstore called Scribner's. Look carefully on the front of the building and you can still see the old sign. Inside, look at how the walls on the upper level were built for bookshelves.

## Dining Without Restaurants

New York has an ample supply of chain supermarkets (Food Emporium, Gristede's, Sloan's, Pioneer, and more) and mini-marts (all over town and often open twenty-four hours a day), but the best groceries come from the City's many gourmet mega-stores. These hybrids of a gourmet store and a super-

# Quick Guide to Food Courts

The glory of a food court is that each family member can choose from a variety of foods, and everybody can still dine together at one of the communal tables. Check out these food courts for painless family dining.

| Food Court | Address | Comments |
|---|---|---|
| Grand Central Station | 42nd St. and Park Ave., MTE | The newly renovated dining concourse is truly something to behold, with a great variety of foods, all from local establishments (no national chains allowed). |
| Manhattan Mall | 33rd St. and Sixth Ave., MTW | A good assemblage of fast food and a few more healthful options, plus a view of the Empire State Building. |
| Pier 17 | At the South Street Seaport, FD | The top floor's food court resembles those in many suburban shopping malls, but you're right on New York's East River. |
| World Financial Center | At Liberty St., adjacent to the World Trade Center, FD | A good selection of snacks and sandwiches in a beautiful setting on the Battery Park City marina. |

market are a unique urban phenomenon, and New York has many wonderful examples of them from which to choose.

### Agata & Valentina
**1505 First Avenue (at 79th St.), UES      212-452-0690**

A relative newcomer with a bright future. Open daily 8 A.M.– 9 P.M.

### ★ Balducci's
**424 Avenue of the Americas      212-673-2600**
**(at Ninth St.), WV**
**Coming soon: Broadway at 66th Street**

Far and away the best gourmet store for the money in New York. Open daily 7:00 A.M.–8:30 P.M.

### Chelsea Market
**75 Ninth Avenue (between      212-243-6005**
**15th and 16th Sts.), CH**

Top-notch marketplace, with many vendors, in Chelsea. Open Monday through Friday 7 A.M.–8 P.M., Sunday 10 A.M.–6 P.M.

### Citarella
**2135 Broadway (at 75th St.), UWS      212-874-0383**
**1313 Third Avenue (at 75th St.), UES**

Originally one of New York's premier fish markets, now also offering first-rate meat, produce, and everything else. Open Monday through Saturday 7 A.M.–9 P.M., Sunday 9 A.M.– 7 P.M.

*Snack time*

### Dean & DeLuca
**560 Broadway (at Prince St.), SH**          **212-431-1691**

Tony, overpriced, gorgeous. Open Monday through Saturday
10 A.M.–8 P.M., Sunday 10 A.M.–7 P.M.

### Eli's
**1411 Third Avenue (between**          **212-717-7664**
**80th and 81st Sts.), UES**

Similar inventory to Vinegar Factory (see p. 373), but in more
luxurious surroundings. Open daily 7 A.M.–9 P.M.

## City Fact
The stone that was used to construct Eli's was imported from Jerusalem by the owner.

### Fairway Downtown
**2127 Broadway (at 74th St.), UWS          212-595-1888**

The best for the price/quality equation. Open daily, 24 hours.

### Fairway Uptown
**2328 Twelfth Avenue                          212-234-3883**
**(at 126th St.), UWS**

Like Fairway Downtown, but larger, better, less crowded, and with free parking (a really big deal for New Yorkers). Because of its inaccessibility (too far to walk; not particularly close to public transportation), you really need a car to shop here. Open daily 8 A.M.–11 P.M.

### Gourmet Garage
**453 Broome Street (at Mercer St.), SH    212-941-5850**
**301 East 64th Street (between              212-535-6271**
**First and Second Aves.), UES**
**2567 Broadway (between                     212-663-0656**
**96th and 97th Sts.), UWS**

A mini-chain of warehouse-style gourmet stores. Some great stuff, but hit-or-miss overall. Open daily; hours vary according to location.

### Grace's Marketplace
**1237 Third Avenue (at 71st St.), UES    212-737-0600**

Lovely Upper East Side store owned by a Balducci family faction. Open Monday through Saturday 7:00 A.M.–8:30 P.M., Sunday 8 A.M.–7 P.M.

### Grand Central Marketplace
**On the Grand Central Station Main Concourse, MTE**
**Each purveyor/stall has its own telephone number**

Elegant new marketplace with dozens of gourmet food stalls. Open Monday through Friday 7 A.M.–9 P.M., Saturday 9 A.M.–7 P.M., Sunday 9 A.M.–5 P.M.

### Union Square Greenmarket
**Union Square Park (along Broadway and**
**East 17th St.), US**

New York's premier farmers market. Go very early for the best selection. Open Monday, Wednesday, Friday, Saturday, early morning until mid-afternoon.

For other area greenmarkets, see the Council on the Environment of NYC's Web site: www.users.interport.net/~conyc/.

### Vinegar Factory
**431 East 91st Street (between          212-987-0885**
**First and York Aves.), UES**

Same owner as Eli's. Warehouse-style gourmet store; expensive with beautiful produce. Open daily 7 A.M.–9 P.M.

### ★Zabar's
**2245 Broadway (at 80th St.), UWS     212-787-2000**

A classic (a temple to some, a homecoming to others, or just a really good place to shop to the rest), and still one of the best. Open Monday through Saturday 8:00 A.M.–7:30 P.M., Sunday 9:00 A.M.–7:00 P.M.

# INDEX TO DINING BY NEIGHBORHOOD AND CUISINE

*Indian*
Kohinoor Indian Cuisine
(p. 348)
Raj Mahal (p. 348)

*Japanese*
★Shabu-Tatsu (p. 352)

*Korean*
Dok Suni's (p. 355)

*Mexican and Tex-Mex*
★Benny's Burritos (p. 355)
Burritoville (p. 356)
Mary Ann's (p. 357)

*Pastries*
De Robertis (p. 358)
★Veniero's (p. 359)

*Pizza*
Patsy's (p. 362)
Stromboli (p. 363)

*Polish*
Christine's (p. 364)

*Southeast Asian and Pan-Asian*
Holy Basil (p. 365)
Penang (p. 366)

*Tibetan*
Lhasa (p. 368)

**FINANCIAL DISTRICT**

*Candy and Nuts*
Neuchatel (p. 332)

*Food Courts*
Pier 17 (p. 369)
World Financial Center
(p. 369)

*Japanese*
Menchanko-Tei (p. 352)

*Mexican and Tex-Mex*
Burritoville (p. 356)

**GRAMERCY PARK/
FLATIRON**

*American*
★America (p. 313)
Chat 'n' Chew (p. 316)
Gramercy Tavern (p. 317)

*Bagels*
★Ess-a-Bagel (p. 320)
Pick-a-Bagel (p. 321)

*Brunch*
Friend of a Farmer (p. 326)

*Chinese*
Mee (p. 335)

*Indian*
Curry in a Hurry (p. 347)

**LITTLE ITALY**

*Deli and Sandwiches*
★Italian Food Center
(p. 338)

*Ice Cream*
Ciao Bella (p. 346)

*Italian*
★Casa Bella Restaurant
(p. 350)

*Pastries*
Ferrara (p. 358)

**LOWER EAST SIDE**

*Bagels*
★Kossar's (p. 320)

*Candy and Nuts*
Bazzini (p. 328)
★Economy Candy (p. 329)
The Sweet Life (p. 330)
Wolsk's Candy (p. 330)

*Deli and Sandwiches*
★Katz's Deli (p. 338)

CHAPTER

7

Shopping

# Shopping

Map shows highlights only. See chapter text for more listings.

**"W**e didn't come all the
way to New York just to shop!" you say. But shopping in New
York City isn't just about buying things; it's an activity and attraction unto itself. Shopping doesn't have to mean spending
money and wasting time like the characters of *Clueless*. New
York City shopping can be just as entertaining (Tannen's
Magic Store), culturally enlightening (Chinatown), and educational (Store of Wonder) as seeing a show, going to a museum (indeed, most of the museums have interesting shops
within), or reading a book (and that's not to mention all of
New York's wonderful independent booksellers!).

It's getting harder and harder to find unique, interesting,
independent stores in most of America. Just about every mall
in every town has exactly the same stores. But New York City,
which isn't a mall town, is the last bastion of the independ-
ents. Department stores, specialty shops, boutiques, street
vendors, and kiosks all offer original New York-esque products
that you'll be hard-pressed to find anywhere else. Even if you

do end up in a chain store in New York City, you may very well be visiting the original—like Saks Fifth Avenue or Barnes & Noble.

Shopping is deeply embedded in the culture of New York. We're a varied bunch, and each of us is accustomed to being able to find anything, whenever we want it, and for whatever price we want to pay. You're in a city with more than 40,000 retail outlets. If you can't find it here, it probably doesn't exist. Whether your children are partial to street fairs (which abound in the City throughout the temperate months), the hip world of second-hand stores in Greenwich Village, or the high-falutin' boutiques on the Upper East Side, even the pickiest, most specialized, most budget-conscious shoppers will find something.

Although rents and sales taxes (8.25 percent, except for shoes and clothes under $110 per item) are high, the enormous volume of sales in many New York stores means there's still plenty of money to be saved by shopping in the City. Then again, though I don't advise it, you can also easily spend more money shopping for your kids in New York City than a full year at Yale or Harvard would cost.

A word to the wise: As with all things, kids—and even the most devoted teenage shoppers—will have limited attention spans for dragging around the City's stores. So set priories for their shopping time (and yours) and save your visits to the Gap, Toys "R" Us, and Footlocker for home.

*Store hours:* Most of the larger stores are open 10 A.M. to 6 P.M. Monday through Saturday (with extended hours until 8 P.M. on Thursday) and Sunday 12 P.M. to 5 P.M. But it's always best to call ahead to make sure a particular store will be open (some of the smaller boutiques, especially, change their hours often).

The following abbreviations are used to indicate the age-appropriateness of each store.

PK: Toddlers and pre-kindergarten; birth–4 years
K: Kids; 5–8 years
PT: Pre-teens; 9–12 years
T: Teenagers; 13 years and older

I've also indicated the neighborhood, using the following abbreviations:

| | |
|---|---|
| BR: Brooklyn | BX: Bronx |
| CH: Chelsea | CT: Chinatown |
| EV: East Village | FD: Financial District |
| GD: Garment District | GP: Gramercy Park/Flatiron |
| GV: Greenwich Village | LES: Lower East Side |
| LI: Little Italy | MT: Midtown |
| MTE: Midtown East | MTW: Midtown West |
| Q: Queens | SH: SoHo |
| SI: Staten Island | TBC: TriBeCa |
| TD: Theater District | TS: Times Square |
| UES: Upper East Side | US: Union Square |
| UWS: Upper West Side | WV: West Village |

# Major Shopping Districts

In New York, no matter where you walk, stores abound. But there are some major shopping districts that every dedicated shopper loves to hit when visiting the City, whether for the first time or the fiftieth. Most of the stores mentioned here are described in more detail in the sections that follow; these neighborhood overviews are intended as a taste of things to come.

**Fifth Avenue:** Starting at FAO Schwarz at 58th Street and down to Saks Fifth Avenue at 49th Street, Fifth Avenue is a main thoroughfare. On this strip you'll find Trump Plaza (worth a look), Tiffany, Disney, NikeTown (around the corner on 57th St.), Coca Cola, H&M, and Rockefeller Plaza. Farther along, at 40th Street, you'll hit Lord & Taylor.

**Madison Avenue:** The whole of Madison Avenue from 58th Street up to 94th Street consists of one high-end boutique after another, many of them flagship stores for designers (which many girls find fascinating). As you stroll up Madison, you'll pass the back entrance to FAO Schwarz, plus Barney's, TSE, BéBé, Jacadi, Polo, Oilily, Tartine et Chocolat, Olive & Bette's, Catimini, Wicker Garden's Children, and Dollhouse Antics.

**Columbus Avenue:** Full of small boutiques, the avenue will have your children wandering happily along Columbus from the Capezio store at 66th Street, to Betsey Johnson, Z'Baby, and the weekend flea market at 77th Street, to Maxilla and Mandible near the Museum of Natural History.

**SoHo:** The streets of SoHo are rife with excellent shopping opportunities, enough to make any young girl squeal with delight—and any parent clutch the credit cards tight. The main drags are along Spring Street, Prince Street, and West Broadway, though there are plenty of other crisscrossing smaller streets to browse. This is an excellent people-watching neighborhood.

**The Village:** 8th Street in the West Village and St. Marks Place in the East Village, this is the stuff that Hollywood movies are made of. Along 8th Street, between Fifth and Sixth Avenues especially, shoe stores abound, as do second-hand stores (like Andy's Cheapies), punk shops, and leather-goods shops. On the other side of Astor Place, between Third and Second Avenues, is where the real show is—tattoo parlors and piercing shops, lots of angry (harmless) youth in black (usually torn) clothing, street vendors with silver jewelry, punk shops selling leather and studs, rock posters—you get the idea. Most kids get a big kick out of this neighborhood, primarily because it's different from what they're accustomed to seeing. This strip is more for the show than anything else.

**South Street Seaport and Pier 17:** This is a great area for a picnic, lunch at the food court, a browse, a break, or all four. South Street Seaport includes different shops, most of which, like Brookstone, Abercrombie & Fitch, and Laura Ashley, you probably have back home. But the setting is lovely (the old cobblestone streets are the originals), there's a worthwhile museum, and, if you wander over to Pier 17 (the Seaport's central fixture), you can check out the sailboats, get a great view of the Brooklyn Bridge, and grab a fresh-squeezed lemonade. It's a great stop to coordinate with a visit to the Statue of Liberty or Wall Street or a ride on the Staten Island Ferry.

**Manhattan Mall:** The Manhattan Mall is not as much a great shopping destination (most of the stores are chains) as it is a great place to have lunch (there's an extensive food court on the top floor, with some more healthful options beyond the regular fast-food scene—salads, Greek food, deli sandwiches), take an indoor break, and get a great

*Commissioning a work of art outside the Met*

(free) view of the Empire State Building. It's also the ideal jumping-off point for a trip to Macy's and a walk down Broadway toward Union Square.

**A Note About Gift Shops**

Nearly every museum and attraction in the City has an extensive and elaborate gift shop where you can browse through a well-chosen selection of everything from books to jewelry, clothes, house gifts, and art. If you are visiting any of the City's zoos, they are also good destinations for gift- and treat-buying for the children. So is, surprisingly enough, the main branch of the New York Public Library at 42nd Street and Fifth Avenue. I have not listed those shops here—they are discussed in chapter 5.

A ★ indicates a particularly noteworthy store for its price range, type, or appeal to kids.

# Clothing

Of the literally hundreds of clothing stores in New York City, these are my favorites.

| *Au Chat Botté* | PK |
|---|---|
| 1192 Madison Avenue (at 87th St.), UES | 212-722-6474 |

Very expensive high-end European infant and toddler clothing—lots of pinks and blues—and baby furniture.

| *The Baby Collection* | PK/K |
|---|---|
| 1384 Lexington Avenue (between 91st and 92nd Sts.), UES | 212-828-8633 |

Top American labels, like Flaphappy, plus prestige imports.

**Baby Gap**                                   PK
341 Columbus Avenue              212-875-9196
(at 76th St.), UWS

Although there are more Gap stores around than you can
shake a stick at, Baby Gaps are rare. This is a particularly nice
and well-stocked one.

**Bambini**                                         PK/K
1367 Third Avenue (at 78th St.), UES     212-717-6742

Excellent selection of shoes and casual and dress clothes for
children 3 months to 8 years. European imports are big here.

**BéBé Thompson**                          PK/K/PT/T
1216 Lexington Avenue               212-249-4740
(between 82nd and 83rd Sts.), UES

Cute, sweet clothes—nothing but the best for the jet-setters.
Designer labels available; prices are high. Infant to 14 years.

**★Ben's for Kids**                              PK
1380 Third Avenue                    212-794-2330
(between 78th and 79th Sts.), UES

One-stop shopping for your infant or toddler (up to 3 years),
including not only clothes, but also furniture, strollers, clothing and toys. A Manhattan favorite.

| *Bloomers* | PK/K/PT |
| --- | --- |
| 1042 Lexington Avenue | 212-570-9529 |
| (between 74th and 75th Sts.), UES | |

Designer clothes for infants 3 months to size 6x, plus children's sleepwear so exquisite it's a shame to use it just for sleeping—the owner prefers to think of it as playwear, too (up to size 12).

| *Bombalulu's* | PK/K/PT |
| --- | --- |
| 101 West 10th Street (between | 212-463-0897 |
| Seventh Ave. and Greenwich), WV | |

Hip, downtown clothing and toys.

| *Calypso Enfant* | PK/K/PT |
| --- | --- |
| 284 Mulberry Street (between | 212-965-8910 |
| Houston and Prince Sts.), EV | |

The downtown crowd has designer labels, too. There's even a line of baby bath products and clothes for mothers at the adult Calypso store, located around the corner. Infant to 12.

| *Catimini* | PK/K/PT |
| --- | --- |
| 1284 Madison Avenue (between | 212-987-0688 |
| 91st and 92nd Sts.), UES | |

Very expensive and beautiful children's clothing. Catimini is the be-all and end-all in children's fashion, and the clothes are exceptionally comfortable. Infant to size 12 girls; up to size 10 boys.

| *CoCo & Z*<br>222 Columbus Avenue<br>(at 70th St.), UWS | PK/K/PT<br>212-721-0415 |

Spiffy clothes for kids. Newborn to size 8 boys and size 10 girls.

| *East Side Kids*<br>1298 Madison Avenue (between<br>92nd and 93rd Sts.), UES | PK/K/PT/T<br>212-360-5000 |

Extensive selection of shoes and sneakers up to adult size 10.

| *G.C. William*<br>1137 Madison Avenue (between<br>84th and 85th Sts.), UES | PK/K/PT/T<br>212-396-3400 |

Casual to formalwear for boys to size 20 and girls to size 16. Also a good selection of girly knick-knacks—funky pads, pens, jewelry, and the like.

| *Good-Byes Children's Resale Shop*<br>230 East 78th Street (between<br>Second and Third Aves.), UES | PK/K<br>212-794-2301 |

Baby and children's gently used clothing, books, toys, and equipment. Newborn to 5 years.

| *Granny Made*<br>381 Amsterdam Avenue (between<br>78th and 79th Sts.), UWS | PK/K<br>212-496-1222 |

The merchandise has a handmade feel to it. Full line of layette plus unique, beautiful, classy sweaters and clothes for infant to age 7.

| *Great Feet (by Stride Rite)* | PK/K/PT/T |
| 1241 Lexington Avenue | 212-249-0551 |
| (at 84th St.), UES | |

An excellent selection of dressy and casual shoes for children of all ages featuring Sam & Libby, Nine West, Adidas, Nike, Kenneth Cole, Sperry, and, of course, Stride Rite.

| ★ *Greenstones & CIE* | PK/K/PT |
| 1184 Madison Avenue (between | 212-427-1665 |
| 86th and 87th Sts.), UES | |
| 442 Columbus Avenue | 212-580-4322 |
| (at 81st St.), UWS | |

A terrific, reasonably priced clothing destination for infants and boys and girls up to size 12. Hats, shoes, and slippers for infants too. This store is new and bustling with customers.

| ★ *Harry's Shoes* | PK/K/PT/T |
| 2299 Broadway (at 83rd St.), UWS | 212-874-2035 |

You'd think they were giving something away at Harry's by the hordes of people who fill the store during operating hours. That certainly isn't the reason (nor is it the brusque service). Rather the crowds come for the incredible selection of fine shoes for the entire family.

| ★ *Infinity* | PK/K/PT/T |
| 1116 Madison Avenue | 212-517-4232 |
| (at 83rd St.), UES | |

Infinity specializes in pre-teen clothing, but also sells for ages 4 to adult. The stock includes casual and dressy and novelty accessories. The store does a lot of mail order (20 percent of its business comes from mail order customers).

| *Jacadi* | PK/K |
| --- | --- |
| 1281 Madison Avenue (between 91st and 92nd Sts.), UES | 212-369-1616 |
| 787 Madison Avenue (between 66th and 67th Sts.), UES | 212-535-3200 |

Upscale French infants' clothing in muted and pastel colors.

| *Jane's Exchange* | PK/K/PT |
| --- | --- |
| 207 Avenue A (between 12th and 13th Sts.), EV | 212-674-6268 |

Children's consignment store (up to size 12), plus maternity clothes.

| *Kids Are Magic* | PK/K/PT |
| --- | --- |
| 2293 Broadway (between 82nd and 83rd Sts.), UWS | 212-875-9240 |

A large, affordable selection of clothes, from soup to nuts, for boys and girls.

| *La Layette* | PK |
| --- | --- |
| 170 East 61st Street (between Lexington and Third Aves.), UES | 212-688-7072 |

Extremely high-end frilly clothing for infants to children's size 2. Also a worthwhile stop for layettes, gifts, hand-painted furniture, and fine European linens.

| *La Petite Etoile* | PK/K/PT/T |
| 746 Madison Avenue (between | 212-744-0975 |
| 64th and 65th Sts.), UES | |

French and Italian clothing lines for newborn to 14 years. Stock includes mostly casual clothes, but there are also some selections for dress up (including christening gowns).

| ★*Lester's* | PK/K/PT/T |
| 1522 Second Avenue (at 79th St.), UES | 212-734-9292 |

A real New York institution, Lester's has been selling to New York parents since 1948. Still a family-run business (with plenty of third-generation customers coming through), Lester's caters to children from newborn up to size 16 girls, size 20 boys. The stock includes top clothing brands—imported and domestic—plus sneakers, dress, and casual shoes. Lester's also has a full layette department—everything the mother needs for her infant, birth to 3 months. They'll even hold onto the merchandise for you if you're superstitious about bringing it home before the baby is born. A good place to stock up for your daughter on accessories, jewelry, hair bits, and bobs, and for kids going to camp with care packages, bunk junk, and camp labels.

| ★*Little Eric* | PK/K/PT/T |
| 1331 Third Avenue (between | 212-288-8987 |
| 76th and 77th Sts.), UES | |
| 1118 Madison Avenue (between | 212-717-1513 |
| 83rd and 84th Sts.), UES | |

An incredible selection of children's dress and casual shoes, all with the Little Eric label. Also name-brand sneakers. Sizes to men's 8 and women's 9.

**Littlestars New York City**      PK/K
968 Third Avenue (at 58th St.), MTE    212-826-7159

Clothes for children up to 8 years old, plus furniture.

**Magic Windows and Magic Windows Baby** PK/K/PT/T
1186 Madison Avenue (between     212-289-0028
86th and 87th Sts.), UES

Everything from casual everyday wear to clothes dressy enough
for weddings. Also a good place to pick up baby blankets and
stuffed animals. Newborn to size 16.

**★Morris Brothers**      K/PT/T
2322 Broadway (at 84th St.), UWS    212-724-9000

You can outfit the whole family, kindergartners through teens,
at Morris Brothers, a favorite destination of New York mothers for casual clothing and summer camp stock.

**Nursery Lines**      PK
1034 Lexington Avenue     212-396-4445
(at 74th St.), UES

Emphasis on Italian imports, hand-knit sweaters and hand-
embroidered clothes for children up to age 4. Also custom-
designed nursery furniture.

**Oilily**      PK/K/PT
870 Madison Avenue     212-628-0100
(between 70th and 71st Sts.), UES

Brightly colored, soup-to-nuts clothing (reminiscent of
Provençal-style fabrics) and accessories for ages newborn to 12.

| *Once Upon a Time* | PK/K/PT/T |
|---|---|
| 171 East 92nd Street (between | 212-831-7619 |
| Lexington and Third Aves.), UES | |

You can outfit your child from infant to size 14 at this UES store, which sells gently used (if used at all) clothing in season.

| *Second Act Children's Wear* | PK/K/PT/T |
|---|---|
| 1046 Madison Avenue (between | 212-988-2440 |
| 79th and 80th Sts.), UES | |

Barely used clothing for infants, boys, and girls up to age 13, as well as toys, dolls, a great selection of books, and sometimes ice skates and inline skates. The range of quality is from very expensive clothing down to Gap and Levis.

| ★*Shoofly* | PK/K/PT |
|---|---|
| 465 Amsterdam Avenue (between | 212-580-4390 |
| 82nd and 83rd Sts.), UWS | |
| 42 Hudson Street (between | 212-406-3270 |
| Duane and Thomas Sts.), TBC | |

If I had to choose one store for kids' shoes . . . I'd have to say that Shoofly is right up there. The best selection in town (includes the largest selection of imported children's shoes in the country). Also good for children's accessories and accoutrements like hats, belts, and socks.

**Small Change**                              PK/K/PT/T
964 Lexington Avenue                      212-772-6455
(at 70th St.), UES

Beautiful, classy floral dresses for girls and babies. Clothes for newborns to size 12 boys and size 14 girls. Also a small selection of shoes and accessories.

**Spring Flowers**                                       PK/K/PT
1050 Third Avenue (at 62nd St.), UES    212-758-2660
905 Madison Avenue (at 72nd St.), UES  212-717-8182

Strictly high-end (with branches in Beverly Hills and Palm Beach) this boutique outfits infants and boys to size 8, girls to pre-teen (approximately size 14 girls). Casual, dressy, and formal wear, plus a selection of shoes for kids.

**Tartine et Chocolat**                          PK/K
1047 Madison Avenue                      212-717-2112
(at 80th St.), UES

A tremendous selection of high-end French import clothing for infants through children's size 10. Tartine also carries a full line of layette accoutrements and baby equipment plus a limited number of furniture items, including cribs, dressers, armoires, nursery items, linens, and accessories.

**Wicker Garden's Children**                    PK
1327 Madison Avenue                      212-410-7001
(between 93rd and 94th Sts.), UES

Very expensive boutique with mostly white and dress-up clothes. Children's furniture is also a big part of the inventory. Newborn to size 4.

| *Wynken, Blynken & Nod* | PK/K |
| 306 East 55th Street (between First and Second Aves.), MTE | 212-308-9299 |

Wonderful retro boutique with a diverse inventory of designer children's wear, and as a bonus, some lovely hard-to-find wooden puzzles and toys. Newborn to age 7.

| ★*Z'Baby and Company* | PK/K/PT/T |
| 100 West 72nd Street (at Columbus), UWS | 212-579-BABY (2229) |
| 996 Lexington Avenue (at 72nd St.), UES | 212-472-BABY (2229) |

High-end, too-cute designer clothes. Infant to age 15.

| *Zitomer* | PK/K/PT/T |
| 969 Madison Avenue (between 75th and 76th Sts.), UES | 212-737-5560 |

This amazing store—nearly a department store—started out as a pharmacy. Over the years, as other tenants moved from the building, Zitomer expanded to include a full selection of mostly European clothing, for children newborn to age 14, with everything from casual to formalwear. Head for the third

## Money-Saving Tip
A few months before you leave home, stop buying the kids things that can wait, like clothes and shoes, and save some of the purchasing for the trip. When kids ask for things, say, "Let's buy that in New York." This will build anticipation and add to the shopping budget, even though it's money you would have spent at home anyway.

floor for the toy (and game) department, and don't overlook
the bath and hair accessories—and school uniforms, too.

## Extras

| | |
|---|---|
| ★*Art & Tapisserie* | PK/K/PT/T |
| 1242 Madison Avenue (at 89th St.), UES | 212-722-3222 |

A delightful selection of wooden toys and puzzles, original
furnishings (step stools, tables and chairs, toy chests), hooded
towels (the cutest you've ever seen), blankets, and clothes
(newborn to 14 years). A great place to buy gifts.

| | |
|---|---|
| *Kids Down the Block* | PK/K/PT/T |
| 490 Amsterdam Avenue | 212-496-1546 |
| (between 83rd and 84th Sts.), UWS | |

This small store, owned by the same folks who own West Side
Kids, has a terrific selection of infant clothes to size 6x, unique
decorations for the bedroom, bedding, small area rugs, books,
jewelry, gifts, animal beanbag chairs, and even nightlights.

| | |
|---|---|
| *Little Extras* | PK/K/PT |
| 676 Amsterdam Avenue | 212-721-6161 |
| (at 93rd St.), UWS | |

The selection of infant mobiles alone is worth the trip to this
store, but they also stock children's furniture, stuffed animals,
infant toys and supplies, and a great selection of birth an-
nouncements.

# Teen Clothing

Teen clothing is a totally different proposition from kids' clothing. For today's hip teens, the downtown scene is where it's at. Although the uptown stores like Barney's, Bendels, and Bloomies carry the latest high-end fashions, and many children's clothing stores market to teens, it's in the Village, SoHo, and even Chinatown—at the grownup stores—where you'll find the funkier clothes most teens really want. Second-hand clothing stores abound in these neighborhoods, as do outdoor markets, up-to-the-minute celebrity status shops, and make-up boutiques. These are some of the best for teens.

| *Alice Underground* | PT/T |
|---|---|
| 481 Broadway (between | 212-431-9067 |
| Grand and Broome Sts.), SH | |

A New York City classic. The stock consists mostly of vintage clothes with a smaller selection of new originals (including imports from around the world).

| *Amsterdam Boutique* | T |
|---|---|
| 454 Broadway (between | 212-925-0422 |
| Grand and Howard Sts.), SH | |

Subtlety is not the name of the game here. Teen girls happily shop for fitted clothes, leather pants, sequins, and anything brightly colored.

| *Andy's Chee-Pees* | PT/T |
|---|---|
| 691 Broadway (between | 212-420-5980 |
| Third and Fourth Aves.), EV | |

An all-time favorite (albeit somewhat overpriced) for cool vintage and second-hand clothes. About one-fourth of the stock is new clothing.

| *Anik* | PT/T |
|---|---|
| 1355 Third Avenue (between | 212-861-9840 |
| 77th and 78th Sts.), UES | |
| 1122 Madison Avenue (between | 212-249-2417 |
| 83rd and 84th Sts.), UES | |

Attractive fashion-forward clothes for teen girls.

| *Anthropologie* | K/PT/T |
| --- | --- |
| 375 West Broadway (between | 212-343-7070 |
| Spring and Broome Sts.), SH | |

A fabulous selection of eclectic, expensive clothes for teens. Expect to find $39 tee shirts and the like. A great place for browsing, and there are tons of gadgets, gift items, and housewares, too.

| *Antique Boutique* | PT/T |
| --- | --- |
| 712-714 Broadway (between | 212-460-8830 |
| 4th St. and Astor Pl.), EV | |

A great place to shop for vintage clothing and mass-market, trendy, fashion-forward styles. Downstairs, look for designer labels.

| *Avirex* | PT/T |
| --- | --- |
| 595 Broadway (between | 212-925-5456 |
| Houston and Prince Sts.), SH | |

Avirex is especially good on casual clothes for boys with tee shirts, pants, bomber jackets, and other sporty wear.

| *Betsey Johnson* | PT/T |
| --- | --- |
| 138 Wooster Street (between | 212-995-5048 |
| Prince and Houston Sts.), SH | |
| 248 Columbus Avenue (between | 212-362-3364 |
| 71st and 72nd Sts.), UWS | |
| 251 East 60th Street (between | 212-319-7699 |
| Second and Third Aves.), UES | |
| 1060 Madison Avenue (at 80th St.), UES | 212-734-1257 |

Full line of the famous Betsey Johnson clothing for girls, teens, and women.

| *Big Drop* | PT/T |
| --- | --- |
| 174 Spring Street (between West Broadway and Thompson), SH | 212-966-4299 |
| 1321 Third Avenue (between 75th and 76th Sts.), UES | 212-988-3344 |

Fashionable, trendy girls' clothes that are sure to delight.

| *Buffalo Chips* | PK/K/PT/T |
| --- | --- |
| 355 West Broadway (between Broome and Grand Sts.), SH | 212-625-8400 |

This is what we call chic Western wear. Huge selection of cowboy boots (including some that have been previously worn), belts, and hats. Who doesn't know somebody that could use a pink cowgirl hat? Also suede cowboy and cowgirl outfits for kids.

| ★*Canal Jean Co.* | K/PT/T |
| --- | --- |
| 504 Broadway (between Spring and Broome Sts.), SH | 212-226-1130 |

As a teen, this classic store was always a stop on my New York City walking circuit, and it remains so for most in-the-know kids with off-beat tastes. With a large selection of jeans, shirts, and casual wear, this store demands a visit, if only for a browse. Also check out the vintage and surplus sections.

| ★*Century 21* | PK/K/PT/T |
| --- | --- |
| 22 Cortlandt Street (at Dey St.), FD | 212-227-9092 |

Excellent brand names at impossible discounts. A favorite shopping destination of New Yorkers for years—so much so that the store is forced to expand regularly to keep up with demand.

SHOPPING

405

*Want to go
for a ride?*

| *Cheap Jack's* | PT/T |
| --- | --- |
| 841 Broadway (between 13th and 14th Sts.), US | 212-777-9564 |

Though nothing at Cheap Jack's is actually cheap, the store does have a great selection of vintage clothes.

| *Chill on Broadway* | PT/T |
| --- | --- |
| 427 Broadway (at Howard St.), SH | 212-343-2709 |

This new store was still stocking their shelves when I popped in, and the contents looked extremely promising for teen shoppers. A fashionable selection of clothes and shoes at affordable prices with a wide range, from baggy linen trousers to colorful dresses, floral prints, and snakeskin-textured red leather shoes.

| *Cinco* | PT/T |
| --- | --- |
| 960 Lexington Avenue (at 70th St.), UES | 212-794-3826 |

A small boutique for the fashion set, the likes of whom want to dress a la *Vogue* and *Mademoiselle*.

| ★ *Conway* | PK/K/PT/T |
|---|---|
| 1333 Broadway (at 35th St.), FD (largest store, including shoes) | 212-967-3460 |
| 151 William Street (between Fulton and Nassau Sts.), FD | 212-374-1072 |
| 45 Broad Street (Exchange-Beaver), FD | 212-943-8900 |
| 201 East 42nd Street (at Third Ave.), MTE | 212-922-5030 |
| 11 West 34th Street (between Fifth and Sixth Aves.), MTW | 212-967-1370 |
| 450 Seventh Avenue (between 34th and 35th Sts.), MTW | 212-967-1371 |
| 225 West 34th Street (between Seventh and Eighth Aves.), MTW | 212-967-7390 |

Conway is a great stop for children from early childhood through the teenage years. Up-to-date fashion knockoffs at extremely good prices should satisfy not-too-picky children and parents. Don't expect to find the highest quality workmanship on these clothes, but they'll last until your child outgrows them or the fashion changes.

| *Daffy's* | K/PT/T |
|---|---|
| 335 Madison Avenue (at 44th St.), MTE | 212-557-4422 |
| 1311 Broadway (at 34th St.), MTW | 212-736-4477 |
| 111 Fifth Avenue (at 18th St.), GP | 212-529-4477 |
| 125 East 57th Street (between Lexington and Park Aves.), MTE | 212-376-4477 |

Name-brand clothing for the family, at discounted prices.

| *Danskin* | K/PT/T |
| 159 Columbus Avenue (between | 212-724-2992 |
| 67th and 68th Sts.), UWS | |

Minimalist clothing, tank tops, workout clothes, leotards, and the like.

| *Da'Vinci* | PT/T |
| 37 West 8th Street (between | 212-674-4746 |
| Sixth Ave. and MacDougal St.), WV | |

A vast selection of Italian imported shoes, belts, and bags.

| *Detour* | PT/T |
| Women's: 154 Prince Street | 212-966-3635 |
| (at West Broadway), SH | |
| Men's: 425 West Broadway | 212-219-2692 |
| (between Prince and Houston Sts.), SH | |

A strong selection of reasonably priced (very hard to find in SoHo), trendy clothes.

| *Dieci* | PT/T |
| 30 West 8th Street (between | 212-614-0248 |
| Fifth and Sixth Aves.), WV | |

For 8th Street, this store qualifies as mellow—halter tops, brightly colored skirts, and sarongs were on display the last time I stopped in.

| *Diesel* | K/PT/T |
|---|---|
| **770 Lexington Avenue (across from Bloomingdale's), UES** | **212-308-0055** |

A huge example of this chain store (lots of jeans and such), Manhattan's Diesel even has a theme-style restaurant that's fun for the kids.

| ★*Dollhouse* | PT/T |
|---|---|
| **400 East 4th Street (at Lafayette St.), EV** | **212-539-1800** |

French and American styles of very chic clothing.

| *8th Street Lab* | PT/T |
|---|---|
| **69 East 8th Street (between Mercer St. and Broadway), EV** | **212-228-9657** |

A gold mine of trendy Village-wear. With loud music pounding all around, your teen will be thrilled to go through the racks of hip downtown clothing, plus sunglasses and funky accoutrements.

| *Energywear* | PT/T |
|---|---|
| **140 East 63rd Street (at Lexington Ave.), UES** | **212-752-5360** |

Predictably skimpy clothes. This fitness-oriented store (most items relate to sports and fitness) is part of the Equinox gym. There's a selection of clothes for working out (and some for going out), and equipment as well.

| Flying A | PK/PT/T |
| --- | --- |
| 169 Spring Street (at West Broadway), SH | 212-965-9090 |

Half the stock in this store is shoes (including fur clogs), and the other half is clothes and accessories, like tiny tee shirts, socks, fun purses, and even a small selection of baby/toddler shirts, too.

| ★ Forréal | PT/T |
| --- | --- |
| 1369 Third Avenue (between 78th and 79th Sts.),UES | 212-396-0563 |
| 1200 Lexington Avenue (between 81st and 82nd Sts.), UES | 212-717-0493 |

| Forréal Basics | PT/T |
| --- | --- |
| 1335 Third Avenue (between 76th and 77th Sts.), UES | 212-734-2105 |

Extremely popular at this moment with teen girls around town, Basics and the dressier uptown stores have racks of something for every occasion. Basics has jeans and tee shirts and casual wear. Often mothers end up shopping for themselves while they wait for their extremely choosy daughters.

| Galo | K/PT/T |
| --- | --- |
| 825 Lexington Avenue (between 63rd and 64th Sts.), UES | 212-832-3922 |

European imported shoes for boys and girls up to size 38 (approximately size 7, American, for men; 8 for women).

| *H & M* | PK/K/PT/T |
|---|---|
| **640 Fifth Avenue (at 51st St.), MTE** | **212-489-0390** |

All the rage since it hit Fifth Avenue (they can't manage to keep the shelves stocked), H&M is a huge Swedish department store with great styles and a lot of variety—and the price is ever so right!

| *Here & Now* | PT/T |
|---|---|
| **56 West 8th Street (between Fifth and Sixth Aves.), WV** | **212-979-2142** |

Fashion-sensitive clothing, leather, and shoes.

| *Intermix* | PT/T |
|---|---|
| **1003 Madison Avenue (between 77th and 78th Sts.), UES** | **212-249-7858** |
| **125 Fifth Avenue (between 19th and 20th Sts.), CH** | **212-533-9720** |

Trendy contemporary clothing that most every girl seems to want to have.

| *Lord of the Fleas* | PT/T |
|---|---|
| **2142 Broadway (at 75th St.), UWS** | **212-875-8815** |

Hip, fun clothing—ideal for the girl who likes to be original (and that doesn't have to mean weird).

| *J.D.* | T |
|---|---|
| **1 West 8th Street (between Fifth Ave. and MacDougal St.), WV** | **212-533-7222** |

With branches in Milan and Paris, this boutique is guaranteed to have skimpy, tight, bright, trendy clothes.

*Joe Stix* PT/T
10 Fifth Avenue (at 8th St.), EV 212-529-7564

Hip clothing for girls, and it won't break the bank.

*Know Style* PT/T
44 West 8th Street (between 212-529-7655
Sixth Ave. and MacDougal St.), WV

A large selection of clothes for guys and girls, at reasonable prices.

*Lucky Brand* PT/T
38 Greene Street (at Grand St.), SH 212-625-0707

Lucky Brand retail store for jeans.

*Marsha D.D.* PK/K/PT/T
1324 Lexington Avenue 212-534-8700 (girls' store)
(between 88th and 89th 212-876-9922 (boys' store)
Sts.), UES

A favorite destination for Upper East Side kids, D.D. has two
stores jam-packed (separated by a tiny unrelated lingerie store)
with casual clothes (including bathing suits) for kids' sizes 4 to
16 for girls, 4 to 20 for boys. Also good for trinkets, gadgets,
and camp packages.

*Medici* PT/T
420 Columbus Avenue 212-712-9342
(at 80th St.), UWS

Up-to-the-minute shoe fashions, primarily featuring the
Medici brand.

### *M. W. Teen*  K/PT/T
**1188 Madison Avenue**  **212-289-0181**
**(at 87th St.), UES**

Next door to Magic Windows, Teen provides upscale clothing to fashion-conscious teens (boys to size 12, girls to teen sizes— approximately age 16) as well as jewelry and accessories.

### *Necessary Clothing*  PT/T
**470 Broadway (between**  **212-966-9011**
**Grand and Broome Sts.), SH**

One of the many giant stores that line Broadway. Full of afford-able, trendy, brightly colored, mostly skimpy clothes for girls.

### *Nelly M.*  PT/T
**1309 Lexington Avenue**  **212-996-4410**
**(at 88th St.), UES**

Fashionable, skimpy clothing is the stock and trade at this UES boutique.

### *Nicole Miller*  PT/T
**780 Madison Avenue**  **212-288-9779**
**(at 66th St.), UES**
**134 Prince Street (between**  **212-343-1362**
**West Broadway and Wooster St.), SH**

The place to shop if you're a fan of Nicole Miller's funky style.

### *Oasis*  PT/T
**138 Spring Street (at Wooster St.), SH**  **212-219-0710**

Fashion-sensitive clothes for girls.

*Old Navy Clothing*  PK/K/PT/T
610 Avenue of the Americas  212-645-0663
(at 18th St.), CH
503 Broadway (between  212-226-0838
Spring and Broome Sts.), SH
150 West 34th Street  212-594-0049
(at Seventh Ave.), MTW

This chain hasn't been around all that long, and many towns still don't have one. For fashionable, affordable casual clothes by the same people who own the Gap and Banana Republic, this is a good stop if you don't have a local branch.

*Olive & Bette's*  PT/T
1070 Madison Avenue (at 81st St.), UES  888/767-8475
252 Columbus Avenue (at 72nd St.), UWS

Expect to pay more than $100 for jeans at this superhip women's clothing store. Featured in the likes of *Mademoiselle* and *Marie Claire,* O & B belongs to the scantily clad club.

*Phat Pharm*  PK/K/PT/T
129 Prince Street (at Wooster St.), SH  212-533-PHAT

Especially good for boys, the store features Phat Pharm brand casual clothes, jeans, jackets, and shoes for the whole family.

*Polo-Ralph Lauren*  PK/K/PT/T
867 Madison Avenue  212-606-2100
(at 72nd St.), UES

You won't find a more beautiful place to stock up on Polo clothing. Although the help can be a bit stiff, the gorgeous surroundings more than make up for the staff's snootiness.

## Learning Tip

Have a peek into the Polo Store at 72nd Street and Madison Avenue. Gertrude Rhinelander Waldo commissioned this beautiful mansion as a personal residence, but she never moved in.

| *Putumayo* | PT/T |
|---|---|
| 147 Spring Street (between West Broadway and Wooster St.), SH | 212-966-4458 |

Featuring understated women's clothes, Putumayo has lots of floral dresses and skirts, simple blouses, seasonal hats, and a few bags. This was always one of my regular stops when I was a teen . . . but then again, I was an innocent.

| *Rampage* | PK/K/PT/T |
|---|---|
| 127 Prince Street (at Wooster St.), SH | 212-995-9569 |

Casual clothes like jeans, tank tops, tee shirts and lots of knitwear.

| *Reminiscence* | PT/T |
|---|---|
| 50 West 23rd Street (between Fifth and Sixth Aves.), CH | 212-243-2292 |

A great selection of vintage clothing for trendy teens who are out to make a statement. A good place to stock up on funky gift items, too.

| *Replay Store* | PK/K/PT/T |
|---|---|
| 109 Prince Street (at Greene St.), SH | 212-673-6300 |

Especially good for jeans for the whole family—you'll never see a more varied selection of fades anywhere.

| *Rugged Sole* | PT/T |
|---|---|
| 7 West 8th Street (between Fifth Ave. and MacDougal St.), WV | 212-477-7555 |

A truly vast selection of sneakers.

| *Sacco* | PT/T |
|---|---|
| 2355 Broadway (at 86th St.), UWS | 212-874-8362 |
| 324 Columbus Avenue (at 75th St.), UWS | 212-799-5229 |
| 111 Thompson Street (between Prince and Spring Sts.), SH | 212-925-8010 |
| 94 Seventh Avenue (at 16th St.), CH | 212-675-5180 |

Whatever shoe styles are hot, they've got them at Sacco, with their own label to boot.

| ★*Scoop* | PT/T |
|---|---|
| 1273-1277 Third Avenue (between 73rd and 74th Sts.), UES | 212-535-5577 |
| 532 Broadway (between Spring and Prince Sts.), SH | 212-925-2886 |

Teen girls go crazy over this place, as do the aspiring teens (they struggle for a find, just so they can purchase anything with the scoop label) who are trying so hard to be with it. The best selection is at the uptown branch, where there are three Scoop stores in a row, all interconnected. Prices are steep, fashions are fleeting, and styles are far too risqué for my taste, but I'm sure these girls don't want my opinion on this one anyway.

| *Screaming Mimi's* | PT/T |
|---|---|
| 382 Lafayette Street (between | 212-677-6464 |
| East 4th St. and Great Jones), EV | |

A mix of vintage clothes, sportswear, shoes, and trinkets from the 1950s through the 1970s, as well as newer, more current items.

| *Shoe Closet* | PT/T |
|---|---|
| 9 West 8th Street (between | 212-529-0840 |
| MacDougal St. and Fifth Ave.), WV | |

A large selection of not-too-crazy shoes.

| *Shoe Plaza* | PT/T |
|---|---|
| 60 West 8th Street (at Sixth Ave.), WV | 212-420-8832 |

Another 8th Street shoe emporium with a giant inventory.

| *Sofia* | PT/T |
|---|---|
| 828 Lexington Avenue (between | 212-207-4370 |
| 63rd and 64th Sts.), UES | |

Retro styles of skimpy, trendy clothes for mature teens with brave—or indifferent—parents.

| *Stella Dallas* | PT/T |
|---|---|
| 218 Thompson Street (between | 212-674-0447 |
| Bleecker and West 3rd Sts.), WV | |

A small, somewhat dingy store packed with a good vintage selection; I almost bought my wedding dress at this old Village gem.

| *Tani* | **PT/T** |
| 2020 Broadway (between | 212-873-4361 |
| 69th and 70th Sts.), UWS | |

An excellent selection of high-quality and fashionable shoes and boots.

| *Trash and Vaudeville* | **PT/T** |
| 4 St. Mark's Place (between | 212-982-3590 |
| Second and Third Aves.), EV | |

Clothing and shoes best described as punk and rocker styles. It's a great stop for a peek at the current European fashions.

| *Urban Outfitters* | **K/PT/T** |
| 162 Second Avenue (between | 212-375-1277 |
| 10th and 11th Sts.), EV | |
| 374 Avenue of the Americas | 212-677-9350 |
| (between Waverly St. and Washington Sq.), WV | |
| 628 Broadway (between | 212-475-0009 |
| Bleecker and Houston Sts.), SH | |

There's no shortage of hip and trendy clothes, gifts, furniture, and trinkets at this home-grown New York City fave (now a national chain).

| ★ *Venus* | **K/PT/T** |
| 382 West Broadway (between | 212-966-4066 |
| Broome and Spring Sts.), SH | |

The stock in this downstairs store is sure to bring a smile to everyone's face. Half crazy-clothes (the Bruce Lee button-down shirt is amongst my favorites) and half gadgets and accoutrements (boas, wigs, etc.), Venus is definitely good for a visit. The staff is a real hoot, too.

| *Village Designer Shoes* | PT/T |
|---|---|
| **1186 Madison Avenue (between** | **212-534-4807** |
| **86th and 87th Sts.), UES** | |

Very fashionable (and expensive) shoes for girls wearing adult sizes 5½ and up. Just because the shoes are nice, don't assume the staff will also be nice; but don't be too put off—they mean no harm.

| *Village Leather* | PT/T |
|---|---|
| **355 Sixth Avenue (between** | **212-352-3105** |
| **West and 4th Sts.), WV** | |

Whether you decide to let your daughter buy the high-heeled boots with glitter is up to you, but rest assured they do have them here. They also have a tamer selection of shoes, leather pants, and jackets, for those not quite up to the red spiked numbers.

| *Warehouse* | PT/T |
|---|---|
| **581 Broadway (between** | **212-941-0910** |
| **Houston and Prince Sts.), SH** | |

On the fringe of SoHo, here's a wide selection of fashionable clothes at reasonable prices.

| *What Goes Around Comes Around* | PT/T |
|---|---|
| **351 West Broadway (between** | **212-343-9303** |
| **Broome and Grand Sts.), SH** | |

This store's stock is based on the premise that fashion repeats itself. It is also a high-end boutique vintage clothing store (with SoHo rent to pay). Don't expect to find many bargains.

## Top Ten Favorite Stores
## for Parents to Stock Up for Kids

1. Lester's (p. 395)

2. Ben's for Kids (p. 390)

3. Harry's Shoes (p. 393)

4. Z'Baby and Company (p. 399)

5. Shoofly (p. 397)

6. Century 21 (p. 404)

7. Morris Brothers (p. 396)

8. Art & Tapisserie (p. 400)

9. Little Eric (p. 395)

10. Conway (p. 406)

| | |
|---|---|
| *XOXO* | PT/T |
| 426 West Broadway (between | 212-334-9450 |
| Prince and Spring Sts.), SH | |
| 732 Broadway (at Waverly St.), GV | 212-995-5858 |

Great fashion-forward teen styles at surprisingly affordable prices.

| | |
|---|---|
| *Yellow Rat Bastard New York City* | PT/T |
| 478 Broadway (between | 212-219-8569 |
| Broome and Grand Sts.), SH | |

Good for boys especially, don't let the name scare you at this very downtown store. Jeans and other casual clothes are the hits here.

| *Zara* | PK/K/PT/T |
| --- | --- |
| 580 Broadway (between | 212-343-1725 |
| Prince and Houston Sts.), SH | |

This Spanish department store carries clothes with flair—good for the whole family.

### Insider's Tip

"Visit SoHo on a weekend, when it's most crowded, for the ultimate in people-watching."
—Billy, father of two

# Bookstores

We have Barnes & Noble and Borders all over town (including the original Barnes & Noble, and the largest one). But, because you've come all the way to New York City, you'll surely prefer to take advantage of our unique local (often family-run) bookstores.

| *Bank Street Books* | PK/K/PT |
| --- | --- |
| 610 West 112th Street | 212-678-1654 |
| (at Broadway), UWS | |

Catering to children and teachers, this one is worth the trip uptown.

| *Bookberries* | PK/K/PT |
| --- | --- |
| 983 Lexington Avenue | 212-794-9400 |
| (at 71st St.), UES | |

A good selection of picture books. One nice feature is that they'll put together gift baskets with a selection of your favorite books.

### Books of Wonder    PK/K/PT/T
16 West 18th Street (between    212-989-3270
Fifth and Sixth Aves.), GP

Specialty bookstore focusing on hard-to-find and collectors' titles. Children are welcome, and story hour at 11:45 A.M. on Sundays is an especially popular time at this neighborhood store. The selection is appropriate for children infant to mid-teens.

### Choices—The Recovery Bookshop    PK/K
220 East 78th Street (between    212-794-3858
Second and Third Aves.), UES

This store is of the self-help variety, but they also have a very good selection of children's books.

### Coliseum Books    PK/K/PT/T
1771 Broadway (at 57th St.), MTW    212-757-8381

A terrific bookstore for any book lover, Coliseum is one of the few New York City classics still standing. A good selection across the board.

### Drama Book Shop    K/PT/T
723 Seventh Avenue (2nd fl.;    212-944-0595
between 48th and 49th Sts.), MTW

A limited selection of drama and theater books geared toward children, including books on children in theater, paper doll books, and paper theater cutouts.

**Forbidden Planet**                    K/PT/T
840 Broadway (at 13th St.), US     212-473-1576

Science fiction and fantasy books, with a good selection of children's comic books, trading cards, and games too.

**Gryphon Bookshop**                    PK/K/PT/T
2246 Broadway (between              212-362-0706
80th and 81st Sts.), UWS

Used books with extensive children's section.

**J. Levine Books & Judaica**          PK/K/PT/T
5 West 30th Street, (between        212-695-6888
Park and Madison Aves.), MTE

A large selection of Jewish books for all ages of children.

**The Julliard School Bookstore**       PT/T
60 Lincoln Center Plaza, UWS   212-799-5000 ext. 237

An extensive selection of music, recordings, and books about music—it's Julliard, what do you expect?

**Librairie de France**                 PK/K/PT/T
610 Fifth Avenue, Rockefeller       212-581-8810
Center Promenade, MTE

A full complement of books in French for all ages of children, as well as adults.

*Logos Bookstore*　　　　　　　　PK/K/PT/T
1575 York Avenue (between　　　212-517-7292
83rd and 84th Sts.), UES

Specializing in religious titles—but not exclusively—Logos carries an extensive selection of Christian, Jewish, and secular books for children and adults. There's even a small outdoor garden, perfect for a quiet break.

*McGraw-Hill Bookstore*　　　　　　PT/T
1221 Sixth Avenue (between　　　212-512-4100
48th and 49th Sts.), MTW

Unequaled in computer book selection.

*Rand McNally Map & Travel Store*　PK/K/PT/T
555 Seventh Avenue (between　　212-944-4477
39th and 40th Sts.), MTW
150 East 52nd Street (between　　212-758-7488
Lexington and Third Aves.), MTE

In addition to the great map selection, these stores also carry games, puzzles, activities for the car, globes, and other interesting travel-related items.

*Rubys Book Sale*　　　　　　　　PK/K/PT/T
119 Chambers Street (between　　212-732-8676
Church St. and West Broadway), FD

Large selection of children's books, all ages.

| *Shakespeare & Company Booksellers* | PK/K/PT/T |
|---|---|
| 716 Broadway (at East 4th St.), EV | 212-529-1330 |
| 939 Lexington Avenue (at 69th St.), UES | 212-570-0201 |
| 137 East 23rd Street (at Gramercy St.), GP | 212-505-2021 |
| 1 Whitehall Street (between Broadway and Bowling Green), FD | 212-742-7025 |

A New York institution, be prepared for brusque service (old New York style), but they carry a good selection.

| *Strand Bookstore* | PK/K/PT/T |
|---|---|
| 828 Broadway (at 12th), US | 212-473-1452 |

| *Strand Annex* | PK/K/PT/T |
|---|---|
| 95 Fulton Street (three blocks east of Broadway), FD | 212-732-6070 |

This is New York's favorite place to browse for second-hand, scarce, and out-of-print books. A New York establishment of long standing, with a slogan that says it all: "Home of 8 miles of books."

| *Teachers College Bookstore* | PK/K |
|---|---|
| 1224 Amsterdam Avenue (at 120th St.), UWS | 212-678-3920 |

The huge selection of educational and children's books is why people are willing to make the trip so far uptown. Offers two floors of children's books in addition to educational toys and extensive teacher's sections.

*West Side Judaica & Bookstore*  PK/K/PT/T
2412 Broadway (between  212-362-7846
88th and 89th Sts.), UWS

Jewish books for adults and children.

## Collectibles, Cards, and Comics

*MVP Cards*  K/PT/T
256 East 89th Street (between  212-831-2273
Second and Third Aves.), UES

A good selection of sports cards; baseball, basketball, football . . .

*It's "A"nother Hit*  K/PT/T
131 West 33rd Street (between  212-564-4111
Sixth and Seventh Aves.), MTW

This is a favorite stop of city boys because they carry everything: Comics, toys, collector's cards, memorabilia, and sports cards (baseball, basketball, hockey, football, soccer, and racing).

*Jim Hanley's Universe*  K/PT/T
4 West 33rd Street (between  212-268-7088
Fifth Ave. and Broadway), MTW

Expect to find a wide selection of comics at this friendly store.

*Roger's Time Machine*  K/PT/T
207 West 14th Street (between  212-691-0380
Seventh and Eighth Aves.), CH

These guys are serious about comics. They carry a broad selection from current to collectibles, underground and alternative. Second floor.

| ★ *The Sleep of Reason* | K/PT/T |
|---|---|
| 47 West 8th Street (between MacDougal St. and 6th St.), WV | 212-982-7901 |

It's well worth the trip up the flight of stairs (second floor) to get to this crowded, friendly comic book store. The selection is vast, everyone is welcome, and the staff couldn't be nicer. If they don't have what you're looking for, they can tell you who does.

| *St. Marks Comics* | K/PT/T |
|---|---|
| 11 St. Marks Place (between Second and Third Aves.), EV | 212-598-9439 |

Don't expect handholding at this Saint Marks Place comic book mecca. They have a tremendous selection, though they don't take very good care of their stock, perhaps because the store occupies such a small space (comics are piled on the floor). Be up on your pricing too, because the prices are somewhat random and often out of line with reality.

In addition to the comic book stores listed, walk along Saint Marks Place, between Second and Third Avenues, for a handful of other shops.

## Consumer Electronics

I've found that kids, especially boys, absolutely love to spend hours upon hours in the gigantic electronics stores of New York City.

| *B & H Photo-Video* | K/PT/T |
|---|---|
| 420 Ninth Avenue (between 33rd and 34th Sts.), MTW | 212-444-6615 |

An extensive selection of camera, audio, and video equipment. Prices are as good as you'll find.

★*Detective Store International*       K/PT/T
173 Christopher Street       212-366-6466
(at West Side Hwy.), WV

Sells all sorts of high-tech gadgets like you see in the movies:
Surveillance equipment, body armor, special alarm systems,
metal detectors . . . a real hit with the boys.

*Hammacher Schlemmer*       K/PT/T
147 East 57th Street (between       212-421-9000
Lexington and Third Aves.), MTE

High-end, high-tech gadgets for the person who has everything, or who just wants to play with toys.

★*J&R*       K/PT/T
Addresses all along Park Row, FD       800-426-6027

Ten related stores on Park Row between Beekman and Anne
Streets carrying every conceivable type of electronic equipment, from computers to cameras.

*The Sony Store*       K/PT/T
550 Madison Avenue (between       212-833-6800
55th and 56th Sts.), MTE

You can see and play with all of the latest Sony gadgets at this
welcoming, high-tech emporium. Perfect to coordinate with a
visit to Sony World of Wonder.

*Spectra*       K/PT/T
903 Madison Avenue (between       212-744-2255
72nd and 73rd Sts.), UES

Home theater electronics store.

## Insider's Tip

"When visiting a department store, it helps to have a plan of attack. Know what you're looking for, or you'll waste all your time wandering. If you separate from your kids, which you might want to do if they're old enough, pick a place and time to meet at regular intervals." —*Addie, mother of two*

## Department Stores

Department stores in New York are an entire culture unto themselves, and each one has a distinctive personality.

| *Barneys* | PK/K/PT/T |
|---|---|
| Madison Avenue (at 61st St.), UES | 212-826-8900 |

Popular with the Hollywood set, Barneys is a status symbol all its own.

| *Bloomingdale's* | PK/K/PT/T |
|---|---|
| 1000 Third Avenue (between 59th and 60th Sts.), UES | 212-355-5900 |

This remains a favorite stop for pre-teen and teenage girls, from the Bloomies undies to the multitudes of make-up counters.

| *Henri Bendel* | PK/K/PT/T |
|---|---|
| 712 Fifth Avenue (at 55th St.), MTE | 212-247-1100 |

A high-end boutique-ish department store with a great make-up department.

| Lord & Taylor | PK/K/PT/T |
| 424 Fifth Avenue (between 39th and 40th Sts.), MTE | 212-391-3344 |

A very extensive children's department is only one of the draws at this New York City classic.

### City Fact

Even in this age of mega-malls and superstores, Macy's remains the world's largest department store: An entire New York City block.

| Macy's | PK/K/PT/T |
| 34th Street (at Broadway), MTW | 212-695-4400 |

You could spend an entire day walking the many floors at Macy's, and many people do. If you happen to be in New York City during Thanksgiving, be sure to watch the Macy's parade, or, at holiday time, you can check out the extensive Christmas windows.

### Learning Tip

Macy's wasn't always the largest department store in the world. Term paper idea: Where was the first Macy's and how did it get its start? How did Macy's differ from any other store of its time (example: Did any store offer a money-back guarantee before Macy's?)?

| *Saks Fifth Avenue* | PK/K/PT/T |
|---|---|
| 611 Fifth Avenue (between 49th and 50th Sts.), MTE | 212-753-4000 |

A good destination for the entire family to shop or browse, S5A also has a very good restaurant with a worthwhile view.

# Dolls and Dollhouses

| *Doll House Antics* | PK/K/PT/T |
|---|---|
| 1343 Madison Avenue (at 94th St.), UES | 212-876-2288 |

Dollhouses for play and collectibles for the connoisseur. One especially great feature at Antics is that they have two incredible dollhouses set up for children to play with.

| *Manhattan Doll House* | K/PT/T |
|---|---|
| 236 Third Avenue (between 19th and 20th Sts.), GP | 212-253-9549 |

Miniatures, dollhouses, and dolls for play and collectors.

| ★*New York Doll Hospital* | K/PT/T |
|---|---|
| 787 Lexington Avenue (2nd fl.; between 61st and 62nd Sts.), UES | 212-838-7527 |

This hundred-year-old business (opened in 1900) is a real New York institution. A tiny space that can hold only three to four people at any given time, it is as much a museum as a store. Here they buy and sell antique dolls and restore animals (of the stuffed variety), toys, dolls, and mechanical toys. They

## Kids' Top Ten Favorite Stores

can also outfit your doll in made-to-order clothes, shoes, and socks. "We can repair it if was made today, yesterday, or thirty years ago, it's just a matter of mechanics," say the owners. Don't mind the piles of heads and headless doll bodies lying on the floor—it's all part of this place's charm.

| *Tiny Doll House* | K/PT/T |
|---|---|
| 1146 Lexington Avenue (between 79th and 80th Sts.), UES | 212-744-3719 |

TDH sells dollhouses, furniture, and accessories. They can outfit you with everything you need for your house (starting at about age 5 and up), but it's not a store for unruly tots because there are lots of collectibles, too.

# Games

| *Chess Forum* | K/PT/T |
| --- | --- |
| 219 Thompson Street (between 3rd and Bleecker Sts.), WV | 212-475-2369 |

Just across the street from the Chess Shop, Chess Forum carries a similar stock with an equal number of enthusiasts.

| *Chess in the Schools* | K/PT/T |
| --- | --- |
| 353 West 46th Street (between Eighth and Ninth Aves.), MTW | 212-757-0613 |

Chess boards, pieces, and instructional materials.

| *Chess Shop* | K/PT/T |
| --- | --- |
| 230 Thompson Street (between 3rd and Bleecker Sts.), WV | 212-475-9580 |

A wide range of chess boards, pieces, and instructional information on display, with devotees playing inside.

| ★ *The Compleat Strategist* | K/PT/T |
| --- | --- |
| 11 East 33rd Street (between Fifth and Madison Aves.), MTE | 212-685-3880 |

This is a popular destination for older boys in search of board games, strategy games, and role-playing games (like Dungeons and Dragons).

| *Dart Shoppe* | PT/T |
| --- | --- |
| 30 East 20th Street (between Broadway and Park Ave. South), GP | 212-533-8684 |

Hard to believe many avid dart players exist, but they do, and this is the place for them to shop.

★*Forbidden Planet*      **K/PT/T**
840 Broadway (at 13th St.), US      **212-473-1576**

An enormous store selling a variety of strategy, board, and video games, books, videos, and tee shirts.

★*Funcoland*      **K/PT/T**
901 Sixth Avenue (at 33rd St.), MTW      **212-868-3156**

Funcoland buys and sells video games. They also have a bunch on display, which are there for play.

*Game Quest*      **K/PT/T**
1596 Third Avenue (between      **212-423-0697**
89th and 90th Sts.), UES

Video games are the specialty of the house, but don't expect to find demos out for play.

*Game Show*      **K/PT/T**
1240 Lexington Avenue      **212-472-8011**
(at 84th St.), UES
474 Sixth Avenue (at 12th St.), WV      **212-633-6328**

Primarily games and puzzles geared toward teens and adults (though they do carry some toys and gadgets that are appropriate for younger kids, especially in the summer, when New York parents are planning packages for sleep-away camp).

*Games Workshop*      **K/PT/T**
54 East 8th Street (between      **212-982-6314**
Broadway and Mercer St.), WV

A full complement of tabletop strategy and war games. The friendly staff will be more than happy to tell you all about this hobby if you let them.

| | |
|---|---|
| *Video Gamesters*<br>244 West 14th Street (between<br>Seventh and Eighth Aves.), CH | K/PT/T<br>212-929-3366 |

A wide selection of video games, with a few on display for play—but mostly a buying destination.

## Gifts and Goodies

| | |
|---|---|
| *Alphabets*<br>2284 Broadway (between<br>82nd and 83rd Sts.), UWS | K/PT/T<br>212-579-5702 |
| 115 Avenue A (at 7th St.), EV | 212-475-7250 |
| 47 Greenwich Avenue (between<br>Sixth and Seventh Aves.), WV | 212-229-2966 |

Teen-appropriate gifts and gadgets. Look for insightful tee shirts, hip messenger-type bags, and other retro cool gift items. Also lunch boxes and stuffed animals.

| | |
|---|---|
| *E.A.T. Gifts*<br>1062 Madison Avenue (between<br>80th and 81st Sts.), UES | PK/K/PT/T<br>212-861-2544 |

This store is packed with original gift items. Look for tasteful piñatas, tee shirts, dolls, umbrellas, mini dollhouse accessories, jewelry, and books. You'll be able to find something for everyone on your list here.

| | |
|---|---|
| ★*girlprops.com*<br>153 Prince Street (downstairs,<br>West Broadway), SH | PK/K/PT/T<br>212-505-7615 |

This store is an absolute bonanza for every girl! There are thousands of items to choose from, which is difficult to believe considering how small the space is. Despite the pricey location, the motto is "Inexpensive . . . we *never* say cheap." One step inside and you'll see it's true: Power bracelets are a mere 99 cents, bead bracelets are twelve for $1.99, and real feather boas (something every family should have) are only $7.99. Whatever a girl's budget, she'll be able to spend it here.

| *It's a Mod, Mod World* | K/PT/T |
|---|---|
| 85 First Avenue (between | 212-460-8004 |
| Fifth and Sixth Aves.), EV | |

A hip Village gift store where they make lots of their own products and also carry some of the usuals, like candles, journals, CDs, salt and pepper shakers, and ashtrays.

| *La Brea* | K/PT/T |
|---|---|
| 1321 Second Avenue (between | 212-879-4065 |
| 69th and 70th Sts.), UES | |
| 1575 Second Avenue (between | 212-772-2640 |
| 81st and 82nd Sts.), UES | |
| 2130 Broadway (between | 212-873-7850 |
| 74th and 75th Sts.), UWS | |
| 2440 Broadway (at 90th St.), UWS | 212-724-2777 |

Unique and funny gifts and gadgets: Tee shirts, cards, candles, bath crystals, glow-in-the-dark finger paints, and other nifty bric-a-brac.

| ★*New York Firefighter's Friend* | K/PT/T |
|---|---|
| 263 Lafayette Street (between | 212-226-3142 |
| Prince and Spring Sts.), LI | |
| www.nyfirestore.com | |

This is a great stop for any firefighting enthusiast in the family. They carry all sorts of firefighter stuff: Fire trucks (the toy kind), tee shirts, caps, teddy bears, books, pajamas, raincoats, and, of course, boots. It's not primarily a toy store, though, but rather a store for people seriously interested in firefighting.

| *One Shubert Alley* | PK/K/PT/T |
|---|---|
| 1 Shubert Alley (between 44th | 212-944-4133 |
| and 45th Sts. at Broadway and Eighth Ave.), MTW | |

A good stop for those looking to buy Broadway souvenirs. Tee shirts, buttons, and posters are at the top of the list for New York City gifts.

*Chinatown is gift central*

| *Popover's Plums* | PK/K/PT/T |
|---|---|
| 555 Amsterdam Avenue | 212-496-9648 |
| (at 87th St.), UWS | |

A wide selection of gift items and trinkets ranging from stuffed animals to jewelry and candles.

**P.S. I Love You**                         K/PT/T
1242 Madison Avenue (between        212-722-6272
89th and 90th Sts.), UES

Best for girls, this store specializes in gifts and trinkets. Look
for campy tee shirts (good for the boys too), silver jewelry,
purses, candles, boxer shorts, pens, cards, and other gifty items.

**Ricky's New York City**                   K/PT/T
590 Broadway (between               212-226-5552
Prince and Houston Sts.), SH

If the wide selection of boas doesn't draw you into this store,
perhaps the strobe lights and pulsing, youthful crowd will.
Originally more of a cosmetics-type store, Ricky's still carries a
wide range of hair care products, along with the newer addi-
tions (key chains, jewelry, kitschy lunch boxes, brightly colored wigs, and other fun stuff).

**United Nations**                          K/PT/T
First Avenue (between 45th           212-963-4465
and 46th Sts.), MTE

Stop in here after your UN visit because this is a great place to
buy meaningful gifts and souvenirs. The complex has multiple
shops within it, but the
most promising for kids
are the post office (for
stamp collecting), book-
shop, and the main gift
shop, on the lower level.
Many children find the
postcards featuring flags of

**Helpful Hint**
Visit busy areas like
Times Square and the
South Street Seaport
first thing in the morning
and midweek to avoid
unpleasant crowds.

all of the participating UN countries a good purchase, as well as calendars, dolls, and books.

## Hobbies and Crafts

| ★*America's Hobby Center* | K/PT/T |
|---|---|
| 146 West 22nd Street (between Sixth and Seventh Aves.), CH | 212-675-8922 |

An excellent destination for an extremely extensive (they do a huge mail order and even an export business) selection of models, including model rockets, boats, trains, cars, airplanes, and even the equipment to upgrade models to remote control.

| *Cinderella Flower and Feather Co.* | K/PT/T |
|---|---|
| 60 West 38th Street (between Fifth and Sixth Aves.), MTW | 212-840-0644 |

This neighborhood is rife with accoutrements for every creative child: Beads, feathers, patches, you name it, they've got it. Wander up and down 37th and 38th Streets and along Sixth Avenue to see the selection and pick your favorite shop. Also try Gampel Supply (39 West 37th St., 212-398-9222) for an exceptional selection of beads, and at a discount to boot.

| *Jan's Hobby Shop* | K/PT/T |
|---|---|
| 1557 York Avenue (between 82nd and 83rd Sts.), UES | 212-861-5075 |

Everything the aspiring or expert model builder needs, including paints, books, brushes, and the models themselves. If your child is a real enthusiast, be sure to spend a minute talking to the proprietor, Fred, who has turned his love for building models into a very successful career.

*Lee's*                                    **K/PT/T**
220 West 57th Street (between              212-247-0110
Seventh Ave. and Broadway), MTW

Lee's sells an enormous collection of supplies for the professional artist and draftsman.

*Mach 1 Hobbies*                           **K/PT/T**
249 West 29th Street (between              212-947-0157
Seventh and Eighth Aves.), CH

Remote control models. First you build them (a huge selection), then you control them.

★*New York Central Art Supply*            **K/PT/T**
62 Third Avenue (between                   212-473-7705
10th and 11th Sts.), EV

A top pick for art supplies, especially paper—both homemade
and commercial. Some fans say they have the best selection in
the United States, others say it's the best in the world. There's
only one way to find out . . .

★*Pearl Paint*                            **K/PT/T**
308 Canal Street (between                  212-431-7932
Church St. and Broadway), CT
www.pearlpaint.com

Pearl Paint is a New York classic. It offers discounted prices on
all tools that any artist, budding or professional, could wish
for. The store has grown over the years and now not only occupies the entire building at 308 Canal, but also has offshoots
(framing, paint, office accoutrements) out the back door and
down the block.

| | |
|---|---|
| *Red Caboose* | PK/K/PT/T |
| 23 West 45th Street (downstairs, between Fifth and Sixth Aves.), MTW | 212-575-0155 |

Everything the young train enthusiast could ever hope for and more. Complete train sets and accessories for the beginner, and collectibles for older kids (and adults). The selection is great, and the prices won't leave you short of breath.

## Learning Tip

Pier 17 and much of the South Street Seaport are built on "reclaimed land." It used to be underwater. Term paper idea: Where was the original shore-front road near the South Street Seaport? What is/was its name? How many extra streets were added by reclaiming land during the eighteenth and nineteenth centuries? When was the South Street Seaport turned into a shopping district and how many years later was Pier 17 added?

# Magic

| | |
|---|---|
| *Abracadabra* | K/PT/T |
| 19 West 21st Street (between Fifth and Sixth Aves.), CH | 212-627-5194 |

Look for everything from make-up and costumes to props, wigs, gags, magic, and hats.

★*Flosso Hornmann Magic Co.*     K/PT/T
45 West 34th Street (6th fl., rm. 606;     212-279-6079
between Fifth and Sixth Aves., ), GD

This shop has been around since 1869, and if that isn't enough to impress you, perhaps this will: It's the oldest magic shop in the world. Amateurs and professionals alike flock to this well-stocked magic museum, and the kind staff puts on little shows for the kids.

★*Tannen's Magic*     PT/T
24 West 25th Street (between     212-929-4500
Broadway and Sixth Ave.), CH

You're just as welcome to stop in for a browse as for a shop at Tannen's, and chances are pretty good that you'll catch a spontaneous show if you hang around. Another of New York's favorite establishments, Tannen's is a perfect stop for magic lovers whether they're beginners or advanced.

## Music

*Colony Record & Tape Center*     T
1619 Broadway (at 49th St.), MTW/TS     212-265-2050

Specializing in hard-to-find titles, of interest mostly to collectors.

*Generation Records*     PT/T
210 Thompson Street (between     212-254-1100
Bleecker and West 3rd Sts.), WV

Specializing in new and used rock, alternative, gothic, industrial, punk, and hardcore music; available on compact disc, vinyl, cassette, and 7-inch singles.

### Other Music
**PT/T**
15 East 4th Street (at Lafayette), EV      212-477-8150

Experimental and independent labels are the attraction at OM. If it's out there, OM is likely to have it, and the staff is extremely friendly so don't be afraid to ask.

### Rocks in Your Head
**PT/T**
157 Prince Street (between      212-475-6729
West Broadway and Thompson St.), SH

They could be friendlier in this well-stocked shop, but they won't bite, and the selection of new and used CDs and LPs is worth the effort. They also carry videos, books, and tee shirts.

### Second Coming Records
**PT/T**
235 Sullivan Street (between      212-228-1313
3rd and Bleecker Sts.), WV

New and used CDs, LPs, and cassettes—don't expect to find the Spice Girls here.

### Tower Records
**K/PT/T**
692 Broadway (at West 4th St.), GV      212-505-1500
### Tower Outlet
**K/PT/T**
20 East 4th Street (at Lafayette), GV      212-228-7317

The largest Tower in the City, this one is a New York City original.

In addition to the record stores listed above, others are along St. Marks Place between Second and Third Avenues. Good for a browse, but know your prices because some of the spots along this street are a bit out of line.

# Out of This World, Science-Related Stuff

| ★*Maxilla & Mandible* | K/PT/T |
|---|---|
| 451 Columbus Avenue (between | 212-724-6173 |
| 81st and 82nd Sts.), UWS | |

More like a museum than a store, M&M never fails to make an impression on those who enter this small shop. The stock ranges from boxed tropical insects (yes, they're dead and they're real) to seashells and skeletons. They even have a "want list" so you can make requests, and they'll see if they can find what you're looking for.

| *Star Magic* | K/PT/T |
|---|---|
| 745 Broadway (at Eighth Ave), EV | 212-228-7770 |
| 1256 Lexington Avenue | 212-988-0300 |
| (at 85th St.), UES | |

All kinds of books, toys, rocks and minerals, plastic dinosaur figures, holograms, stars and sparkles, music, planetarium kits, rockets, and dragon figurines. "Space age gifts," they say.

| *Store of Knowledge WNET* | PK/K/PT/T |
|---|---|
| 1091 Third Avenue (at 64th St.), UES | 212-223-0018 |
| 153 World Trade Center Concourse | 212-321-2855 |
| (on the concourse by the Gap), FD | |

A fabulous educational store that doesn't feel like education, full of toys, books, and science- and nature-related goodies; good for a browse or a buy. This one is sure to delight every child.

| *Unique Science* | PT/T |
|---|---|
| 410 Columbus Avenue (between 80th and 81st Sts.), UWS | 212-712-1899 |

Good enough to satisfy any curious kid, this place has all sorts of science stuff including experiment kits, rocks, minerals, anatomical models, and dinosaur figures.

### Helpful Hint

If shopping is becoming too time consuming, set a time limit per store or per day so that the entire visit to New York City isn't spent inside stores.

# Sports

| ★*Ballet Shop* | K/PT/T |
|---|---|
| 1887 Broadway (between 62nd and 63rd Sts.), UWS | 212-581-7990 |

As a young girl, this store was my absolute favorite stop on trips into the City to see the New York City Ballet and American Ballet Theater. Full of tee shirts, books, collector's items (signed toe shoes), music, and ballet trinkets. Any aspiring dancer will be in heaven in this one-of-a-kind store.

| *Blades Board & Skate* | K/PT/T |
| --- | --- |
| 120 West 72nd Street (between Broadway and Columbus Ave.), UWS | 212-787-3911 |
| 659 Broadway (between Bond and Bleecker Sts.), EV | 212-477-7350 |
| 128 Chambers Street (at West Broadway), FD | 212-964-1944 |
| Chelsea Piers, West 23rd Street (at West Side Hwy.), CH | 212-336-6299 |
| 160 East 86th Street (between Lexington and Third Aves.), UES | 212-996-1644 |
| 1414 Second Avenue (between 73rd and 74th Sts.), UES | 212-249-3178 |

The name says it all.

| *Capezio* | PK/K/PT/T |
| --- | --- |
| 1650 Broadway (2nd fl.; at 51st St.), MTW | 212-245-2130 |

There are a handful of Capezio stores throughout the City, but this one is the largest and stocks dancewear of all kinds.

| *Eastern Mountain Sports* | K/PT/T |
| --- | --- |
| 20 West 61st Street (between Broadway and Columbus Ave.), UWS | 212-397-4860 |
| 611 Broadway (at Houston St.), EV | 212-505-9860 |

A regional chain, EMS carries a full line of outdoor gear and equipment.

## Learning Tip

Before there were cars, people got around New York City by horse. There are still stables in Manhattan and, amazing as it may sound, they're vertical—just like apartment buildings, but for horses. Term paper idea: Discuss the history, importance, and decline of the horse in the development of New York City.

| ★*Miller's* | K/PT/T |
|---|---|
| 117 East 24th Street (between Park and Lexington Aves.), GP | 212-673-1400 |

Every time my husband's teenage niece visits the City from Seattle, Miller's is the first place she wants to go to check out the full line of equestrian equipment.

| *Modell's* | K/PT/T |
|---|---|
| 1535 Third Avenue (between 86th and 87th Sts.), UES | 212-996-3800 |
| 200 Broadway (between Fulton and John Sts.), FD | 212-964-4007 |
| 280 Broadway (at Chambers), FD | 212-962-6200 |
| 901 Sixth Avenue (lower level; at 33rd St.,) MTW | 212-594-1830 |
| 51 East 42nd Street (between Vanderbilt and Madison Aves.), MTE | 212-661-4242 |

The reasonable prices at this sporting goods store should leave you with enough left over to take the kids on that tour of Madison Square Garden. Modell's, or Mo's as it is known locally, is reputed to be the oldest family-owned and operated sporting goods chain store in the country.

| *Paragon Sports* | K/PT/T |
| --- | --- |
| 871 Broadway (at 18th St.), US | 212-255-8036 |

Paragon started out as a small-time sporting goods store and has expanded to include everything from hiking and camping gear to equipment for tennis, skiing, and in-line skates. Certainly not the cheapest (expect to pay retail), but it's the most extensive selection of so many items in any given place in the City.

| *Peck and Goodie* | K/PT/T |
| --- | --- |
| 917 Eighth Avenue (between 54th and 55th Sts.), MTW | 212-246-6123 |

A New York institution for skaters, Peck and Goodie stocks ice skates, inline skates, and even skateboards.

| *Soccer Sport Supply Company* | K/PT/T |
| --- | --- |
| 1745 First Avenue (between 90th and 91st Sts.), UES | 212-427-6050<br>800-223-1010 |

The best (highest quality and best selection) soccer and rugby gear around. This store does a tremendous amount of mail-order business both nationally and internationally.

| *Tent & Trails* | K/PT/T |
| --- | --- |
| 21 Park Place (between Broadway and Church St.), FD | 212-227-1760 |

By far the best camping store in the City. I have outfitted myself for many weekend camping outings as well as intense Himalayan treks and backpacking trips here. They have everything you need, a knowledgeable if somewhat ornery staff, and amazingly low prices. They pack into three floors what suburban stores would display in twenty. If you don't see it, ask for it because it's probably hidden behind three other items.

| | |
|---|---|
| *Yankees Clubhouse Shop* | K/PT/T |
| **393 Fifth Avenue (between** | **212-685-4693** |
| **36th and 37th Sts.), MTE** | |
| **110 East 59th Street (between** | **212-758-7844** |
| **Park and Lexington Aves), UES** | |
| **8 Fulton Street (at South** | **212-514-7182** |
| **Street Seaport), FD** | |

This is the place to outfit yourself for a ball game or to buy souvenirs.

## Money-Saving Tip

Set an allowance for children in advance—and tell them about it—so that they know they can make a finite number of New York City purchases on the trip and they can plan accordingly. This will save you money and stress; it will save your children from raised expectations and tantrums.

## Theme Stores

| | |
|---|---|
| *Coca-Cola Fifth Avenue* | PK/K/PT/T |
| **711 Fifth Avenue (between** | **212-418-9260** |
| **55th and 56th Sts.), MT** | |

Fully stocked with Coca-Cola wear and gifts.

| *The Disney Store* | PK/K/PT/T |
|---|---|
| 711 Fifth Avenue (at 55th St.), MTE | 212-702-0702 |
| 39 West 34th Street (between | 212-279-9890 |
| Fifth and Sixth Aves.), MTW | |
| 141 Columbus Avenue | 212-362-2386 |
| (at 66th St.), UWS | |

It speaks for itself—the largest store is on Fifth Avenue.

| *NBA Store* | K/PT/T |
|---|---|
| 666 Fifth Avenue (at 52nd St.), MTE | 212-515-6221 |

A full complement of National Basketball Association clothing and accessories.

| *NikeTown* | K/PT/T |
|---|---|
| 6 East 57th Street (between | 212-891-6453 |
| Fifth and Madison Aves.), MTE | |

This is more of a Nike museum than a store, though everything is for sale, including all the most recent styles.

| *Warner Bros. Studio Store* | PK/K/PT/T |
|---|---|
| 1 East 57th Street (at Fifth Ave.), MTE | 212-754-0300 |
| 1 Times Square (at Broadway | 212-840-4040 |
| and 42nd St.), TS | |

The Fifth Avenue emporium is the larger of the two Warner Bros. establishments.

*See the Quick Guide to Theme Restaurants in chapter 6 for related theme stores.*

# Toys

| *A Bear's Place* | PK/K |
| --- | --- |
| 789 Lexington Avenue (between 61st and 62nd Sts.), UES | 212-826-6465 |

A good selection of wooden toys and puzzles, unique puppets, games, and furniture. The emphasis here is on toys that are unique or very distinctive.

| *Big City Kite Co.* | K/PT/T |
| --- | --- |
| 1210 Lexington Avenue (at 82nd St.), UES | 212-472-2623 |

A small store with a big inventory of kites and every kite-flying accessory imaginable: Books, videos, and other simple flying objects.

| *Children's General Store* | PK/K |
| --- | --- |
| 2473 Broadway (at 92nd St.), UWS | 212-580-2723 |
| 107 East 42nd Street (Grand Central Terminal), MTE | 212-682-0004 |

A nice selection of children's toys that you won't find everywhere else.

| *Chimera* | PK/K/PT/T |
| --- | --- |
| 77 Mercer Street (between Spring and Broome Sts.), SH | 212-334-4730 |

Chimera is full of nifty novelties of all sizes and shapes. The merchandise is mainly geared toward older children and adults, but there's a good inventory of stuffed animals for younger kids.

Union
Square
Greenmarket

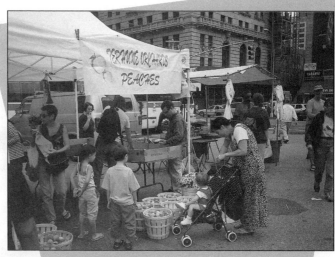

| *Classic Toys* | PK/K/PT/T |
|---|---|
| 218 Sullivan Street (between | 212-674-4434 |
| Bleecker and West 3rd Sts.), WV | |

Great for children who are into vehicles, this store specializes
in toy soldiers, cars, and airplanes for play and for collecting.
Also stuffed animals.

| ★*Cozy's Cuts for Kids* | PK/K |
|---|---|
| 1125 Madison Avenue | 212-744-1716 |
| (at 84th St.), UES | |
| 448 Amsterdam Avenue | 212-579-2600 |
| (at 81st St.), UWS | |

The primary purpose of most visits to Cozy's is haircuts, but
there's also a nifty selection of toys, bath toys and products,
hair care items and accessories, puzzles, bubbles, dolls, and
books.

**Dinosaur Hill**                       **PK/K**
306 East 9th Street (between            212-273-5850
First and Second Aves.), EV

Dinosaur toys, stuffed animals, and puppets are the theme of the house, but don't be discouraged if your child isn't in the dinosaur craze—plenty of other enchanting options are available, with an especially quirky appeal. The store is particularly hospitable to browsers.

**★Enchanted Forest**                   **PK/K**
85 Mercer Street (between               212-925-6677
Spring and Broome Sts.), SH

When your children walk into the Enchanted Forest, it's as if they're walking into a fantasy land. There are tin toys and stuffed toys, toys that evoke past eras, and toys straight out of the imagination. Don't expect to find things that you'd see in chain toy stores; everything about this store is unique, especially the toys. A good place to stop for a break from the City.

**★FAO Schwarz**                        **PK/K/PT/T**
767 Fifth Avenue (between 58th and 59th Sts.), MT

This is more of a destination than a place to shop (though you certainly can buy plenty of incredible stuff here). People literally line up at the entrance to get in at busy times of the year, and they find it well worth the wait. Full of every kind of stuffed animal (half a floor's worth), multitudes of board games, books, infant toys and accessories, a candy department, a whole line of Barbie dolls and accessories, not to mention the $19,500 mini-Range Rover! Every child is sure to delight in a visit to this store. Allow plenty of time to explore.

**Geppetto's Toybox**  PK/K/PT
10 Christopher Street (between  212-620-7511
Greenwich and Gay Sts.), WV

A unique selection of new (for newborn to 12) and collectible toys, including Teddy bears, dolls, party favors, rocking horses, and others.

**Homboms**  PK/K
1500 First Avenue (between  212-717-5300
78th and 79th Sts.), UES

Carries a wide variety of toys, including some specialty toy store items (including the entire line of Thomas the Tank toys and Brio) and some mass market (like Fisher-Price) too. The selection is primarily aimed at children 5 and under.

**Kidding Around**  PK/K/PT
68 Bleecker Street (between  212-598-0228
Broadway and Lafayette), EV
60 West 15th Street (between  212-645-6337
Fifth and Sixth Aves.), US

Runs the gamut from developmental toys for your infant to science experiments for the older kids. Also a good collection of dolls, complete with ethnic selections, music toys, and art sets and supplies for budding da Vinci's.

**Mary Arnold Toys**  PK/K/PT/T
1010 Lexington Avenue (between  212-744-8510
72nd and 73rd Sts.), UES

Toys for all ages of children and also adults. Also a small selection of baby equipment and furniture, like rockers and chairs.

454

| *Penny Whistle Toys* | PK/K/PT |
|---|---|
| 448 Columbus Avenue (between 81st and 82nd Sts.), UWS | 212-873-9090 |
| 1283 Madison Avenue (between 91st and 92nd Sts.), UES | 212-369-3868 |

Very popular with neighborhood kids, Penny Whistle carries a good selection of quality toys neatly packed into tight surroundings.

| *West Side Kids* | PK/K |
|---|---|
| 498 Amsterdam Avenue (at 84th St.), UWS | 212-496-7282 |

A great neighborhood toy store with a promising selection of toys, games, dolls and furniture, books, book-related videos, plush animals, and other tantalizing treats.

## Money-Saving Tip

Before you visit stores like FAO Schwarz, explain to your children that it's not about buying, but rather it's about the experience—sort of like an interactive museum, only better. They can play with, touch, read, and experiment with toys without buying them, which isn't possible at most other toy stores. Much of the merchandise at fancy toy stores is available elsewhere for less.

# INDEX TO SHOPPING
# BY NEIGHBORHOOD

SHOPPING

**459**

# Index
# by Neighborhoods

# Index